**WITHDRAWN
UTSA Libraries**

RENEWALS 458-4574
DATE DUE

New Mexican Spanish Religious Oratory, 1800-1900

New Mexican Spanish Religious Oratory, 1800–1900

☦

Edited and
with an introduction by

THOMAS J. STEELE, S.J.

☦

University of New Mexico Press
Albuquerque

© 1997 by the University of New Mexico Press
All rights reserved. First Edition

Library of Congress Cataloging-in-Publication Data
New Mexican Spanish religious oratory:1800-1900
edited and with an introduction by Thomas J. Steele, S.J.
first edition   p. cm.
Includes bibliographical references and index.
ISBN 0-8263-1768-5
1. Preaching—New Mexico—
History—19th century.
2. Sermons, Spanish—New Mexico.
I. Steele, Thomas J.
BV 4208.U6N48   1997
251'.009789'09034—dc20   96-10115
CIP
DESIGNED BY SUE NIEWIAROWSKI

Contents

Preface VII

Introduction 1

I Franciscan Christianity on the Northern Frontier 5
  Anonymous Franciscan 8

  Superstición 10
  Superstition 11

  Manuel Antonio Garcia del Valle 19

  Viernes Santo 22
  Good Friday 23

II Three Orations of Padre Antonio José Martínez 41
  Primer Misa 46
  First Mass 47
  Panegirico por El Padre Hidalgo 60
  Panegyric on Padre Hidalgo 61
  El cuatro de julio 80
  Fourth of July 81

III The French Clergy 89
  Joseph P. Machebeuf 91
  Sermon on the Passion 93

  Viernes Santo 96
  Good Friday 97
  El sacerdocio 110
  The Priesthood 111

  Jean Baptiste Lamy 120

  Profesión Religiosa 124
  Religious Profession 125
  Navidad 130
  Christmas 131
  Instrucción sobre la Pasión 136
  Instruction on the Passion 137

IV **Addresses at Religious Schools**   143

    Rafael Romero   148

    Distribución de Premios del Colegio de las Vegas   150
    Distribution of Prizes, College of Las Vegas   151

    Vito Tromby, S.J.   160

    La Escuela Nueva de San Felipe Neri   162
    The New School Building at San Felipe Neri   163

V **Presbyterian Christianity on the Western Frontier**   173

    José Vicente Ferrer Romero   176

    Necesidad de Cultivar la Mente y el Corazón   178
    The Necessity of Cultivating the Mind and the Heart   179

    Elijah McLean Fenton   182

    Las Ovejas del Christo   184
    Christ's Sheep   185

VI **Methodist Christianity on the Western Frontier**   193

    Thomas Harwood   197

    Transfiguración de Cristo   198
    Transfiguration of Christ   199

    Blas Chávez   205

    Fúnebre del Niño   206
    A Child's Funeral   207

    Lauriano Vargas   211

    Falsas Dioses   212
    False Gods   213

Conclusion   Old World and New World   216

Sources of Religious Oratory in Spanish from Nineteenth-Century New Mexico   219

Index of Biblical References   223

Index of Topics   225

Preface

Since there may be some information useful to philogists, I transcribed the Spanish texts as carefully as I could, ignoring only the occasional—and now obsolete—accent on the preposition *á*.

My English version of each speech is very free. Since the original is right next to the translation, most readers will be perfectly aware how many liberties I have taken. My main goal was to express in English that is readable today the personality and literary style of each speaker as best I was able to discern them in the Spanish original. Footnotes to the sermons run across the bottom of each pair of pages, usually with numerals in both the Spanish text and the English.

I wish to thank many persons who helped me with this book: anonymously, the many librarians and archivists of the collections noted in "Sources of Spanish Religious Oratory," and the helpful editors at the University of New Mexico Press; and by name my friends William García, Enrique Lamadrid, and Miguel Leatham.

Introduction

Religious Oratory in Nineteenth-Century New Mexico

As the Gospel of John presents him, Jesus is the Word Incarnate, an utterance of the divine mind and will transformed into human flesh who expresses himself by speaking in human words. Though his words are definitively recorded in scripture, every culture and every age must express this divine wisdom anew in its own language so that it can apply it in practice to its own problems. This is the act of teaching that Jesus commands of his followers as individuals and of his church as his corporate body for as long as history shall continue.

In the Acts of the Apostles, Saint Luke enshrined some proven patterns of preaching in the proclamations of Peter and Paul (Acts 2:14–40; 3:12–26; 10:28–43; and 13:16–41). But as the proclamation of the good news moved out of the first Christian century and out of the eastern Mediterranean into all the diverse thought-patterns of mankind's many cultures, different preaching traditions arose in Christian history. We will experience several different ones in the various sermons in this book. Franciscans traditionally quoted the dying Poverello as sending them to "preach and proclaim to sinners, 'Reward, glory, hell, virtue and vice, and penance for all.'"[1] Frenchmen looked back to Bossuet as an archetype of sophisticated Christian eloquence, Jesuits from Naples might emulate Saint Francesco de Hieronimo, and the Methodist and Calvinist traditions in England and America could model themselves on John Wesley and Jonathan Edwards. The Reverend Arthur Dimmesdale's election sermon near the end of *The Scarlet Letter* reminds us that in the seventeenth and eighteenth centuries the English colonies knew no Jeffersonian separation of church and state any more than New Mexico did, for in New Mexico many if not most formal occasions of state (like those of the Grito de Dolores in 1832 and

---

1. "Hijos mios muy amados, corred el mundo, por la gloria del nombre del Señor, predicando, y anunciando a los pecadores. Premio, Gloria, Ynfierno, virtud, y vicio, y a todos Penitencia"; fray Manuel Antonio García del Valle, sermon on the occasion of the First Mass of Father Rafael Ortiz, 4 October 1823, Santa Fe; Archives of the Archdiocese of Santa Fe, loose documents 1823, no. 16, p. 10; microfilm reel 54, frame 608.

the Fourth of July in 1860) sounded just about as religious as the academic festivals of religious education and even actual church services themselves.

In this light, we can see more clearly that political oratory, church sermonizing, and even scholastic addresses are nearly always persuasive, attempts to get people to *act* in a particular way. In such speeches, as a result, *in*formation (the content of the communication) is subordinated to *form*ation (instilling in the listener the end and purpose the speaker intends).

For a sermon is usually not a content-oriented but an event-oriented mode of discourse, especially if "event" includes the entire occasion: the feast day with its readings, for example. In Charles Briggs's six-level scale of contextuality-textuality, the average sermon—not written out word for word but delivered from notes (or a fortiori, just off the top of the head)—would probably fall into the fourth or fifth spot along with jests, anecdotes, humorous tales, legends, and treasure tales. Such a sermon is less contextual than historical discourse and proverb and scripture performances, but it is not as text-dominated as hymns and prayers, which are seldom or never altered so as to respond to the congregation's reaction or so as to reflect the concrete life-situation of the moment.[2] By contrast to a sermon-delivered-from-notes or a sermon-off-the-top-of-the-head, the sermons presented in this book were all composed ahead of time, and (with the obvious exception of Fr. Machebeuf's "etc. etc. etc." cadenzas) they were probably delivered pretty much as written. Hence they were as textual as prayers and hymns, and the preachers performed them like one-man plays, with no deviation from the written text despite any developments in the context—babies bawling, parishioners yawning, intolerable heat or cold, Indian attacks, or the roof falling in.[3]

---

2. Assuming that most of the clergy and laity represented in this book came from residually-peasant families, we can speculate that the content of the oral tradition (proverbs, for instance) merely gave way to the copybook nuggets of the commonplace (*topoi*) tradition: verses taken from Scripture and supplemented by quotable quotes and illustrative illustrations from the Fathers of the Church, church history, and other respectable sources.

3. Charles Briggs, *Competence in Performance: The Creativity of Tradition in Mexicano Verbal Art* (Philadelphia: University of Pennsylvania Press, 1988).

There was a widespread tradition of publishing sermons until about seventy-five or a hundred years ago. Arthur Rimbaud made the remark, true as it was snide, that every little cleric in France had a notebook of his own poetry, and he must have known that every cleric big or little had a half a dozen notebooks of his own sermons and prayed for a publisher to descend upon him like a heavenly angel. Vastly fewer readers and publishers today are partial to such books, so our experience of sermons on the printed page occurs in English classes: Jonathan Edwards' "Sinners in the Hands of an Angry God," Father Mapple's homily in *Moby Dick*, the Jesuit retreat-master's two sermons on Hell in Joyce's *Portrait of the Artist as a Young Man*, the black preacher's Easter panegyric in Faulkner's *Sound and the Fury*, and Tosamah's "Word" sermon in Momaday's *House Made of Dawn*.

By the time our nineteenth-century New Mexican speakers had crafted their addresses, rhetoric had migrated from the oral world of oratory into the handwritten and typeset world of alphabetic literacy. The persuasive, behaviorist purpose of most of the speeches that follow—"Do as I tell you" rather than "Think as I think"—takes us into the realm of authority, whether it is the authority of the Roman Church or the authority of the Bible, to which the Presbyterians and the Methodists appeal. This may be neither a familiar nor a user-friendly world for a reader of the late twentieth century, who will probably have to make a concerted effort to become vicariously a believing member of some nineteenth-century New Mexican faith community in order to get on the speaker's wave length, much in the way that any modern reader must become (fictionally) an educated and sophisticated Elizabethan gentleman, a member of the coterie in-group, in order to read Shakespeare's sonnets or Donne's love poetry as they were intended to be read.[4] So fictionalize yourself, and read on!

---

4. Walter J. Ong, S.J., "The Writer's Audience Is Always a Fiction," *Interfaces of the Word* (Ithaca: Cornell University Press, 1977), pp. 53-81, implies a methodology for examining how a preacher structures his congregation, signaling them who and what they must become for the purposes of listening to his sermon.

PART I

Franciscan Christianity on the Northern Frontier

✠

✣

Saint Francis of Assisi founded the Order of Friars Minor, the Franciscan priests and brothers, in the early thirteenth century. The Cistercian monk Joachim of Fiore (d. 1202) triggered apocalyptic hopes that spread into the Franciscan order that strict poverty would quickly bring an end of human history and usher in the Millennial Kingdom. With the discovery of the New World—and some confusion between newly-discovered and newly-created—the Observant Franciscans, heirs of Joachim's ideals, hoped that their missionary work among the innocent inhabitants of the Valley of Mexico would bring about the thousand-year paradise of the Messiah. In the late sixteenth century, when it had become obvious that New Spain had not gone as it should, many Franciscans had perhaps begun to hope for a new Mexico where their plans could go right.[1]

When they traveled up into New Mexico to be missionaries to a new set of unspoiled American Adams and Eves, the Franciscans so strongly resisted becoming mere parish priests that they founded only three parishes for the rapidly growing population of Spanish settlers prior to the 1820s; but still the end-times refrained from arriving. When diocesan priests replaced them in New Mexico, the Franciscans replaced exiled Jesuits on the northwest frontier of New Spain, soon moving into Alta California under the leadership of fray Junípero Serra. California did not become the millennial kingdom either, by the way.[2]

The Franciscan friars, who had staffed New Mexico almost exclusively up to the end of the eighteenth century, brought with them their mainstream late-medieval spirituality, the gift of Saint Bernard of Clairvaux and Saint Francis of Assisi, a spirituality that tried above all to arouse a tender compassion for the humanity of Jesus in his birth and in his death. Hence Franciscans opposed anything such as superstition that drew a Catholic away from Christ (the first sermon), and they fostered an especially devout observance of Holy Week (the second sermon).

1. John Leddy Phelan, *The Millennial Kingdom of the Franciscans in the New World* (Berkeley: University of California Press, 1970), especially pp. 44-58. Delno C. West, "Medieval Ideas of Apocalyptic and Early Franciscans in Mexico," *The Americas* 45 (1989), 293–313.

2. Phelan, p. 1, states that "the Middle Ages sang its swan song in the New World in the Sixteenth Century." Since he adds on page 54 that after New Spain became subject to the bishop-centered decrees of the Council of Trent "the friars were left with but two alternatives—to retire peacefully to their monasteries or to transfer their missionary enthusiasm to the colonial frontiers," we might say that the medieval world sang its first swan-song encore in New Mexico in the early nineteenth century and its second in California a few decades later.

See Juan de Montoya, *New Mexico in 1602*, trans., ed., George P. Hammond and Agapito Rey (Albuquerque: Quivira Society, 1938), p. 12; fray Alonso de Benavides, *The Memorial of 1630*, trans., ed., Mrs. Edward E. Ayer et al. (1916; reprint Albuquerque, Horn and Wallace, 1965), pp. 66-68; fray Jerónimo de Zárate Salmeron, *Relaciones*, trans. Alicia Milich.(Albuquerque: Horn and Wallace, 1966), pp. 54-56; and especially Marc Simmons, *The Last Conquistador: Juan de Oñate and the Settling of the Far West* (Norman: University of Oklahoma Press, 1991), pp. 61-64, 183-84.

On the residual medievalism of traditional New Mexican religious culture, see Thomas J. Steele, S.J., *Santos and Saints* (Santa Fe: Ancient City Press, 1994), pp. 1-2, 13n1, 21, 35, 57-58n4, 93, 106-8, and 111.

Anonymous Franciscan

This sermon survives in a late nineteenth-century copy in the Martínez-Sandoval Papers at the New Mexico State Records Center and Archives. It fills the four pages formed by a single folded sheet of lightly-lined blue paper. It was probably copied in the latter third of the nineteenth century by someone who did not know Latin (he misconstrued Latin quotations) and who especially did not understand the system of Latin abbreviations the author used to refer to his various authorities.

But the sermon itself must be quite a bit older than the late nineteenth century, for at that date a Catholic priest in New Mexico would probably have spent some time defending certain Catholic devotions against Protestant charges of being themselves superstitions. The preacher's mentality seems to me quite essentialist, making it earlier than the late-eighteenth- and nineteenth-century developmental or processual world-view characteristic of Condorcet, Comte, Darwin, Marx, Newman, and Freud, which can be characterized as existential or historicist. Furthermore, because the speaker describes the Inquisition as still in operation and uses the word "México" to name the city rather than the nation, it seems best to date the work from the first two decades of the nineteenth century, but it could be even older than that. Some priest of the diocese of Durango might have written it, but there were many more Franciscans in the colony, and among them fray Santiago Fernández de Sierra and fray Manuel Antonio García del Valle can be shown to have written equally scholarly orations.

We possess, it seems, only the first half of the sermon, for the beginning of the second paragraph formally divides the whole of the subject of superstition into two parts, and what remains of the sermon treats only the first of those parts. After a brief, vigorous introduction (*exordium*) followed by the statement of parts (*divisio* or *partitio*) just mentioned, our orator begins the body of the sermon (*narratio*, *confirmatio*, and *refutatio*), offering a very brief conclusion to wrap up the first half of the announced subject matter before the manuscript breaks off.

The speaker divides his sermon in precisely the way the subject of superstition was divided in moral theology as it was taught and written about in the Latin tradition of seminary education which has come to be called—somewhat insultingly, and justly so—"textbook theology." The long his-

tory of Catholic thinking and writing about morality, which began with the New Testament and the Fathers and continued with the great medieval scholastic theologians, eventually settled down into the dry and predictable tomes which served Tridentine seminaries, the diocesan schools for clergy mandated by the Council of Trent (1545–63).

Not only does the sermon's structural development into generic divisions and specific subdivisions stem from the tradition of textbook theology, but absolutely all the examples of specific superstitions come from those books as well. The author's trail is easy to follow; he marked it very clearly by giving his references, which are duly recorded in the footnotes. Like each specific example, the textbook-theology tradition as a whole was anything but original; in those days, a substantively innovative author was asking for trouble with the Holy Office of the Inquisition—and he would get it.

The whole sermon attacks what could well be called magic—the age-old human tendency to try to "capture" the power of the holy and manipulate it for one's own selfish purposes. Unfortunately, then, we do not learn anything trustworthy about New Mexican life during the period of the sermon. None of the superstitions attacked can on the basis of this sermon be asserted to have been practiced in New Mexico—or, for that matter, in the France of Thomas Aquinas, the Portugal of Fagúndez, the Spain of Sánchez, the Germany of Laymann, or the Italy of Tamburelli. They belong to that never-never land of Titius and Bertha, the John Doe and Mary Roe of moral theology; they belong to the la-la land of textbook theology.

But even if our diligent cleric crafted his sermon by plundering textbooks rather than by gleaning his teeming personal brain, his sermon is not just some dry-as-dust classroom lecture. From the textbook-theology building-blocks, he crafts a lively sermon with a vigorous style: there is humor in the tale of the white cat that falls into the ink, there is strength in the plain speaking about the nonsense of superstition, and there are even some nice rhetorical flourishes like the apostrophe to the superstitious Señora at the start of the second-last paragraph. Anyone who attends church regularly hears far worse sermons on a regular basis. *Ars celat artem*, the Romans said, art conceals art; and few of the preacher's listeners could have guessed that there is nothing original in the sermon except the cat.

Superstición

Que facilidad veo en introducirse novedades con capa de devocion, tan sin reparo hasta en las devociones quieren que aya usos. O valgame Dios!

Esplico primero lo que sera superticion en el modo despues dire lo que toca ala superticion en el objeto.[1] Hablo por suma dicha nuestra entre Catolicos. Adoramos a nuestro verdadero Dios, en si mismo, y le adoramos en sus Santos, en esto jamas podemos tener peligro de porte de lo que adoramos, pero si podemos tenerlo de porte de el modo, con que ofresemos estos cultos, esto es peligro de que nosotros con el modo de haserlos los hagamos superticiosos

y podra suseder esto de dos maneras, la primera si reverenciamos a Dios dandole cuto falso y mentiroso. Como si alguno obserbara aora alguna, o algunas de aquellas ceremonias de los Judios,[2] que si entonces eran de verdadera Religion por que significamos al Mesias que que abia de venir; aora que lo adoramos ya venido para nuestro remedio, son ceremonias falsas son y mentiroso, y siempre pecado mortal y grabisimo, si alguno hisiere con advirtencia.[3] Asi tambien comete superticion y gravisimo sacrilegio por culto falso el que sin ser Saserdote, ni tener orden Sacro, o dixera misa o exercitara con los ornamento[s] sagrados algun acto de los que solo pueden haserlos ya por el orden Sacro estan consagrados para ministros de la yglecia.[4] Esto no ay quien lo ignore pero si acuerdo que qualquiera que supiere que alguno ha hecho esto, esta obligado debaxo de excomunion a delantarlo luego al santo tribunal de la inquisicion.[5]

---

1. In question 92, article 2, of the Secunda Secundae of his *Summa Theologiae*, Thomas Aquinas asserts that there are different species of superstition and that they result either from showing inappropriate worship to an appropriate object (the true God) or from showing any worship to an inappropriate object (some creature). This initial division by manner and object is a standard feature of the "textbook theology" tradition.

2. St. Thomas Aquinas, *Summa Theologiae* II-II q. 92, 2 ad 3 and q. 93, 1 corp. refers to "ceremonies of the old law" and "a ritual of the old law" as examples of superstition, as do Paul Laymann, S.J. (1574–1635), *Theologia Moralis Quinque Libris Partita Complectens* (Mainz: Nicholas Heinrich, 1630), Tomás Sánchez, S.J. (1550–1610), *Opus Morale in Praecepta Decalogi* (Paris: Michael Sonnius, 1615); Tommaso Tamburini, S.J. (1591–1675), *Opera Omnia* (Venice: Niccolò Pezzana, 1692), Estêvão Fagúndez, S.J. (1577–1645), *In Quinque Priora Praecepta Decalogi* (Lyons: Laurence Anisson and the Heirs of G. Boissat, 1640), and Januario Bucceroni, S.J., *Institutiones Theologicae Moralis* (Rome: Forzani and Co., 1892). Furthermore, a book that Martínez used in the seminary, Vincent-Luigi Cardinal Gotti's *Theologia Scholastico-Dogmatica* (Venice: Balleoni, 1750), 1:100, informs the reader that "A person would practice the second mode of superstition by adoring the true God with a false and outmoded ritual, as for instance if somebody honored Him with a pagan or Jewish religious ritual." And Lucio Ferrari's *Prompta Bibliotheca Canonica, Juridica, Moralis, Theologica, nec non Ascetia* (Rome: Remondini, 1767), 7: *sub verbo* "Superstitio," says that "The superstition of false cult is worshiping God with Jewish or Muslim ceremonies such as circumcision, immolating a lamb, and suchlike, which signify that Christ is yet to come and that he has not already come."

3. The Spanish here is ambiguous. "Con advirtencia" [advertencia] can be translated "openly, publicly," "with full knowledge," or "after a warning."

Superstition

What ease I see in introducing novelties with a veneer of piety, so heedless that even in performing their devotions people want to make innovations. O Lord deliver us!

I will first treat what superstition is according to its *manner*, then speak of what superstition is according to its *object*.[1] I speak for our great joy in being among Catholics. We adore our true God in Himself, and we adore Him in His saints. In this we never run the risk of being misled by *what* we adore, but we can run a danger of being misled according to the *manner* in which we offer these devotions, that is, the danger that by the mode of our performing them we make them superstitious.

Now we can do this in two ways. The first comes about if we reverence God but give Him a false and lying worship—for example, if someone were to observe today one or more of those Jewish ceremonies[2] that were once part of the true religion because we prophesied the Messiah who *was* to come. They are now false ceremonies and a lying worship, now that we adore him who has already come and saved us, and they are a most serious mortal sin, if anyone does them with full knowledge.[3] Further, he also is guilty of superstition and a most grave sacrilege for false cult who without being a priest or ordained in any way either says mass or performs with the sacred vestments any ceremony of the sort that can only be performed by those who are already consecrated by Holy Orders to be ministers of the church.[4] There's nobody who doesn't know this, but I do remind you that whoever knows of someone doing this is obliged under pain of excommunication to denounce the guilty party right away to the Holy Tribunal of the Inquisition.[5]

Since Stanley M. Hordes helped me with this thorny passage in the Spanish text, I would like to thank him both for that aid and for calling my attention to this fascinating sermon to begin with.

4. Valentín de la Madre de Dios, O.S.C.O., *Fuero de la Conciencia* (Madrid: Pantaleón Aznar, 1771), 1:154, names this mode of superstition along with various others the sermon employs: "False cult . . . using the ceremonies of the Old Testament to venerate God, or giving absolution or saying mass without being ordained, or faking miracles, or faking relics of the saints, or propagating false revelations. . . . . Superfluous cult is...adding to the ceremonies of the mass or placing the mass candles in such and such rank, position, and order."

Bucceroni, *Institutiones Theologicae*, 1:165, defines false cult, a variety of superstition, as happening when "a layman worships God as a public minister of the Church." On the same page Bucceroni mentions old-law ceremonies and refers to insisting on hearing Mass before dawn, Mass with a certain number or order of ceremonies or prayers, or Mass in a certain place.

Bucceroni's book is obviously too late to have been a source for the present sermon, but it is a representative later example of the Jesuit "textbook theology" represented by the four older moralists, all Jesuits, cited in notes 11-14.

5. The Inquisition closed shop in the Spanish Empire in 1820; see Richard Greenleaf, "The Inquisition in Eighteenth-Century New Mexico," *New Mexico Historical Review* 60 (1985), 56; he refers to AASF l.d. 1820 no. 11, a letter of Bishop Castañiza.

/11

Peca tambien mortalmente por este culto falso y superticioso que finge reliquias de santos donde por reliquia lo que sabe que no lo es peca mortalmente. El que finge milagros le dice o cuenta o los escrive[6] como si la verdad de nuestra fe necisitara de esas mentiras o yentes mios mucha facilidad ay de esto ay muchos milagros y milagreros, sepan que es pecado fingir milagros y contarlos. Y que diremos de el que da una medalla o cruz a otro diciendole que tiene indulgencias quando sabe el que aquella medalla es de las que venden en el baratillo y que no tienen indulgencia alguna materia es de muy grave escrupulo, que si aquel suponiendo que asu medalla tiene indulgencia reduce solo a ganar estas indulgencias la satisfacion de sus culpas. Y despues de la muerte se halla engañado que no ha ganado indulgencia alguna y que le restan muchos años de purgatorio sera poco engaño este [que] alla [l]leveran los que asi fingen indulgencias

pecan tambien por este culto falso, y superticioso los hypocritas las que fingen que tienen revelaciones y raptos. Tal puede suceder entre Christianos o pluguera a Dios, y nunca sucedera los que o las que vistiendose el exterior trage humilde y penitentes afectan solo en lo exterior austeridades, disciplinas, ayunos; y alla en lo escondido, el diablo, y ellos saben quanto se regalan: "Simulata sanctitas duplex iniquitas," dise San Agustin[7] Dos veses iniquos en lo esterior, por mentiroso, y en lo interior, por lleno de pecados. Hablo, de los que solo coge el exterior de virtud, el trage humilde, porque les den limosna por tener entrada en las casas, por tener con que pasar la vida.

Miren, tenia uno de gato, todo blanco, y como lo descubrian los ratones, apenas podia casar tal vez alguno sucedio que el gato cayo en una olla de tinta y salio ya de blanco, todo negro, los ratones viendolo que pensaron que no era el y que hera perro salen todos libremente a jugar, y el gato entonses: o que pesca. Bien, hubo menester todas sus uñas, con que pesco en una dia mas que en ciento, Ha! Si se quedan todavia las uñas, que importa, que se mude solo el trage: Señores y Señoras, no tengan en solo exterioridad las creederas tan faciles, cuantos engaños de estos ha visto descubiertos Mexico? que no quiero dezir al Mundo; Revelaciones, extasis, arrobos, y todo mentiras, y falcedad, por el aplauso, por las comodidades; y aun se si diga por las torpezas. Dios lo descubrira.

---

6. Sánchez, *Opus Morale*, no. 9, p. 305, mentions the faking of relics and miracles, as do Tamburini, *Opera Omnia*, and Fagúndez, *In Quinque Priora*.

7. The exact quotation is "Simulata innocentia non est innocentia: simulata aequitas non est aequitas, sed duplex iniquitas; quia et iniquitas est, et simulatio—Pretended innocence is not innocence, pretended justice is not justice but a double wickedness, for it is both wickedness and pretense"; *Enarratio in Psalmum LXIII* 11 (verse 7), in *Patrilogium Latinum* (Paris: J.-P. Migne, 1845), 36:765.

Moreover, he sins mortally by this false and superstitious cult who fakes relics of the saints where instead of a relic he knows that it is no such thing. He [is equally sinful] who fakes miracles, either by making statements or telling stories or writing them[6]—as if the truth of our faith needed these lies. Oh, my people, this is very easy to do. There are many "miracles" and "miracle-workers." Realize it's a sin to fake miracles and publicize them. And what shall we say of a person who gives a medal or a cross to somebody, telling him it carries indulgences, when he knows that that medal is just one of the ones sold in some cheap shop and that it carries no indulgence? Such a matter is extremely serious, for what if someone supposes that his medal carries an indulgence [illegible] only to gain from those indulgences satisfaction for his sins, and then after death finds himself deceived, finds that he has not gained any indulgence, finds that many years of purgatory remain for him? This will be a small surprise compared to that waiting for those who thus fake indulgences.

Moreover, by means of this false and superstitious cult, these hypocrites sin who pretend to have revelations and raptures. Such a thing can occur among Christians. Oh, pray God to thwart men and women who on the outside wear humble and penitential attire and exteriorly mimic austerities, scourgings, and fasts; and there in hiding is the devil. And they know how much they please each other. "Simulata sanctitas duplex iniquitas—pretended holiness is a double wickedness," says St. Augustine;[7] it is two times as wicked: on the outside for being mendacious and on the inside for being full of sins. I speak of those who take on a virtuous exterior, a humble dress, only to be given an alms, gain entrance into homes, to get something to survive on.

Behold, there was once a man who had a cat, a perfectly white cat, and since the mice could see it, it was barely able to catch even one of them. Then it happened that the cat fell into a jar of ink and came out totally black instead of white. The mice, seeing it in this condition, thought that it was not the same cat, that it was some dog, and they all went out carelessly to play; and then the cat—oh what a catch! Well, the cat made use of all its claws, for with them it caught more in one day than it could have in a hundred days. Ha! If the claws still remain, what does it matter if the clothing changes? Señores and señoras, credulous people should not judge by the exterior only. Think how many of these deceits have been discovered in [the City of] Mexico—for I do not want to talk about the whole world: revelations, ecstasies, trances, and all the lies and falsity for applause, for profit, and you might even say for turpitude. God will disclose this kind of thing!

La segunda especie de superticiones, que consiste solo en el modo, es quando aunque reverenciamos a nuestro verdadero Dios, o sus santos, pero es ofreciendole un culto superfluo, impropio, y vano, que ni sirve para la gloria de Dios, ni para excitar la piedad, y la devocion. Pongo por exemplo, que para conseguir, lo que pedimos, se ha de encender tanto numero de velas, deste, o de aquel tamaño, y no mas, ni menos Conc Trid. sess. 22, Decr de ob. & evit en Miss Sacr.[8] y a eso quieren que este obligada la mano de Dios para favoresernos:

quien no ve que esto es superticion: que para tener buen parto la preñada ha de oir una Misa en pie y no de rodias. ¡Ay tal engaño! y porque la oyga de rodias dexara Dios de favorserla. Que ha de ser la Misa de un sacerdote que se llame Juan.[9] ¡Ay tal unigaridad [vulgaridad]! Y si se llama Pedro o Francisco, dixara por eso de ser Sacerdote? que se han de rezar tanto numero de oraciones, y ni una mas ni menos: ¡Ay tales cuentos de viejas!

Anden, Señora, Regla general, en poniendo la devocion para que valga ha de ser a tal hora en tal dia con tantas velas, con tantas oraciones, etc., todo esto es superticion y sera pecado venial; sino es, que por haserce con desprecio de los ritos de la iglecia o con escandolo, lo hasen pecado mortal (Divus Thomas [Aquinas, *Summa Theologiae*] 2–2, q. 91, art. D Thom 2.2.Q.O.2. Art 2;[10] Laym t.2.l.4. tr.10. c.1;[11] Thom Sanch.[12] apud tamb.[13] fagundez 5. ad Ep 6)[14] como seria tambien pecado mortal si la musica, que

---

8. The Council of Trent's "Decree on What Is to Be Observed and What Is to Be Avoided in Celebrating Mass—Decretum de Observandis et Evitandis in Celebratione Missae" notes: "Finally, lest any room be made for superstition, there should be decrees and penalties announced to keep priests from celebrating [Mass] at any but the suitable hours and from using any other rites, ceremonies, or prayers except those approved by the church and accepted due to frequent praiseworthy use. Priests should rid the church of any set number of masses or candles, which smack more of some superstitious cult than of true religion." *Canones et Decreta Concilii Tridentini* (Madrid: Gabriel de Leon, 1662), pp. 176-77. Sánchez, *Opus Morale*, no. 7, p. 304, also refers to this decree of the Council of Trent.

9. In New Mexico, anyone named Juan or Juana was reputed to have special powers against witches; see Marc Simmons, *Witchcraft in the Southwest* (Lincoln: University of Nebraska Press, 1980), pp. 47-49; Nasario García, *Recuerdos de los Viejitos—Tales of the Ro Grande* (Albuquerque: University of New Mexico Press, 1987), pp. 166, 215-18. But the source of the sermon's reference to the priest named John is doubtless, directly or indirectly, Laymann (note 11) or Sánchez, *Opus Morale*, 12), who says at no. 4, p. 304: "Exemplum autem prioris cultus superflui est . . . audiendae missae Sacerdotis, qui tali nomine appelletur, v.g. Ioannes—An example of this first kind of superfluous worship is . . . hearing mass said by a priest named some particular name, for instance John." Fagúndez, *In Quinque Priora*, refers only to "a priest of some certain name" (no. 5, p. 176).

10. The text says on one line "D. Thom. 2. 2. q. 0" and on the next line "1. art 2." This may well be a copyist's error for "2. 2. q. 91, art. 2," assuming that the copyist was more accurate than usual in his rendering of Latin abbreviations.

The second species of superstition, which consists wholly in the *manner*, occurs when, although we reverence our true God or His saints, we rather offer Him an improper, superfluous, and vain devotion which does not give any glory to God and does nothing to arouse our piety and devotion. Take for instance when in order to get what we want, we have to light a certain number of candles of such and such a size and no more and no fewer (Council of Trent, session 22, Decr. de ob. et evit. in Miss. Sacr.)[8] and by doing so we hope to force the hand of God to grant us a favor.

And who does not see that this is a superstition, that in order to achieve an easy childbirth, the pregnant woman has to hear one mass standing up and not kneeling? Oh, such a fraud! And if she hears it on her knees, why should God refuse to favor her? What about a mass by a priest named Juan?[9] Oh, such a vulgarity! And if he is named Pedro or Francisco, does he cease for that reason to be a priest? Or that such and such a number of prayers have to be said, not one more or less? Oh, such old wives' tales!

People usually go about, Señora, supposing that a devotion in order to be efficacious has to be performed at such and such an hour on such and such a day of the week, with such and such a number of candles, with such and such prayers, and so forth. All this is superstition, and it's a venial sin unless it goes so far as to hold church rites up to derision or to give scandal, and then it becomes a mortal sin. (Divus Thomas [Aquinas, *Summa Theologiae*] 2–2, q. 91, art. 2;[10] Laymann tom. 2, bk 4, tract 10, ch. 1;[11] Thomás Sánchez[12] apud [Tommaso] Tamburini;[13] Fagúndez, 5 ad Ep. 6).[14]

This article states that since humans ought to praise God aloud and in public so as both to reinforce their own devotion and to edify others, music is a most suitable addition to the spoken word. This whole set of references is more appropriate to what follows than to what precedes it.

11. Laymann, *Theologia Moralis Quinque*, 1:733-34, names the sacrifice of the Pascal Lamb and the practice of other Jewish ceremonies as implying that the Messiah (the Christ) has not yet come.

12. Lib. 1, ch. 37, nos. 7, 9, 11, and 12, pp. 304-5. Tamburini quotes Sánchez with regard to faking relics, faking miracles, playing or singing inappropriate music in church, and fasting on Sundays.

13. Tamburini, *Opera Omnia*, vol. 1, p. 66; lib. 2, ch. 6, no.1, divides superstition in the broad sense into worship of a creature as God (idolatry, magic, divination, vain observance, and witchcraft) and giving God an inappropriate worship (superstition in the strict sense), which might be either basically false (Jewish or Muslim rites) or true but superfluous, such as adding prayers to the Mass (only a venial sin unless it involves serious irreverence or contempt), playing corrupt music or singing profane songs in church, creating false relics, falsely claiming miracles or favors, or fasting on Sundays. Tamburini cites Sánchez three times.

14. Fagúndez, *In Quinque Priora*, pp. 175-80; lib. 1, ch. 34, nos. 1-15. Fagúndez mentions Jewish ceremonies (nos. 3, 15), Muslim ceremonies (no. 15), false relics and miracles (nos. 3, 15), exact number and color or candles (no. 5), exact number of prayers (no. 5), mass before sunup (no. 5), and mass by a priest of some certain name (no. 5). The Latin abbreviation "5 ad Ep. 6" seems to refer to Paul's Epistle to the Ephesians 5:6, "Let no one seduce you with empty words, on account of which the wrath of God comes upon the children of unbelief."

/15

se introduxo en la iglecia, para alentar con espirituales jubilos el fervor y piedad de los corazones,[15] hubiese quien la profañara con sonecillos provocativos de lascivia pues tal atrevimientos avia de aver? Bueno es que quede dicho cantantes et psallentes en cordibus vestris Domino nos dize San Pablo; "audiate bac": espone San Geronimo: "quibus pesallendi in Ecclesia officium est, Deo non voce, sed corde pesallendum, ne en Ecclesia tebeatralis modali audiantur, et cantica."[16] En la yglesia no se pueden tocar los sones que se tocan en los teatros.[17] Miren, como tendrian los santos por culto suyo esas musicas, que se avian introducido, y esas danzas en los que llamaban incendios?

Este, pues, que aun las obras de piedad, y de devocion las podemos viciar, y haserlas superticiosas por el modo, ó con lo falso, y mentiroso de las seremonias, ó con lo superfluo, vano, o ilegitimo. Quereis quitaros de peligros? Pues seguir siempre las devociones, las oraciones, los cultos que estan aflentados ya con el uso comun dela yglesia, no ande buscando novedades, que siempre la novedad es peligrosa, unos modos de devociones particulares y esquisitos. Paraque asi tenemos tantos tan aprobados, tan seguros, y tan ciertos. . . .

—*fin*—

15. Thomas Aquinas, *Summa Theologiae* II-II, q. 91, 2 ad 2 gives a correct reply to an objection he had posed at the beginning of the article which used the quotation from Jerome in our footnote 16. The use of music "non propter devotionem excitandam—not for the sake of arousing [appropriate] devotion" is forbidden in church.

16. St. Jerome, *Commentarium in Epistolam ad Ephesios* [5:19] *Patrilogium Latinum* (Paris: J.-P. Migne, 1866), 7:561-62: "Audiant hi quibus psallendi in ecclesia officium est, Deo non voce, sed corde cantandum; nec tragoedorum modum gutter et fauces dulci medicamine colliniendas, ut in ecclesia theatrales moduli audiantur et cantica—Let those whose task it is to sing songs in the church pay attention to this, that God is to be sung to not with the voice [only] but with the heart; nor should the throat and mouth be defiled with a sweet medicine according to the practice of tragic actors so that theatrical ditties and songs should be heard in the church." Aquinas quotes this passage in *Summa Theologiae* II-II, q. 91, 2, obj. 2, as does Sánchez, *Opus Morale*, in no. 7, p. 304.

17. A common Anglo accusation against New Mexican church music was that the musicians played the same songs in church that they had played the night before at the fandango. Perhaps the critics had no better an ear for music than President Ulysses Grant, who maintained that he only recognized two pieces of music; one was "Pop Goes the Weasel" and the other one wasn't.

Just so, it would also be a mortal sin if the music which was played in church, instead of encouraging with spiritual joy the fervor and piety of hearts,[15] instead profaned the place with little songs that provoke lust—but what insolence such a person would have! There's a good old saying, "Cantantes et psallentes in cordibus vestris Domino—Singing songs and psalms in your hearts to the Lord" [Eph. 5:19], St. Paul tells us. "Audiant haec," St. Jerome explains, "quibus psallendi in Ecclesia officium est, Deo non voce sed corde psallendum; ne . . . in Ecclesia theatrales moduli audientur et cantica—Let them listen to this, those people whose duty it is to sing in the church: God is not to be praised with voice [alone] but with the heart; nor . . . should theatrical ditties and songs be heard in the church."[16] In the church the same songs cannot be performed as are performed in the theaters.[17] Look, how could the saints like for their feast day those concerts which have been introduced, and those dances, in those so-called conflagrations?

Let it be known, then, that even works of piety and devotion can become corrupt and turn into superstitions either by the false manner or the fraudulent manner of the ceremonies or by some excessive, vain, or illegitimate manner. You want to be freed from dangers? Well, always follow the devotions, the prayers, the cults which have been encouraged for a long time by the common usage of the church. Don't go around looking for novelties, for innovation is always dangerous, [or looking for] various modes of peculiar and exquisite devotion. And it is for that reason that we have so many that are approved, secure, and authentic . . .

—end—

Manuel Antonio Garcia del Valle

In an 1833 letter to the famous Padre Martínez of Taos, the author of this sermon introduced himself as "fray Manuel Antonio García del Valle of the regular observance of Our Holy Father Saint Francis, former master of philosophy in the College of Tlatelolco in Mexico, exempt definitor, general preacher, honored father of the Province of the Holy Gospel of Mexico, former vice-custos, former custos, and present custos of the Custody of the Conversion of Saint Paul of New Mexico." Born in the City of Mexico about 1784, García came to New Mexico in 1810 as a newly-ordained Franciscan priest and spent time in various of the Pueblo churches, being stationed in Nambé when he delivered the sermon printed here. He died at Sandía Pueblo in June 1834.[1]

In 1821, the pastor of the parish church of San Francisco de Asís in Santa Fe, Cura don Francisco Ignacio de Madariaga, invited the Franciscan to deliver the solemn sermon on Good Friday afternoon. He probably chose him both because he had a reputation as an excellent preacher and because, as a Franciscan, he had inherited the mainstream medieval spirituality of Bernard of Clairvaux and Francis of Assisi, a spirituality that focused on the humanity of Christ both at birth and especially during his passion and death. This sermon is especially remarkable because, at the end, it turns into the ritual text of the very moving ceremony of dismantling the life-size crucifix set up in the sanctuary: removing Pilate's inscription, the crown of thorns, the three nails, and the body of Christ, and bringing each item to the statue of Our Lady of Solitude, the bereaved Mother, thereby forming the tableau known as the Pietà.

---

1. The letter, in the Ritch Paper microfilms, reel 8, pp. 126, 190, appoints Martínez temporary director of the Third Order of Saint Francis in northern New Mexico; see Thomas J. Steele, S.J., and Rowena A. Rivera, *Penitente Self-Government* (Santa Fe: Ancient City Press, 1985), pp. 10-11n11; William Wroth, *Images of Penance, Images of Mercy* (Norman: University of Oklahoma Press, 1991), pp. 172-73. In a province of an exempt religious order, a definitor is one of several assistants to the provincial superior who share with him in governance.
John Kessell, *Kiva, Cross, and Crown* (Washington: National Park Service, 1979), pp. 426-28, 503; fray Angélico Chávez, *Archives of the Archdiocese of Santa Fe* (Washington: Academy of American Franciscan History, 1957), p. 247.

Such dramatic episodes were widely practiced in New Spain. In his recent *Images of Penance, Images of Mercy*, William Wroth describes such a combination of preaching and ritual in New Spain with the help of a 1596 book by the Dominican fray Agustín Dávila Padilla that recounts the Good Friday events in the Dominican church in Mexico City:

> On Christ the Lord's cross hangs a very much venerated image.... To the right of the holy crucifix stands an image of the Queen of the Angels [as Our Lady of Solitude] dressed in mourning, with only a linen cloth in her hands as if to wipe the tears from her face.... All this augments the people's devotion when the deposition is performed.... The preacher proposes some points about the cross and Christ's death as an introduction.... Then he begs permission from the Queen of the Angels to take her son down; he asks in very tender words with which God inspires him.... When the nail is removed from one hand, the arm hangs loose and is held only by a white cloth that a priest has tied around it hold it up.[2]

Early nineteenth-century inventories of the parish church in Santa Fe described the main statues involved, precisely those necessary for presenting a New Mexican passion play:

> An image of the Crucified Lord the size of a man, and on either side a Lady of Sorrows and a Lady of Solitude somewhat smaller, all three of them statues.... A statue of the Holy Buried Body [of Christ], about the size of a man.[3] ... A statue of Jesus the Nazarene a vara and three quarters (58 inches) tall.[4]

---

2. Wroth, pp. 20-23, 47-48, 74, 77, 174-76; Fray Agustín Dávila Padilla, O.P., *Historia de la Fundacion y Discurso de la Provincia de Santiago de México, de la Orden de Predicadores* (1596, reprint Mexico City: Editorial Academia Literaria, 1955), pp. 563-64.

3. This is probably the statue seen by Josiah Gregg in the 1830s and described in *Commerce of the Prairies*: "An image of Christ large as life, nailed to a huge wooden cross, is paraded through the streets, in the midst of an immense procession, accompanied by a glittering array of carved images, representing the Virgin Mary, Mary Magdalen, and several others; while the most notorious personages of antiquity ... may be seen bestriding splendidly caparisoned horses, in the breathing reality of flesh and blood. Taking it all in all, this spectacle ... [is] calculated to produce impressions of a most confused description, in which regret and melancholy may be said to form no inconsiderable share" (Cleveland: Arthur H. Clark, 1905), 20:48.

4. These statues and their wardrobes are tallied in the 1817-18 inventories of don Juan Bautista Ladrón Niño de Guevara and recur, usually word for word, in those of don Agustín Fernández de San Vicente in 1826; Archives of the Archdiocese of Santa Fe, Accounts LXXII, microfilm 45:11-12, 21-22; Accounts LXIV and LXV, 45:488-89, 500.

And until the 1950s, the people of the Tomé parish performed a full-scale passion play in and around the church on the town plaza, then in recent years they resumed it under Edwin Berry's guidance on the nearby Cerro de Tomé. Hence on Good Friday afternoon in 1821, when fray Manuel Antonio García del Valle began to read his sermon, no one would have been surprised to see that the sanctuary of Saint Francis of Assisi Church in Santa Fe was decorated to resemble Calvary just after Jesus died. The life-size Santo Entierro wore a crown of thorns and was held to the cross by three nails, the I.N.R.I. dangled above his head, and his bereaved mother stood nearby in tears.

The sermon's theology is careful and correct enough, not highly technical. It is very rich, especially because of the two dozen direct quotations from the Bible—plus an even greater number of biblical allusions—all providing a solid scriptural foundation for the end, an imaginative dramatization that will go well beyond the inspired text in order to bring the members of the congregation into a very close—and very medieval—union of empathy with the Sorrowful Mother and her dead Son.

For an older description of the Santa Fe holdings, see fray Francisco Atanasio Domínguez, *The Missions of New Mexico, 1776*, trans., ed. Eleanor B. Adams and fray Angélico Chávez (Albuquerque: University of New Mexico Press, 1956), p. 18. A recently-discovered manuscript account of the Albuquerque parish in the same year as the Santa Fe sermon describes items in the San Felipe Neri west transept evidently intended for a passion play; see Thomas J. Steele, S.J., "Alburquerque in 1821: Padre Leyva's Descriptions," *New Mexico Historical Review* 70 (1995), 51. San Miguel Church in Socorro used to own a life-size Santo Entierro and a life-size Soledad now in the International Folk Art Museum, Museum of New Mexico.

Viernes Santo

Unus militum lancea latus eius aperuit, et continuo exivit sanguis, et aqua.
San Juan al Cap 19. v. 34.

¡Que recuerdo, CC nos trayen a la memoria estas palabras de mi texto! Jesus padeciendo, y muerto en el arbol de una Cruz, Pasemos con el pensamiento y concideracion hasta el Golgota ó Monte Calvario; ¿Que descubren nuestros ojos en aquel funesto, triste, y lugubre lugar? Por todos sus angulos se escuchan gritos, lamentos y vozes de dolor. Aqui la Sangre, lagrimas, y crueles dolores del mejor Hijo; la compacion de una, y mas la fina de las Marias, la rabia de los enemigos, Escribas, y Fariseos, los Ayes de unas mugeres piadosas, la consternacion [de los] Discipulos, las blasfemias e improperios que. . . . Hebreos, la voz de un Ladron que pide. . . . -gre que solicita clemencia, la voz de m. . . . vuestros que provoca la Justicia Divina. . . . vinemos pasar en el citio en que mi Justo. . . . -do.

Si los sagrados Historiadores no. . . . de perpetuar en el mundo la memor[ia]. . . . -fante, si la Religion Sancta que proclama. . . . -na, de un modo que no permite la menor du[da]. . . . jamas huviera podido persuadirce, que el M. . . . de los Sanctos debia morir sobre la cumbre a. . . . que ha un lugar destinado al suplicio. . . . quantos? ¿Que un hombre Dios debia aca. . . . mortal por el tormento, y oprobrio del. . . . se atreviera a excogitas que sus enem[igos]. . . . impios, que aun no contentos con. . . . todavia vengasen el costado de. . . . cadaver?—Esto es no obstante, lo que el Evangelio nos representa; *Vnus militum &c*

Si se me permite el discurrir, si se concede ami corto ingenio el conferir sobre el Mysterio de la muerte del Amabilisimo Jesus, que el dia de hoy veneramos; me parece que en él es donde se hace aquella maravillosa alianza de que habló el Profeta Coronado David: quando dixo: que la Justicia y la Misericordia se havian reunido, y que por un feliz enlace se hallaban, una, y otra enteramente satisfechas: *Justicia, et Pax osculate sunt* (Psalm. 84 [85]:11).

Desde el instante que peco el hombre quebrantando el precepto de Dios huvo entre esta Justicia, y Divina Misericordia, una especie de combate. La una estaba armada. . . . a nosotros, disponiendose á vengar los inte. . . . reparar su gloria, por una eterna perdi. . . . -sin olvidar la misma gloria, ni. . . . Todo-Poderozo, compasiva de nuestra. . . . la espada, que amenasaba

Good Friday

One of the soldiers opened his side with his lance, and immediately there came forth blood and water. John 19:34

What recollections, my fellow Christians, these words of my text introduce into our minds! Jesus suffering and hanging dead on the tree of the cross! Let us travel by meditation and contemplation to Golgotha, also called Mount Calvary. What do our eyes see in this sad, ill-fated, and mournful place? From every direction come the cries, laments, and voices of sorrow. Here the blood, tears, and cruel sorrows of the best Son, the compassion of one of the Marys, the finest of them, the fury of enemies, scribes and Pharisees, the lamentations of a few pious women, the consternation of the disciples, the blasphemies and insults the . . . . [The rest of page is torn so that only half of each line remains. The passage seems to describe the voice of the good thief and the voices of Christ's enemies and to emphasize our need to remember what Christ did for us by his death] . . . corpse?—This is, notwithstanding, what the Gospel describes for us: "One of the soldiers etc."

If I may be allowed to elaborate, if it be permitted to my limited understanding to treat of the mystery of the death of the most beloved Jesus which we reverence today, it seems to me that here we find that wonderful union of which the royal prophet David spoke when he said, "Justice and Mercy have met"; and by a happy marriage we find both the one and the other completely fulfilled: "Justice and Peace have kissed" (Ps. 84 [85]:11).

From the moment man sinned by breaking the precept of God, there had been a sort of combat between justice and divine mercy. The one took weapons against us, ready to take revenge . . . .[Again, half of each line for the remainder of the page is torn away. The text speaks of God's decision at the time of the crucifixion to restore his glory, injured by human sin, and asserts that both the justice and the mercy of God were at work in the death of Christ.] [My sermon will treat] Jesus Christ dead upon the cross as a victim of God's justice (first part), and as a victim of the mercy of the same God (second part). This will be the subject we will meditate on, if you grant me your esteemed attention and if at the same time you assist me in attaining the graces of the Divine Spirit, directing to the Holy Wood of the Cross the words the Holy Church provides us this very day, greeting it by reciting: "O Crux Ave."[5]

a nuestra. . . . el golpe á que estabamos expuestos, . . . lo de reconciliarlas? ¡O Secreto. . . . prudencia humana! ¡O Abismo de la. . . . y concejos del Altisimo! El gran medio SS. y. . . . [Jesu]cristo aun desde la Eternidad, y verifica. . . . [ple]nitud de los tiempos una que J.C. Hijo de Dios é. . . . [h]ombre, y verdadero Dios y hombre, derrama . . . . diose su vida, muriose, y con su muer[te]. . . . [m]ismo tiempo sacrificado a la Justicia del. . . . es, y a la Misericordia del Dios de la. . . . -das; J.C. muerto en la Cruz como victima de la Justicia de Dios *1ª. parte* y como victima de la Misericordia del mismo Dios *2ª. parte*. Este sera el asunto que meditaremos, si me dais vuestra respetable atencion, y al mismo tiempo me ayudais a conseguir las gracias del Espiritu Divino dirixiendo a ese madero Sancto de la Cruz las vozes con las quales la Santa Yglesia el dia presente, la saluda diciendo: O Crux Ave[5]

Unus militum aperuit latus eius, et continuo exivit sanguis, et agua. Joanes Cap et v. jam citatis.

Si, despues del nacimiento del mundo—Decia SS. que si despues del nacimiento del mundo fue quando el hombre rebelde, y delinquente se atrevio á rebelar contra el orden de su Criador, y su Dios, despues de este primer pecado, esperaba la Justicia del Cielo una victima capaz de aplacarle, y pedia un Sacrificio digno de la Magestad del Señor profanada, y ultrajada. Aunque en la serie de tantos siglos como pasaron despues de esta caida fatal á toda la humana naturaleza, ofrecian los hombres diversos sacrificios, y holocaustos á Dios para reconocimiento de su Grandeza, y para honrrarle. Mas aquellas hostias eran solo, ó fructos de la tierra, ó viles animales; tales sacrificios no eran proporcionados a la dignidad del Señor cuyo honor se procuraba reparar, y cuyos intereses se intentaba indemnizar. Solo una persona divina, solo la sangre, y muerte de un Dios podia borrar, y lavar enteramente la ofenza echa a un Dios. Esto fue lo que se verificó en el Calvario; y aqui fue donde esta Justicia tan rigorosa é inflexible en defender sus derechos, hallo al fin toda la satisfaccion, que por tanto tiempo havia exigido sin haverla recivido, y que le era por tantos titulos de vida. ¿Que victima, se le sacrificó sobre el Altar de la Cruz? un hombre Dios el Hijo Eterno de Dios que era igual a su Padre y que poseia como él toda la plenitud de la Divinidad; *In ipso inhabitat omnis plenitudo Divinitatis* (Colos. 2:9); como lo testifica el Apostol de las Naciones. Desde el instante de su

---

5. One of many variants of the stanza "O Crux Ave Spes Unica," a later addition to the sixth-century hymn "Vexilla Regis Prodeunt" by Fortunatus, is part of Good Friday Vespers: "O Cross! hail, only hope / In this time of suffering: / Grant grace to the devout, / And forgive the sins of the guilty."

[it is said]

"One of the soldiers opened his side with his lance, and immediately there came forth blood and water." John, chapter and verse as above.

Yes, after the creation of the world—Yes, as I was saying, after the birth of the world, it happened that man rebelled and in his delinquency dared rebel against the commandment of his Creator and God; it happened that after this first sin, the heavenly justice awaited a victim able to placate it, and it demanded a sacrifice worthy of the majesty of the Lord which had been profaned and outraged. In the course of so many centuries as passed after this fall, fatal for all human nature, men indeed offered various sacrifices and holocausts to God acknowledging his greatness and honoring him. But those victims were merely the fruits of the earth or brute animals, and such sacrifices were scarcely proportional to the dignity of the Lord to whose honor they were trying to make reparation and in whose interests they were trying to make compensation. Only a divine person, only the blood and death of a God, could blot out and wholly wash clean the offense committed against a God. This came to pass on Calvary. For it was here that this justice so rigorous and inflexible in vindicating its rights finally found the complete satisfaction which for so long a time it had demanded without having received it, and which was due for so many reasons.

What victim was sacrificed to God upon the altar of the cross? A man-God, the eternal Son of God who was the equal of his Father and who possessed like him the whole plenitude of the Godhead: "In him dwells all the fullness of the Divinity" (Col. 2:9), as the Apostle of the Gentiles attests. From the instant of his incarnation he began this great sacrifice, for he only descended to earth in the capacity of Victim, he only took a mortal body so as to pay homage to the Creator of the universe and offer himself as a holocaust.

In the Temple at Jerusalem he continued and perfected, as it were, this very sacrifice when Simeon took him in his arms, presented by the hand of Mary, the illustrious mother and wonderful creature. Nevertheless, this pledge was no more than the morning sacrifice, and now the evening sacrifice is before us, that is to say, the one in which the victim should altogether be consumed, a purpose to which our loving Redeemer directed all his actions, steps, and intentions, so that in this way he might make reparation for all the glory of the Lord and restore the rights of his justice.

Encarnacion empezo este gran sacrificio, pues solo bajo a la tierra en qualidad de victima, y solo vistio de un cuerpo mortal para tributar homenage al Criador del universo, y ofrecersele en holocausto.

En el Templo de Jerusalen continuo, y como que perfeccionó este mismo sacrificio, quando Simeon lo llevó en sus brazos, presentado por las manos de Maria Ynclita madre y admirable criatura. Empero esto no era mas que el sacrificio matutino, y ahora se nos presenta el vespertino; esto és, aquel en el qual la victima debe consumirse toda entera; puncto a donde se dirijian todos los echos, pasos, y designios de Nuestro Amoroso Redemptor; para por esto reparar toda la gloria del Señor y restablecer los derechos de su Justicia.

¿Que deuda sujetó a este Cordero de Dios a este Cordero sin mancha, a esta inexorable justicia? ¿De que ofenza pudo ser culpable? ¿Que causa le atraxo toda la colera del Cielo, y le expuso a un oprobio, y muerte semejante? ¡Ah, CC. Este és un Mysterio que no debeis ignorar, y que supungo que estais en el impuesto, pues es el fundamento y base principal de nuestra Religion y nuestra creencia. Este hombre Dios que ahora contemplamos exanime, era por naturaleza, la Santidad por Exelencia; en la Celestial morada recive las adoraciones de las Angelicas Ynteligencias y demas tropas predestinadas; aun en este valle de lagrimas en que havito entre los hombres no conoiso [conocio] el mal sino era para confundirlo; y en fin este es a quien por mas de una vez se da aquel publico testimonio que resono por todas las riberas del Jordan, y cumbre de Tabor, que decia: Este mi hijo querido, y el objecto de mis complacencias; *hic est filius meus in quo mihi bene complacui* (Math. 17:5); A pesar de esto, siendo este Salvador Sancto por si mismo para la expiacion de la culpa tomó la forma de pecador; no haviendo jamas cometido pecado, y aun siendo incapaz de cometerlo, quiso no obstante, llevar sobre su cuerpo todas nuestras culpas; *Qui pecata nostra ipse pertulit in corpore suo* (1 Petr. 2:24): nos ensena [enseña] la carta del Principe de los Apostolos, San Pedro. Su Eterno Padre le cubrio de todas ellas, y por tanto mirandolo como pecador, y como satisfactor de ellas tomo con su muerte, é ignomias la venganza que estas iniquidades merecian; *Posuit in eo iniquitatem omnium nostrum* (Isai. 53:6); asi lo havia vatisinado Ysaias.

¿Como se presenta en el Calvario? ¿Como el garante de todas las Naciones, y hombres; De modo que podemos comparle [compararle] a aquella nube que conducia a los Ysraelitas en el Desierto, que estando brillante, y clara de una parte estaba enteramente obscura, y tenebrosa de la opuesta. Testamento bajo este aspecto tan asombroso le concidera hoy el Cielo, y bajo esta lepra del pecado le mira hoy la Justicia de Dios como un objeto digno de todas sus venganzas. Por esto se arma contra él, le persigue espada en mano, y pronuncia contra el la sentencia de muerte, que lla sufrio.

What debt obliged this Lamb of God, this Lamb without blemish, to this inexorable justice? Of what offense could he have been guilty? What cause drew down on him all the wrath of Heaven and laid him open to disgrace, to such a death as that? Ah my dear Christian people, this is a mystery of which you should not be ignorant and which I am certain you are quite clear about, for it is the foundation and main base of our religion and our belief. This God-man whom we contemplate today in death was, by his nature, Holiness *par excellence*; in his heavenly dwelling he receives the adoration of the angelic intelligences and the other throngs of the predestined. Even in this valley of tears where he lived among men, he did not know evil except for the purpose of confounding it; and to sum up, this is the One for whom more than once God the Father gave public testimony which resounded on both sides of the Jordan and on the summit of Tabor when he said, "This is my beloved Son, the object of my satisfaction—here is my Son in whom I am very pleased" (Matt. 17:5). In spite of this, the Savior, since he was holy in and of himself, took for the expiation of sin the form of a sinner—never himself having committed sin, and indeed being unable to commit it—"He chose nevertheless to take upon his body all our transgressions, he who bore our sins in his body" (1 Pet. 2:24), as the letter of the Prince of the Apostles, Saint Peter, instructs us. His Eternal Father covered him with all of our sins and thereby, looking upon him as a sinner and as the Redeemer of those sins, took with his death and ignominy the vengeance those iniquities deserved: "He placed on him the iniquity of us all" (Isa. 53:6), as Isaiah prophesied.

How does he present himself on Calvary? As the master of all the nations and races, so that we can compare him to the cloud that conducted the Israelites in the desert, the cloud which though brilliant and luminous on the one side was so dark and shadowy on the other (Exod. 14:20). The Testament under this amazing aspect Heaven considers him today, and under this leprosy of sin the justice of God looks on him today as an object worthy of all its vengeance. Therefore Justice arms himself against [his Son], he pursues him sword in hand, and he pronounces against him the sentence of death that he suffered.

That victim of whom Saint Paul wrote to the Hebrews was he on whom all the sins of the people were loaded so he might expiate them, and they drove him outside into the fields to kill him and consume him with fire.[6] And what was this, says the same Apostle, but the image and picture of what in the fullness of time is realized in the Anointed of the Lord, that is, Jesus Christ? They take him from the city, they lead him to Golgotha, the stage where the justice of the Eternal Father awaits his death and degradation to satisfy the decree of reprobation against stained and delinquent mankind.

Aquella victima de que hablaba San Pablo a los Hebreos era sobre la qual se ponian todas las iniquidades del Pueblo para expiarlas, y por esto la arrojaban fuera del campo para darle muerte, y consumirla en el fuego;[6]

¿Y que era esto dice el mismo Apostol, sino una imagen y figura de lo que en la plenitud de los tiempos se versa en el ungido del Señor, esto es J.C.? Le sacan de la ciudad, le subir al Golgota, que es el teatro donde le espera la Justicia de su Padre Eterno para con su muerte, y afrenta aplacar el decreto de reprobacion contra el hombre, manchado, y delinquente.

No es el furor solo de los Ministros, la crueldad de los Soldad(os), y la rabia de los Escribas; los que aqui obran es tambien la Justicia de Dios. Asi los sienten muchos interpretes de texto sagrado.

¿O Justicia de mi Dios! Aun no basta esto? ¿Aun no estais satisfecho? ¿Sobre que parte de este Sagrado Cuerpo herireis, que no este toda cubierta de heridas? Ved sus ojos del todo apagados, su boca, y su semblante acardenalado, el pecho despedazado, ved sus pies y manos enclavados convertidos en manantiales de sangre. Mas la Justicia del Padre aun decreta para complemento de sus designios adorables, que haviendo expirado, lleno de dolor, su costado sea razgado con una cruel lanza. *Vnus militum etc.*

¡Que terror SS. que consternacion? solo el aspecto de esta Justicia del Padre sobre su hijo divino basto para poner toda la naturaleza en movimiento; La tierra tiembla, se rasga el velo del Templo, el Sol eclipsa sus luces, la luna muestrase roja, las piedras chocan unas con otras, parece que la noche há tendido su negro manto, todo se halla desconsertado; De suerte que al Senador Areopajita, ahora San Dionicio le obligo a pronunciar esta sentencia; O el universo se disuelve, ó su Autor padece.[7] Habeis escuchado como J.C. fue en su muerte victima del Padre Eterno; vais a oir, como tambien fue victima de Misericordia, que es mi

2ª Pte.

Es caracter de las obras de Dios y de todos designios, que formaron siempre acompañados de su misericordia, para lo que respecta a la salvacion, y predestinacion del hombre. *Universe viae Domini, Misericordia* (Psalm. 24 [25]:10) asi se expresa David. De tal suerte observa este Profeta, que aun en

---

6. The Petrine and synoptic writings of the New Testament use the four "Songs of the Suffering Servant of Yahweh" in Isa. 42-53 as a basis for verbalizing the vicarious redemptive death of Jesus. Here, the preacher reads both a scapegoat connotation and a little of Heb. 9:28 into Heb. 13:12, which echoes Isa. 53:11, the last of the four Songs of the Suffering Servant of Yahweh.

7. Directly or indirectly, Fray Manuel Antonio got this from the *Legenda Aurea* of Jacobus de Voragine, who relied on Peter Comestor's *Historia Scholastica* (Ch. 175; *PL* 198:1631). The tradition confuses three different figures: Dionysius the Areopagite, a convert St. Paul made in Athens

The fury derives not only from the executioners, the cruelty of the soldiers, and the hatred of the scribes, for the dynamic at work here is the justice of God. Such is the sense of the majority of the interpreters of Holy Writ.

Oh the justice of my God! Even this is not enough? Are you not yet satisfied? What part of the sacred body would you wound that is not already totally covered with wounds? See his eyes totally blinded, his mouth and his countenance lacerated, his chest torn into. See his feet and hands pierced with nails and turned into fountains of blood. Moreover, the justice of the Father even decrees, as a complement to its adorable designs, that having died in great pain, his side should be torn open by a cruel lance: "One of the soldiers etc."

What fear, my listeners, what consternation! The mere frown of the Father's justice upon his divine Son was enough to set all of nature into motion. The earth quakes, the veil of the temple tears, the sun darkens its light, the moon turns red, the rocks grate one upon another, the night seems to have spread her black mantle, everything is distraught in such a way that the senator of the Areopagus, now known as Saint Dionysius, was compelled to pronounce this judgment: "Either the universe is destroying itself, or its Author is suffering."[7] You have heard how Jesus Christ was in his death the victim of the Eternal Father. We shall now hear how he was also the victim of mercy, which is my

Second Part.

It is the character of God's works and all his designs for the salvation and destiny of mankind to appear always accompanied by his mercy. "All the paths of the Lord are mercy" (Ps. 24 [25]:10), as David states. Therefore, this prophet observes that even in the midst of his greatest anger and most severe chastisements of his justice, he does not forget this infinite mercy. Listen to the prophet Habakkuk: "Even when you are angry, you do not forget your great mercy" (Hab. 3:2). Only from Hell is it absent, only thither does his benevolence not flow, for those unfortunate ones who have perished are incapable of redemption: "For in Hell there is no

---

(Acts 17:34); St. Denys of Paris, a dim figure said to have converted that area in the late third century; and Pseudo-Dionysius, a Greek Neo-Platonic theologian of the fifth or sixth century who pretended to be the first-century Areopagite so successfully that his writings had an inordinate authority for about a thousand years. Thomas Aquinas spent about half his psychic energy confuting him. The quotation from Pseudo-Dionysius serves as a commentary on Matt. 27:45, 51-53.

See also Steele and Rivera, *Penitente Self-Government*, pp. 196-97, Appendix F, "Some Tinieblas Symbolism."

medio de su mayor enojo, y los mas severos castigos de su Justicia no olvida esta infinita Misericordia; oidselo al Propheta Habacú: Aun quando estuvieras airado, no olvidaras tu grande Misericordia—*Cum iratus fueris misericordie recordaveris* (Habac. 3:2); De solo el infierno esta separada solo alli no corren sus beneficencias, por ser incapaces de redempcion aquellos infelizes perecidos, Quia in inferno nulla es Redemptio, nos dice Job.[8] Mas por qualesquiera otra parte le és tan natural el manifestarse, que en todas las obras del Señor, siempre ha tenido la mejor parte. Sobre exede a sus juicios, su Misericordia, nos acuerda la Epistola de San Tiago: *Superexaltat Misericordia judicium* (Jacob. 2:13):

¿No es innegable que esta misericordia, si alguna ocasion ha derramado sus riquezas con abundancia fue en el Mysterio de la muerte de este Jesus? El hombre por si mismo era incapaz, ni por su esencia, de reparar la injuria cometida contra la Magestad del Altisimo. De donde se infiere por consequencia necesaria, que sin los meritos de un hombre Dios no podia salvarse. A esto vino J.C. este fue el fin de su Mission y el fruto de su muerte.

Este Verbo de Dios debia venir, y tomar una carne semejante a la nuestra. En esta carne mortal debia padecer, y morir; ¿pero como? Debia morir, mas en la supocision en un todo gratuito de su parte y de toda su eleccion, esto es, que queria salvar al mundo; Podia dexar al hombre en el estado de su perdicion, y por este medio escusarse de su Encarnacion, Pasion, Cruz, y muerte ignominiosa. Si SS. asi podia hacerlo, segun todas las leyes de su Justicia. Mas esto fue lo que no pudo veer su Misericordia, sin oponerse a ello; todas sus Caridad y Compacion se conmovieron: Entrañas tiene de Misericordia nos dice en el Santo Evangelio de San Lucas: *Viscera Misericordie* (Luc. 1:78): Siguio sus impulsos, y no pudo (si se permite decirlo asi) resistir a unos sentimientos tan tiernos;

Por lo que pudiendo elegir entre dos partidos, o el de abandonar la salvacion del hombre, ó el sujetar se él mismo a toda la infamia de un suplicio tan cruel; quiso mas bien rescatarnos, al precio de su Sangre, de su vida, y trabajos, que consentir en nuestra eterna desgracia. Su amor para con el hombre es infinito; Porque me amó, se entregó asi mismo por mi; exclama el Apostol: *Dilexit me, et tradidit seipsum por me* (Galat. 2:20): Preguntad al mismo San Pablo, que hizo J.C. en el Calvario donde le condujeron, los verdugos, y sus enemigos, quienes executaron en él con tanta barbarie, é inhumanidad las ordenes que havian recivido; Atender a su respuesta.

Ponen en la Cruz a este Mediador de los hombres, pero él entre tanto,

---

8. "For in the underworld there is no redemption"—a paraphrase of Job, no particular passage, Office of the Dead, response to 7th lesson of the 3rd nocturne of Matins.

redemption," as Job tells us.⁸ But on the other hand, this self-manifestation is so natural to him that in all the deeds of the Lord it always has been the greater part. His mercy always exceeds his judgments, as the Epistle of Saint James reminds us: "His mercy surpasses his justice" (James 2:13).

It is undeniable that this mercy, if on any occasion its riches have rained down in abundance, lay in the mystery of the death of this Jesus. Man in himself, by his very essence, is incapable of healing the insult committed against the majesty of the Most High. From this fact we can infer as a necessary consequence that, without the merits of a God-man, man could not be saved. For this came Jesus Christ; this was the purpose of his mission, and this was the fruit of his death.

This Word of God had to come and take a body like unto our own. In this mortal flesh he had to suffer and die. But how? He had to die, but on that premise it would be completely gratuitous on his part and altogether his own free choice—that is, he wanted to save the world. He could have left mankind in the state of damnation and by that means freed himself from his incarnation, passion, cross, and shameful death. Yes, thus he could have done, by all the rules of justice. But [mankind's damnation] was the kind of thing he could not in his mercy see without opposing himself to it: all his love and compassion were aroused. "He has bowels of mercy," Saint Luke tells us in his Holy Gospel, "Viscera Misericordiae" (Luke 1:78). He followed his impulses, and he simply could not (if I may be allowed to say it thus)—he *could* not resist feelings so tender.

Thus he was able to choose between two options, either to forgo the salvation of the human race or to subject himself to all the infamy of so cruel an execution. He truly preferred to rescue us at the cost of his blood, of his life and labors, rather than consent to our eternal ruin. His love for the human race is infinite. "For he loved me; he delivered himself over for me," exclaims the Apostle (Gal. 2:20). Ask Saint Paul what Jesus Christ was doing on Calvary whither he was led by the executioners and his enemies, who implemented against him, with such barbarity and inhumanity, the orders they had received. Listen to Paul's response: "They nail to the cross the Mediator of mankind, but he meanwhile, with an invisible hand, by an impulse of mercy, fastens to the cross the condemnation written against us. He blotted out and annulled with his blood and with his death the sentence condemning us, blotting out the document given against us, removing it and nailing it to his cross—deleting what was written against us, taking it out of the way, affixing it to the cross" (Col. 2:14). He gave his

con una mano invisible, y por un afecto de Misericordia, ligaba a ella, el proceso, escrito contra nosotros; borraba, y anulaba con su Sangre y con su Muerte, la Sentencia que nos condenaba; Borrando la escriptura otorgada contra nosotros, quitandola, y afigandola a su Cruz: *Delens quod adversus nos erat chrirographum, et ipsum tullit de medio, afingens illud cruci* (Colos. 2:14): Dio la vida, y con su muerte, nos dio, vida, remission, y remedio a todas nuestras culpas. Estando vosotros muertos en delitos, os vivifico, condonaros todos vuestros excesos: *Et vos cum mortui essetis in delictis, convivificavit donans vobis omnia delicta* (Colos. 2:13):

¿No debemos SS. admirarnos, de los prodigios de amor, y misericordia, que manifestó en aquella hora terminando su carrera, y consumando su Caridad para con los pecadores? Quanto mas se acercaba al fin de su vida, tanto mas se enternecia su corazon solo respiraba Misericordia.

En efecto, ¿quales fueron sus ultima palabras ya mui cerca de entregar su Espiritu en las manos de su Padre Eterno? El pedir perdon para sus atormentadores; conceder aun con ciertas palabras de juramento al buen Ladron que le pidio en su Reyno, confesando su Divinidad: *Memento mei cum veneris in Reinum tuum* (Luc. 23:43): *Amen, dico tibi quia mecum eris in Paradizum* (Joan. 19:26). Dexarles a los pecadores como en legado a su misma Madre que era lo que mas ama en este mundo *Ecce Mater tua Ecce Fillius tuus*;[9] Manifestar que aun apetecia el padecer mas por el remedio, de los desgraciados hijos de Eva.

¿No son todas pruebas convincentes, de su Caridad, Amor, y Misericordia para con los hijos del inobediente Adan? De esta suerte SS. amo Dios al mundo, que no dudo el darles a su mismo hijo unigenito, por Medianero, a pezar que en él tenia puesto todo el furor de la ira Divina pues que le veia encargado, y abrumado con el peso de tantas culpas agenas. *Sic Deus dilexit eos ut fillium suum etc*[10]

Mirad si con efecto en esta muerte dolorosima de mi Maestro Divino Jesus, no se halla la venganza contra el pecado, en el Padre Eterno, que lo vindica en la persona de su hijo, y la Clemencia, de este Pacientisimo Nazareno en beneficio de los hombres. He concluido.

Sole [Solo] me resta el dirijirme a vos, Aflixidisima Señora Madre y Virgen Ymmaculada, Criatura la mas llena de gracias, mas tambien la mas llena de tormentos, y dolores. Vuestro mayor desconsuelo és, el veer ese Deifico

---

9. García del Valle's citations are confused; he refers to Luke 23:43 and John 19:26 when he should refer to Luke 23:42 and John 19:26-27. The Spanish text that ends the paragraph, "los desgraciados hijos de Eva," strongly echoes a phrase from the traditional prayer "Dios te salve, Reina y Madre" ("Salve Regina—Hail Holy Queen"), "los desterrados [banished] hijos de Eva."

10. John 3:16: "God so loved the world that He gave His only-begotten Son, so that everyone who believes in Him will not perish but will have eternal life."

own life, and so by his death he has given us life, the remission and cure for all our sins. "When you were dead in your transgressions, he revived you, remitting all your excesses" (Col. 2:13).

We should not be surprised at these prodigies of love and mercy which Christ demonstrated in that final hour, ending his race while consummating his charity toward sinners? The nearer he came to the end of his life, the more his heart softened; it breathed only mercy.

And indeed, what were his final words immediately before he gave his spirit into the hands of his eternal Father? He begged pardon for his tormentors; he granted with a few words of solemn promise to the good thief who asked him . . . in his kingdom, acknowledging his divinity: "'Remember me when you come into your kingdom,'—'Amen I say to you that you will be with me in paradise.'" He left those sinners as a legacy to his own mother, the person he loved most in this world: "Behold your mother. Behold your son."[9] He showed that he still desired to suffer further as a remedy for the wretched children of Eve.

Are not all of these convincing proofs of his charity, love, and mercy toward those children of the disobedient Adam? In this manner, dear people, God loved the world. He did not hesitate to give his only-begotten true Son as Mediator, even though on him would fall all the fury of the divine wrath, for God saw him laden and overcome under the burden of the many sins of so many others. "God so loved them that [he gave] his [only-begotten] Son etc."[10]

See if, in effect, in this most sorrowful death of my divine Master Jesus there is not found both the Eternal Father's vengeance against sin, which he vindicates in the person of his Son, and this most patient Nazarene's clemency on behalf of mankind. I have finished.

[At this point, the preacher turned to the cross with the life-size figure of Christ hanging upon it and to the bulto of Nuestra Señora de la Soledad standing nearby, beginning a text for the deposition from the cross during which the two other priests present, don Francisco Ignacio Madariaga and fray Francisco Hozio, took the parts of Joseph of Arimathea and Nicodemus and removed the various *Arma Christi*—the weapons of Christ, the implements of the passion which he allowed to be used against himself—and placed them one by one onto the cloth hanging over Mary's arms. García continues from the pulpit:]

There remains for me only to say some words to you, most afflicted Lady Mother and Virgin Immaculate, the creature most full of grace but at

Cadaver de vuestro hijo pendiente en esa Cruz, y no tener vos, ni quien os lo baje, ni sabana en que cubrirlo, ni Sepulcro en que depositarlo;[11] !O que angustias! ¡O Que conflictos os cercan por todas partes!

Mas Divina Reyna, Madre de los pecadores, é aqui que yo os presento esos fieles Ministros del Santuario, para que con vuestro permiso, con sus sagradas manos, pongan en las vuestras, esos instrumentos, que han servido en su modo a nuestro rescate. No os detengais subid presurosos esas escalas; Arrancad esa inscripcion, que como causa, ó pregon contra Nuestro Adorable Maestro fixo en ese madero la atrevida, y sacrilega ignorancia de los venenosos Escrivas; Señora esa es la inscripsion, que aun a pezar de la resist[enci]ª del Pueblo amotinado, dispuesto por alta, y particular Providencia, publica que el que ha muerto en esa Cruz és el verdadero y lexitimo Señor de ese rebelde Pueblo Hebreo. Jesus Nazareno Rey de los Judios; el timido Precidente Pilatos ignorando la causa del movimiento de su corazon há dado el testimonio mas autentico del Deicidio, y Regicidio, que esos alevosos Phariseos, y Principes de ese Pueblo han executado.[12]

Esa Corona formada de juncos marinos,[13] es la que los Sayones por escarnio, y para burlarse de vuestro Pacientisimo Jesus, colocaron en la sagrada Cabeza del Rey de los Reyes, y Señor de los Señores. He dicho mal Dolorida Virgen; nosotros somos los que hicimos por nuestros desarreglos pensamientos vanos, soberbios, y presuntuosos, nosotros, sí, nosotros somos la causal, que penetrasen esas espinas, casco, crines, celebro [cerebro], y frente de aquel rostro, en que los Angeles desear el veerse.

Esos clavos, que en algun dia seran el remache, o de una eterna, salvacion, ó eterna condenacion para los hombres impios: han taladrado, aquellas manos sacrosantas, que obraban los prodigios a millares, lastimaron aquellas plantas, que presurosas caminaban, para conceder gracias, beneficios, y milagros estupendos, no solo a los cuerpos caducos, y perecederos, sino aun mas a beneficios de las almas oprimidas, o con las aflixiones, ó con la ignorancia culpable, y reprensible stigna [estigma] de reprecion en el conocimiento de sus peculiares deberes.

En fin Madre y Señora mia, Corredemptora del genero humano, como

---

11. A private devotional text in Spanish from the same general period speaks to Mary of "the cruel helplessness you endured having no one to lower Him from the cross, no shroud in which to wrap Him, no tomb in which to bury Him"; and the *alabados* "Dulcísimo Jesús Mio" and "Ayudemos Almas" both speak of Mary's "three necessities." See Juan B. Rael, *The New Mexican Alabado* (Stanford: Stanford University Press, 1951), p. 75; Thomas J. Steele, S.J., *Holy Week in Tomé* (Santa Fe: Sunstone Press, 1976), p. 171.

12. "President" is the common New Mexican title for Pontius Pilate, whose wife had a dream (Matt. 27:19) warning against her husband's sitting in judgment on Christ. Fray Manuel Antonio implies here that just as God inspired the High Priest Caiaphas to prophesy against his will,

the same time the fullest of torment and sorrow. Your greatest distress is to see that divine body of your Son hanging on that cross and have neither a way to take him down, nor a shroud to wrap him with, nor a grave to lay him in.[11] Oh what anguish! Oh what conflicts surround you on all sides!

But Divine Queen, Mother of Sinners, behold! I present you these faithful ministers of the sanctuary so that with your permission their sacred hands will place into your hands those instruments which have served in their way as your ransom. [fray Manuel speaks here to the two priests:] Do not tarry. Quickly ascend those steps. Tear down that inscription, the cause or publication against our adorable Master which nailed to this tree the insolent and sacrilegious ignorance of the venomous scribes. [Then when they have brought it and placed it on the cloth lying over Mary's outstretched arms, he again speaks to Nuestra Señora:] Lady, that is the inscription which, in spite of the resistance of the rebellious people, nevertheless announces by a high and particular providence that he who died on this cross is the true and rightful Lord of this rebellious Hebrew people: "Jesus of Nazareth, King of the Jews." The fearful President Pilate, unaware of the cause of the movement of his heart, has given the most authoritative testimony of the deicide and regicide the treacherous Pharisees and leaders of this people have perpetrated.[12]

[The two priests remove the crown of thorns:]

This crown, woven of marine reeds,[13] is the one that the executioners, to deride your most patient Jesus with mockery, placed on the sacred head of the King of kings, the Lord of lords. I said incorrectly "Sorrowing Virgin." We ourselves accomplished it by our disordered, vain, proud, and presumptuous thoughts—we, yes, we are the cause why these thorns penetrated the skull, hair, brain, and forehead of that countenance which the angels desire to look upon.

[They tie the arms to the crossbar with pieces of cloth to support the body, then they remove the three nails:]

Those nails—which one day will be the fastening either of eternal salvation or, for impious men, of eternal condemnation—have pierced these

---

"Can you not see it is better for you to have one man die [for the people] than to have the whole nation destroyed?" (John 11:50), so He inspired Pilate to prophesy by identifying Jesus as King of the Jews.

13. *Juncos marinos* (or *marineros* or *marítimos*) are large wild reeds with very sharp spikes on their leaves. They are described by Petrus Comestor in his *Scholastic History* (ch. 168) and by Jacobus de Voragine in his *Golden Legend*; their occurrence in poetry dates back to Ovid's *Metamorphoses*, 4:299. In New Mexico, they turn up in alabados, ballads that narrate the passion, such as "Por el Rastro de la Sangre" and "Ay Mi Corazón Amante," and Gregg calls them "sea grass" in *Commerce of the Prairies*, p. 49.

os intitula el Padre San Bernardo[14] disponeos a recivir el golpe del cuchillo, mas cruel para vuestro puro, casto, amoroso, y afligidisimo corazon. Tomad en vuestros brazos el yerto cadaver del mejor de todos los hijos de las Madres. Dadle el ultimo abrazo de a Dios [adios] pues que es la ultima ocasion que tocais con vuestras adorables manos, la humanidad de ese cuerpo Sacrosancto.

¡O vida muerta! ¡O lumbre oscurecida! o hermosura afeada, ¿y que manos han sido aquellas, que tal han puesto vuestra Divina figura? que corona fue aquella, que mis ojos vieron en vuestra cabeza? ¿Que herida esta que veo en vuestro costado? O Sumo Sacerdote de mundo! Quien ha manchado el espejo, y hermosura del Cielo? ¿Quien ha desfigurado la cara de todas las gracias? ¿Estos son aquellos ojos que obscurecian al Sol con su hermosura? ¿Estas son las manos, que resucitaban los muertos a quien tocaban? Esta es la boca por donde salian los cuatro rios del Paraiso? Tanto han podido las manos de los hombres contra Dios? Hijo mio y Sangre mia ¿de donde se levantó esta fuerte borrasca? ¿Que dia ha sido esta [sic], que asi te me ha llebado? Hijo mio, ¿que hare sin ti? Adonde iré, quien me remediara? Los Padres y los hermanos afligidos venian a rogarte por sus hijos, y sus hermanos difunctos, y tu con tu infinita virtud, y clemencia los consolabas, y socorrias. Mas yo que veo muerto a mi hijo y mi Padre y mi hermano y mi Señor, a quien rogaré por él? ¿Quien me consolara, Donde está el Buen Jesus Nazareno, hijo de Dios Vivo, que consuela a los vivos, y da vida a los muertos? Donde está aquel gran Profeta Poderoso en obras, y palabras [Lucas 24:19]?

Hijo antes mi descanso, y ahora cuchillo de mi dolor, ¿Que hiciste para que los Judios te crucificasen? ¿Que causa hubo para darte muerte? ¿Estas son las gracias de tantas buenas obras? ¿Este es el premio que se da a la virtud?[15] ¿Esta es la paga de tanta doctrina? ¿Hasta aqui ha llegado la maldad del mundo? ¿Hasta aqui la malicia del Demonio? ¿Hasta aqui la bondad, y clemencia de Dios? ¿Tan grande es el aborrecimiento que Dios tiene al pecado? ¿Tanto fue menester, para satisfacer por la culpa? ¿Tan grande es el rigor de la Justicia Divina? ¿En tanto tiene Dios la salud de los hombres?

O Dulcisimo hijo mio, que haré sin ti? Tu eras mi hijo, mi Padre, mi Esposo, mi Maestro y toda mi compañia. Ahora quedo como huerfana sin Padre viuda sin Espozo, y sola sin tal Maestro, y tan dulce compañia; Ya no te veré mas entrar por mis puertas cansado de los discursos, y predicacion

---

14. The notion that Mary cooperated actively and materially with Christ in redeeming the human race is a now-discredited theory of "maximalist" Mariology—Marian devotional speculation that occurred in blissful isolation from scripture and dogma. Bernard never intended to go as far as García del Valle suggests.

holy hands which worked miracles by the thousands, offended those feet which traveled so readily to bestow graces, benefits, and spectacular miracles not only upon feeble and perishing bodies but also and even more to bestow benefits upon souls oppressed either with afflictions or with culpable ignorance and the disgrace of refusing to know their proper duties.

[Finally the two priests remove the body of Jesus and hold it above the outstretched arms of the Lady of Solitude:]

And finally, my Mother and Lady, Co-Redemptrix of the human race as Father Saint Bernard titled you,[14] ready yourself to receive the stroke of the sword, more cruel for your pure, chaste, living, and all-suffering heart. Take in your arms the lifeless body of the best of all the sons of all mothers. Give him the final embrace of farewell, for this is the final chance to touch with your adorable hands the humanity of that most holy body.

[Now at this point, the preacher speaks in the person of the Lady of Solitude, expressing, as best he can, her feelings at this poignant moment of her life:]

"Oh dead life! Oh obscured light! Oh defaced beauty! And what hands were they that have done so to your divine form? What crown is this that my eyes see on your head? What other wound do I see in your side? Oh High Priest of the world! Who has disfigured the mirror and beauty of heaven? Who has disfigured the countenance of all graces? Are these the eyes that blinded the sun with their beauty? Are these the hands that raised to life the dead they touched? Is this the mouth from whence the four rivers of paradise flowed? Have human hands such power against God? My Son and my blood, whence rose this powerful storm? What kind of day has this been that you should be taken from me? My Son, what shall I do without you? Where shall I go? Who will care for me? Fathers and brothers came in their affliction to beg for their dead sons and brothers, and you with your infinite virtue and clemency consoled and assisted them. But I who see my Son and my Father, my Brother and my Lord lying in death—whom can I implore to help him? Who will console me? Where is the good Jesus the Nazarene, Son of the living God, that he might console the living and grant life to the dead? Where is that great Prophet, powerful in works and words [Luke 24:19]?

"My Son, formerly you were my repose, and now you are the sword of my sorrow. What have you done that the Jews should crucify you? What

---

15. Augustine's "Commentary on Psalm 64," excerpted in the Second Nocturne of Matins in the Good Friday office, quotes John 10:32: "Many good deeds I have shown you from the Father. For which of them do you stone me?"

del Evangelio. Ya no te limpiaré mas el sudor de tu rostro asoleado, y fatigado de los caminos, y trabajos. Ya no te veré a mi meza, comiendo, y dando de comer a alma con tu Divina Presencia.

Fenecida es ya mi gloria, hoy se acaba mi alegria y comienza mi Soledad.[16]

No prosigais Madre Dulcisima, permitíd, que ese despedazado cuerpo de mi Maestro, y Salvador, lo muestren, esos Venerables Ministros, del Dios de los Exercitos, a este Pueblo, y que en el vea hasta que puncto han llegado sus desordenes, sus trasgreciones, y la malicia de nuestras culpas.

Pecadores hai teneis a vuestra vista el fructo que haveis conseguido con vuestros pecados &c.
O.S.C.S.M.E.C.A.R.[18]

—*Fin*—
Predicado en la Parroquia de la Villa de Santa Fee
de la Provincia del Nuevo México a 20 de Abril del 821
por el Padre Fray Manuel Antonio García del Valle.

---

16. Compare Charles L. Briggs, *Competence in Performance* (Philadelphia: University of Pennsylvania Press, 1988), pp. 336-38.

17. Dávila Padilla, p. 567, describes the funeral procession in late sixteenth-century Mexico City: "Four priests carry the body of Christ our Lord on their shoulders on an *andas* covered with a striking cloth of embroidered black velvet on which lies the shroud in which the priests received the body as it was taken down from the cross. The body remains on the andas, covered only with a veil of net picked with black and silver thread. Then comes a banner with the royal arms of Christ—the implements of his passion. The image of the most holy Virgin comes right after—the widow who most feels the absence of her sweet spouse, beloved son, and true God."

Descriptions of the deposition and burial appear in Steele, *Holy Week in Tomé*, pp. 140-53.

18. These initials stand for the Latin "Opiniones subjectae censurae sanctae matris Ecclesiae Catholicae apostolicae Romanae—The opinions [expressed in this sermon] are subject to the censure of holy mother the apostolic Roman Catholic Church." My thanks to Felipe Mirabal for figuring most of this out for me.

need was there to kill you? Is this the reward for your many good works?[15] Is this the payment for so much teaching? Has the world's wickedness come to this? Has the devil's malice come to this? Have God's goodness and clemency come to this? Does God have such a great abhorrence for sin? Was it so necessary to make satisfaction for sin? Is such the severity of the divine justice? Does God set so high a value on the salvation of the human race?

"Oh sweetest Son of mine, what shall I do without you? You were my Son, my Father, my Spouse, my Master, and my only companion. Today I am left like an orphan without a parent, a widow without a husband; I am alone without such a teacher or so dear a companion. From now on I shall never again see you come through the door, tired from your teaching and your preaching of the Gospel. Never again shall I wipe away the sweat from your face, sunburnt and tired from walking and working. Never again shall I see you eating at my table while I feed my soul with your divine presence.

"My glory is now dead. Today my happiness has ended and my solitude begins."[16]

[Mary's apostrophe ends, and the preacher resumes in his own person:]

Do not continue further, Mother most sweet. Allow the venerable ministers of the Lord of Hosts to exhibit that mutilated body of my Master and Savior to this people. [At this point the two priests carry the body to the front of the sanctuary, turn it so it faces the congregation, and hold it up in full view of the people.] Now seeing it, they will see what our disorders, our trespasses, and the wickedness of our sins have come to. [And he speaks to all the people:]

Sinners, here you have before your eyes the fruit you have pursued with your sins etc.

[Next, the body is placed in an open latticework coffin which some pallbearers raise to their shoulders, a funeral cortege forms, and the congregation files out of the church, walks in procession through some nearby streets, and returns to the church for a brief burial ritual.[17]]

O.S.C.S.M.E.C.A.R.[18]

Preached in the Parish Church of the Villa of Santa Fe in the Province of New Mexico on 20 April 1821 by

Padre Fray Manuel Antonio García del Valle.

—end—

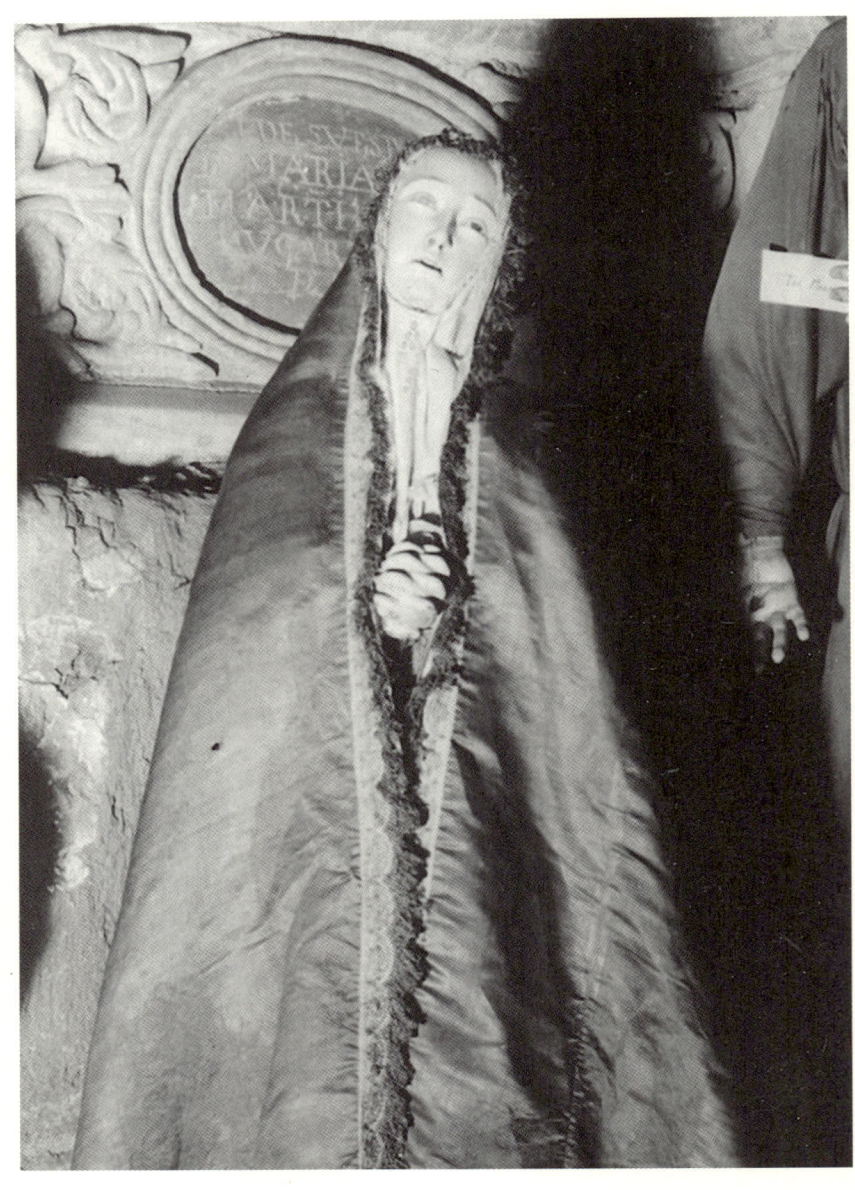

1. Bulto. Our Lady of Solitude.
La Parroquia Museum, St. Francis Cathedral.
Santa Fe, New Mexico.
Courtesy of the Museum of New Mexico,
negative number 129519.

PART II

*Three Orations of
Padre Antonio José Martínez*

✣

✢

Antonio José Martínez was born in the frontier town of Abiquiú on 17 January 1793, grew up in Taos, and married in young manhood only to be widowed. He shortly entered the Tridentine Seminary of the Diocese of Durango, evidently taking as his model the revolutionist and martyred priest-hero Miguel Hidalgo. Martínez's seminary studies also instilled in him a passion for the life of the mind which he never lost. Ordained in 1822, he traveled to Taos a year later to celebrate his first solemn Mass (the first sermon). After a few years in other parishes, he returned to Taos to spend the rest of his long life. He opened a school for boys and girls and a minor seminary to prepare young men for the Durango seminary. Twenty-two of his pupils were ordained, and many others became noted lay leaders of New Mexico Territory. Martínez bought a printing press for the intellectual uses of school and church and for politics, in which he was always involved (second and third sermons).

Martínez appears to have accepted as irreversible the 1846 conquest of New Mexico. He neither incited or approved the Taos uprising of 1847 when Governor Charles Bent was assassinated. For seven years after the 1848 peace treaty, Martínez was a dominant figure in the conventions and legislative sessions that constructed the new order of territorial politics.

Martínez was initially in favor of the new ecclesiastical order that began in 1851, supporting Bishop Lamy until his letter of January 1854 withholding the sacraments from Catholics who did not tithe. In early 1856 Martínez offered his conditional resignation; Lamy accepted the resignation while failing to fulfil the condition upon which it was couched. The new pastor was insulting to his predecessor, so Martínez admitted the parishioners of Taos to the private chapel at his home and resumed their pastoral care. On 27 October 1856 Lamy suspended him. Martínez fought with the next pastor, continued writing annoying letters to Lamy, drew a neighboring pastor into his orbit, and gained the allegiance of about a third of the people in the two parishes. Thus on Sunday 11 April 1858 Lamy's vicar-general, Joseph P. Machebeuf, pronounced Martínez's solemn excommunication in Taos, and the next Sunday in Arroyo Hondo he pronounced the same fate for the other priest.

Father Martínez had been cordial to non-Catholic clergymen from the time they had entered New Mexico with the invading army, but now he became interested, and he even flirted with, Episcopalianism. From 1858 to 1862, Martínez wrote a series of tracts, published as broadsides on his press, but mainly he continued to minister to his third of the parishioners and to work with the penitential Brotherhood of Our Father Jesus the Nazarene until his death on 27 July 1867.

Martínez the preacher was outstanding in New Mexico not merely because he set high standards for himself but because so few priests preached regularly. Pedro Sánchez, one of his former pupils, concluded a brief biography by writing, "In the pulpit he [Martínez] was so acute that with the force of reason, which was second nature to him, he was always able to persuade, to please, and to prove whatever he might wish through his highly creative mind."[1]

---

1. Fray Angélico Chávez, *But Time and Chance: The Story of Padre Martínez of Taos* (Santa Fe: Sunstone Press, 1981), pp. 31, 63; Chávez suggests that the Pueblo-Indian-centered Franciscans normally limited themselves to "simple catechetical instructions." Pedro Sánchez, *Memorias sobre la Vida del Presbítero don Antonio José Martínez* (Santa Fe: Nuevo Mexicano, 1903), pp. 41-42.

For further biographical background, see also Myra Ellen Jenkins, "New Mexico—1863," *Historical Magazine of the Protestant Episcopal Church* 32 (1963): 221-23; E.A. Mares, ed., *Padre Martínez: New Perspective from Taos* (Taos: Millicent Rogers Museum, 1988); Thomas J. Steele, S.J., "Kit Carson and Padre Martínez," *Folk and Church in Nineteenth Century New Mexico* (Colorado Springs: The Hulbert Center for Southwest Studies, 1993), pp. 73-80.

Antonio José Martínez

The Roman Catholic seminary of the nineteenth century was in many ways another world, the moral equivalent of outer space. When young Padre Martínez arrived in Taos in 1823 fresh from the Durango seminary, even though he had grown up in that northern New Mexican town, he and the townspeople must initially have been pretty incomprehensible to each other.

Young Fr. Martínez came down from the ivory tower soon enough, but the initial experience probably stood the Taoseños in good stead in the long run, helping them to survive the arrivals of Charles Bent the Anglo North American, Beaubien and Saint-Vrain the Frenchmen, Father Dámaso Taladrid the Spaniard, Father Gabriel Ussel the Frenchman, Mabel Dodge, D.H. Lawrence, Dorothy Brett, Arthur Manby, and a million later *extranjeros*. But when the familiar hometown boy returned from the heady seminary experience with the philosophical worldview and the academic vocabulary of abstractions and Latinisms that he shows off in this sermon, we can almost imagine the people of Taos echoing the people of Nazareth: "Where did he get all this?" That is, if they got further than asking, "What in the *world* is he talking about?"

Gravid with the new order of things, Father Martínez here utters his joyful Magnificat—"*Quam mihi et vobis*: The nations will say, 'The Lord has done great things for me,' and he will do the same for you. The Lord has done great things for us; we are glad indeed."

2. *Guadalupe Church, Taos, New Mexico.*
Courtesy of the Museum of New Mexico, negative number 93086.

Primer Misa

"*Cantabo Domino qui bona tribuit mihi*" ex. Psalm. 12, v. 6.

 Hermanos y compaisanos mios carisimos y deseadisimos: llegó por ultimo el dichoso día en que desapareciendo, por disposicion divina el denso velo, que por tanto tiempo habia ofuscado vuestros buenos deseos, y propositos, para tener en el Altar un ministro de vuestros hijos; refiramos ya las gracias a nuestro Dios, por ver constituido a este en el sublime estado del Sacerdocio. Si, llenos de juvilo tributemosselas a este Señor, como que es el único autor de tan grande empresa. Nada obra sin fin, ha distribuido desde lo eterno, segun el orden de su alta providencia, el buen suceso, el progreso, y proporcion que cada causa ha de tener, con su respectivo efecto, assí lo sabemos es verdad; pero muy en particular, y con mayor esmero, lo ha hecho en las predeterminaciones correspondientes al fin supremo, ó ultimo, que es el sobrenatural. Assi lo ha hecho me atreveré a decir. . . . Mientras protegiendonos hasta vencer todas las dificultades, ha puesto para vuestro espiritual consuelo este ministro en vuestras manos. Sí, amados compaisanos, aquí me teneis y me ofresco a vuestra disposicion. No me movió desde el principio hasta el ultimo termino de mi carrera, otro fin, despues de servir a nuestro Dios, que hacer y procurar por vuestra felicidad. Assí lo confieso ingenuamente; y no permita Dios, me moviera por algun interes particular; desde luego me apartaria del verdadero fin, a que debo ordenar todas mis acciones.

 Los felices sucesos, los aciertos adecuados para obtenerlo, aun en un tiempo, en que por un justo motivo pudo faltar, y tanto otro beneficio como para obtenerlo, esperimentamos, son una prueba nada equivoca de que por altas determinaciones, nos ha venido esto como un don del cielo.[1] He aquí, con cuan justos motivos debe nuestra gratitud volver las gracias a nuestro Dios, por unos tan singulares beneficios. Esta proposicion sera pues el eje, sobre que rodarán mis desatinadas reflexiones. Pero no las daré movimiento, hasta que no invoquemos la proteccion de nuestra Señora, saludandola y diciendola con el Angel, Ave Maria.[2]

---

 1. The nineteenth-century translation of this sentence reads as follows: "The happy events, the adequate success in attaining it, even at a time in which even for a just motive it might have failed, and the success in having attained it, which we experience, is a proof unmistakable that by other [the Váldez-Ritch ledger reading *otras*, the Read draft reading *altas*] determinations, but [Váldez-Ritch giving *más*, Read giving *nos*] it has come to us as a gift from heaven."

 2. This seems to be a very eighteenth-century image, deriving from the mechanical worldview that produced Paley's watchmaker, Rittenhouse's orrery, "this universal frame," and so forth. It is at the opposite pole from romantic, organic, evolutionary images such as the world tree.

First Mass

"*Cantabo Domino qui bona tribuit mihi*—I will sing to the Lord who has given good things to me" (Psalm 12:6).

My most beloved and longed-for brethren and fellow countrymen:
Finally the beautiful day has arrived when by divine disposition the dense veil has disappeared that for so long a time has obscured your hopes and expectations of seeing at the altar a minister from among your own sons. Let us express our gratitude now to our God to see such a one constituted in the sublime state of the priesthood. Yes, full of jubilation, let us return thanks to the Lord as the unique author of so great an enterprise. Nothing happens without its purpose. God has determined from all eternity, according to the disposition of his holy providence, the good outcome, the progress along the way, and the part each cause would play in terms of its proper effect, as we know to be the case. But in a most particular manner and with the greatest care, God always works all this out in predetermining the highest and most ultimate end, which is the strictly supernatural. I will venture to say that he has done so here.

After protecting us until we overcame all difficulties, God has given this minister into your hands for your spiritual consolation. Yes, my beloved fellow countrymen, here you take possession of me; I place myself permanently at your disposal. No other motive moved me from the start to the finish of my course of studies except the service of our God performed so as to bring about your happiness. Thus I declare it as plainly as I can, and may God never allow me to be motivated by any merely personal interest; I would immediately prove unfaithful to that true goal toward which I ought to direct all that I do.

The happy outcome and the efforts to obtain it, even at a time when for just cause it might have failed (and along with it the successful attainment we are now experiencing), are unequivocal proof that for His lofty purposes God has given us this gift purely as a boon.[1] Behold now for what just motives our gratitude should return thanks to our God for these outstanding benefits. This proposition will indeed be the axle upon which my half-formed reflections will revolve. But I will set them in motion only after we invoke the protection of Our Lady, addressing ourselves to her and saying with the Angel, "Ave Maria."[2]

"Cantabo Domino, qui bona tribuit mihi!" ut supr.

Siempre ha sido la gratitud, siempre ha sido el reconocimiento al bienhechor, una de las primeras funciones, que debe ocupar la atencion de las almas nobles, y agradecidas. Por esto cuando Dios sacó a su antiguo pueblo, de las servidumbre de Egipto, este viendose en libertad, entonó su canto al Señor. Tomó pues, dice la Escritura, Maria Profetisa hermana de Aaron el timpano en su mano, y salieron tras ellas las demas mugeres, con timpanos é instrumentos de cuerda, diciendo, "*Cantemus Domino, gloriose enim magnificatus est*—Cantemos himnos al Señor pues gloriosamente es engrandecido" [Éxodo 15:21]. Que igual al demostracion de cariño y agradecimiento debamos nosotros hoy tributar al Señor de la magestad, al Principe de las eternidades, al Rey supremo de los cielos, y de la tierra, que para gloria de su nombre, para recreo de su amor, para bien de nuestras almas, y para medio de nuestra salud espiritual, por la operacion sensible de sus ministros,[3] y por la secreta efusion de su divino espiritu sobre nosotros; ha hecho que poseamos ya, de esto util, provechoso y necesario bien, rompiendo las dulces y tenaces cadenas, que por tanto tiempo, nos habian tenido aprisionados, é impidiendo alcanzar un tan dichoso fin. Que igual demostracion de cariño y agradecimiento, vuelvo a decir, debamos hoy tributar a nuestro Dios, que aquellos Israelitas en otro tiempo; ninguno lo duda. Por eso os advierto, que inundados de gozo habeis concurrido a este santo Templo, a ofrecer en mi compania, y por medio del sacrificio, vuestros corazones, vuestros votos, y vuestros buenos sentimientos en accion de gracias a nuestro Dios.

Claramente hemos visto, sensiblemente hemos palpado que la cortesa y poderosa mano del Todopoderoso, nos ha protejido, nos ha ayudada admirablemente. Inconvenientes hubo, dificultades de presentaros desde el principio hasta el fin de esa mi carrera. Diganlo los rigores de los frios contra las Haciendas, las langostas, y demas epidemias contra los sembrados, las continuas guerras destructivas de tan propias vidas, y de los bienes destinados para su conservacion. Diganlo, por ultimo, las detracciones y sátiras con que algunas personas imprudentemente quisieron desanimar, constituyendo la nobleza y aptitud para tan honroso estado en la riqueza, ó

---

3. By "the palpable operation of God's ministers," Martínez means the sacraments in general and, given the occasion of the sermon, especially Bishop Juan Francisco de Castañiza's conferring on him the Sacrament of Holy Orders some months earlier.

An Aristotelian analysis by causes, a method Martínez was very fond of, would have worked everything out like this: God is the principal and primary efficient cause of the sacramental effect (Martínez's priesthood). The humanity of Christ is the secondary principal efficient cause. The church and the minister (the ordaining bishop) are conjoined instruments in the order of efficient

"Cantabo Domino qui bona tribuit mihi—I will sing to the Lord who has given good things to me" (as above).

Gratitude—the acknowledgement of the benefactor—has always been one of the fundamental activities occupying the attention of noble and thankful souls. Therefore, when of old, God brought his chosen people out of Egyptian slavery and they found themselves freed, they struck up their canticle to the Lord. Scripture tells us that Miriam the Prophetess, sister of Aaron, took her tambourine in her hand, and that the rest of the women followed her with tambourines and stringed instruments chanting, "*Cantemus Domino, gloriose enim magnificatus est*—Let us sing to the Lord, for he displays his glory and greatness" [Exodus 15:21].

We should address a similar outpouring of affection and gratitude to the Lord of Majesty today, to the Eternal Ruler, to the Supreme King of the heavens and the earth. For the glory of his name, for the exercising of his love, for the benefit of our souls, and for the sake of our spiritual salvation, through the visible operation of his ministers[3] and the secret outpouring of his divine Spirit upon us, he has brought it about that we are now possessed of this useful, beneficial, and necessary good, breaking the seductive and tenacious chains which for so long a time had held us imprisoned and impeded us from attaining such a splendid goal. The suitable demonstration of affection and gratitude that we should offer today to our God, I repeat again, is what those Israelites did in days of old, as everyone is aware. Thus it is, I perceive, that you are suffused with joy, having come to this holy temple to offer, in company with me and with the Sacrifice [of the Mass] as our vehicle, your hearts, your vows, and your best wishes in thanksgiving to our God.

We have clearly seen, we have palpably felt how the subtle and powerful hand of the Allpowerful has protected us and wonderfully aided us. Obstacles and difficulties presented themselves from the beginning to the end of my course of studies. I could speak of what the stock suffered from the cold, of what the crops suffered from the grasshoppers and other plagues, of how many human lives and how much property meant to preserve life

---

causes. The oil of anointing and the gestures and motions of the ritual are also conjoined instruments as well as being material causes of the sacrament-as-action, of which the formula of words is the formal cause. The final cause, as Martínez stated at the end of the first paragraph, is the strictly supernatural intention of the primary and principal efficient Causes (the Trinity, including the Incarnate Word).

Martínez's next sermon will treat the reader to a lot more analysis by causes and effects, means and ends, and so forth.

abundancia de los bienes temporales, como sino vieramos, que el modelo de la perfeccion, Christo Señor Nuestro, abomina tan desemejantes expresiones, y pareceres, dandonos exemplos de todo lo contrario. Pero, como el Señor no[s] ha obligado el ejercicio de su virtud a las proporciones naturales, como se gloria haciendo ostentacion de su infinito poder, donde aparecen las mayores dificultades; como sus eternos decretos son irrevocables y estos no se acomodan al antojo de cualesquiera, nos ha dado a entender en esta obra, por la que placenteros le magnificamos, que sus designios, que sus determinaciones, giran por otra parte mas decorosa, mas noble, y mas contentanea a los deberes de cada uno;[4] nos ha dado a entender, que no busca, sino aquellos corazones, cuyos sentimientos estan despuestos, y ordenados por su misma acertada providencia, para tan alto fin. Siendo así, en vano se multiplicaron entorpecer. Habrá quien consuele, habrá quien anime, habrá quien se preste por protector: y cuando no se hubiere, el mismo Señor, por una accion admirable, efecto de su misericordia, y poder infinito, lo ejecutará. ¡O si así fuera en nuestro caso! O si habiendo superado todas las dificultades que contra esto se anteponian; victoriosos cantaremos unos tan gloriosos triunfos! ¿Pero, quien duda que el efecto, que el resultado ha sido de este modo? Quien no advierte, quien no examina las circunstancias, sin concluir al punto, que estas rectamente nos lo prueban? A la verdad segun me parece, la consecuencia es inconcusa: Por tanto, O Señor, ya te damos los parabienes, y a te referimos las gracias: hemos experimentado ya, que como en aquel tiempo, que como en aquella Ley Antigua convertiste en favor de los Israelitas las turbias y nocivas, en cristalinas y saluberrinas: en este para con nosotros, te habeis manifestado con igual Liberalidad, y con igual franqueza: ¿Pero que duda, que para nosotros no ha sido, sin con una notable diferencia? alla lloviá un manantial perenne, y aunque indirectamente se ordenaba para su consecusion del fin espiritual, para la consecusion de la vida eterna, directa é inmediatamente supeditaba los medios a la conservacion natural. Aquí en nuestro caso, ha sido de otro modo, su primer fin, su inmediata y directa intencion, ha sido el ultimo fin para que nos crio, para el que nos rescató, a costa de tantas solicitudes, y afanes, a costa de su misma preciosisima sangre. Aquí lo ha hecho con el fin de tengais quien inmole y ofresca los sacrificios de un valor incalculable, que es infinito: quien os instruya en sus misterios, leyes, y preceptos, y os de con enteresa y justo la direccion de la carrera del espiritu. Por lo mismo, debeis con igual proporsion exeder a aquellos en vuestras congratulaciones y obsequios al Señor.

---

4. The Spanish text is "y mas contentanea a los deberes de cada uno," surely a slip of the copyist's pen for the Latin borrowing *consentanea*—in keeping with, attuned to.

were lost in wasteful wars. Finally, I could speak of the calumnies and satires by which some persons impudently tried to discourage me, identifying the degree of nobility and the level of aptitude needed for so honorable an estate as consisting in riches, in an abundance of the goods of this world—as if we did not realize that the very model of perfection, Christ our Lord, abominated such unseemly expressions and opinions and exemplified for us the exact opposite.

But as the Lord is not obliged to exercise his virtues in the proportions natural to himself, as he only glories in showing his infinite power upon the appearance of great difficulties, and as his eternal decrees are inalterable and refuse to bend to anyone's caprices, so he has given us to understand by this work, which we are pleased to praise him for, that his plans, his decisions, on the other hand revolve around each person's duties, to make them more decorous, more noble, and more agreeable. 4 He has given us to understand that he seeks only those hearts whose values his own settled providence has disposed and ordered for a purpose so exalted, for a goal so sublime. Since this is the case, the obstructions that intended to paralyze it multiplied themselves in vain. Will there be anyone who can console us, anyone who can lift our spirits, anyone who will offer himself as our protector? And when there was no one else who would, the Lord performed the deed himself by an admirable action that stemmed from his mercy and infinite power.

Oh that it had been so in our case! Oh, if having overcome all the difficulties put in the way, we will sing in our victory of some such glorious triumphs! But who doubts that the outcome, the result, has been just that? Who does not know, who does not examine the circumstances and conclude at once that they righteously prove it to us? It truly seems to me that the conclusion is beyond question. Therefore, O Lord, we are already welcoming you and returning thanks to you. We have already experienced that both now and during the time of the Old Law you transformed, for the Israelites' sake, the turgid and harmful into the crystalline and healthgiving. In your dealings with ourselves, you have shown yourself to possess equal liberality, equal frankness. But who can doubt that as to ourselves you have acted with a noteworthy difference? Then, the showers were perennial, and though they were indirectly intended to achieve a spiritual outcome, to issue into eternal life, they directly and immediately subordinated the means to natural survival.

Here in our case it has been quite different, for God's first end, his immediate and direct intent, has been the ultimate end for which he cre-

Yo creo, que vuestras oraciones, y buenos propositos han hecho mucho al caso para obtener este nuestro exito feliz: pues cuando me hallaba fatigado en mil laboriosas tareas, circundado de los trabajos escolares, y tanto otra congoja como en ello[s] se presenta, todo era despues de despachar mis suplicas a nuestro Dios, poner mi corazon a este mi pais, contemplando las necesidades en que yaciais, quando sentía un animo resuelto a continuar, un aliento y un nuevo fervor para proseguir. Quiza, quiza, decia vuestros continuos ruegos, en union de aquellos mis sentimientos piadosos, se remontaban precuros [sic] hasta lo mas encumbrado de Ympireo, para ser atendidos.

En tal hipotesis me veo presisado a tornaros los afectos carinosos de este mi corazon agradecido, y adeudado para con vosotros. Muy en particular doy los gracias a mis amados padres, que revestidos de una constancia inflexible, de una confiansa firme, piadosa, é inalterable, sostuvieron intrepidos el duro peso que intentaba desgraciarles de sus _____ intentados. Muy en particular las doy a los Ministros Ecclesiasticos seculares, personas suponentes, y demas que para lo mismo concurrieron.

En fin, vengamos todos unanimes con tonos y accentos deliciosos a nuestro Dios, a ofrecerlo los esquisitos frutos que con su auxilio hubemos cosechado: presentemonos en su benigna y respetable presencia con unos semblantes risueñas y placenteros, heridos con la penetrante flecha de su amor ardentisimo. Empuñemos con rapides la cortante espada de las buenas obras, y de los virtuosos sentimientos, contra la maledicencia.[5] Frequentad fervorosos y a menudo la penitencia y Eucaristia, que son aquellos remedios espirituales que nuestra vida Christo puso para nuestra salud, é interior consuelo.

En lo que yo pueda aliviaros me prestaré gustoso. Esto sea pues vuestra accion de gracias; en la ejecusion de esto se llena el padre de las luces de las mayores complacencias; y de este modo los levantemos todos desde aora con las afectos del corazon, el remontoso buelo a la gloria eterna. *"Quam mihi, et vobis."*[6]

—*fin*—

---

5. The fiery arrows and the sword are all that Martínez saved when he totally rewrote the Pauline image in Ephesians 6:10-17.

6. This Latin phrase was capable of many applications; the translation here tries to fit it into the actual context. It has some affinity to Galatians 4:12, and I have obviously made a little Taoseño Magnificat of it (Luke 1:49).

ated us, for which he ransomed us at the cost of so many cares and anxieties, even at the cost of his own most precious blood. Here he has done what he has done so that you might have someone who can immolate and offer sacrifices of inestimable and even of infinite value, someone to instruct you in God's mysteries, laws, and precepts, someone to be for you an accurate and thorough guide for the journey of your spirit. Consequently, you should in like proportion exceed the people of the Old Testament in your expressions of gratitude and reverence to the Lord.

I believe that your prayers and good intentions have done a great deal in my case to assure this happy outcome of ours. Whenever I found myself tired of a thousand laborious tasks, hemmed in by scholarly duties and the anxieties that accompanied them, I simply directed my prayers to our God, set my heart on this land of mine, and contemplated your condition of need, and I always felt my spirit strengthened to continue, strengthened and fervent to endure. Probably, probably, let me say, your constant prayers, united with my own pious feelings, mounted up as harbingers that insisted on being heard at the highest pinnacle of the Empyrean.

On that hypothesis, I find myself compelled to return to you the warmest affection of my grateful heart, which is so deeply in your debt. Most especially I give thanks to my beloved parents. Endowed with an unbending constancy and a staunch, holy, and unchanging trust, they supported without faltering the heavy burden that tended to make them fail in their commitment to their [original] purposes. Very much in particular, I give thanks to the priests of the secular clergy, to other persons of note, and to everyone else who assisted in this enterprise.

Finally, let us all come to our God in unanimity, with delicious tones and accents, offering him the precious fruits we have harvested by his aid. Let us make ourselves present to his benign and august presence, our countenances smiling and happy, wounded with the piercing arrow of his most burning love. Swiftly let us flourish the sharp sword of good works and virtuous feelings against slander.[5] Receive often with all fervor the sacraments of Penance and the Eucharist. These are those spiritual remedies which Christ our Life provided for our salvation and our inner consolation.

In any way I can assist you, I will cheerfully do so. Let today be your way of thanking me. Your doing so will fill the Father of Light with great satisfaction, and in this way let us rise all together with good hearts in soaring flight to eternal glory.

Quam mihi, et vobis—As [God has done great things] for me, so [He has and will] for you.[6]

—end—

Antonio José Martínez's 1832 Panegyric

In the spring of 1831, Antonio Barreiro moved from the southern part of the Mexican Republic to Santa Fe to serve as the *asesor* (legal advisor) to the New Mexican government. To further his own political career, he shortly gained the presidency of the fledgling "Patriotic Society" to sponsor an elaborate public celebration of the Sixteenth of September, the fiesta of Nuestra Señora de los Dolores in 1810 on which Padre Miguel Hidalgo, pastor of Dolores in Guanajuato, began the war for Mexican independence by uttering the "Grito de Dolores." The next year, 1832, Barreiro was again the president of the "Grand Patriotic Commission" to arrange even bigger and better festivities, so he invited Santiago Abreu, Juan Esteban Pino, and Agustín Duran—three very important men about town—to be members of a subcommittee appointed to invite the people to decorate their houses for the evenings of the fifteenth and sixteenth of September.[1]

Since on 7 November 1830 Padre Antonio José Martínez of Taos had been elected one of the *vocales propietarios* of the departmental assembly, he had traveled to Santa Fe for the sessions in 1831 and 1832. Barreiro and he would surely have known each other, and it was probably Barreiro who invited Martínez, on behalf of "The Grand Patriotic Commission," to sing the High Mass on the morning of the Sixteenth of September and deliver a formal panegyric in honor of the great patriot Hidalgo.[2] Along with

---

1. The "Sociedad Patriotica" had been founded in Santa Fe on 1 July 1829; see "Los asuntos pendientes ante el Supremo Govierno, y camaras de la Yn[ter]ior," 15 April–1 September 1831, MANM reel 13, frame 628. Lansing Bartlett Bloom, "New Mexico Under Mexican Administration, 1821–1846," *Old Santa Fe* 1, no. 4 (April 1914), 271, 364. Barreiro to Santiago Abreu and reply, 20–21 August 1832, MANM 14:962-64 with Barreiro adding the rationale: "That such adornment might contribute to the magnificence and the enthusiasm that all should show on such a happy day." On the function of the *asesor*, see Daniel Tyler, "New Mexico in the 1820s: The First Administration of Manuel Armijo" (Ph.D. diss., University of New Mexico, 1970), pp. 243-44.

2. Martínez was evidently absent from Taos 14–21 September 1832, for there are no baptisms, marriages, or burials listed in the parish books between the 13th and the 22nd; see Taos Baptism Book 1830-33, p. 31v (Archives of the Archdiocese of Santa Fe microfilms, reel 20, frame 260), Taos Marriage Book 1827–33, p. 91r (reel 32, frame 807), and Taos Burial Book 1827–50, p. 116r (reel 42, frame 236).

3. Drawing. La Parroquia. Santa Fe, New Mexico.
Courtesy of the Museum of New Mexico,
negative number 10054.

Barreiro's other strategies—which included writing the *Ojeada* (1832) and gaining control of the first printing press in New Mexico to publish *El Crepúsculo* as a campaign newspaper—the Dolores celebrations he fostered seem to have aided Barreiro's political career, for he was elected to the Mexican National Assembly in February 1833 and reelected in the fall of the next year.³

Padre Miguel Hidalgo y Costilla was born 8 May 1753 near the city of Guanajuato and died 30 July 1811 in Chihuahua. He studied with the Jesuits until they were expelled from the whole Spanish empire in 1767, then at the Colegio de San Nicolás and at the Universidad de México. After a few years in a Tridentine seminary, the type mandated by the sixteenth-century Council of Trent, he was ordained in 1789. He taught philosophy and theology at San Nicolás and served as rector, but after some brushes with the Inquisition on account of his interest in contemporary thought, he turned to parish work. Hidalgo worked less for the spiritual than for the economic and cultural betterment of his parishioners, especially by introducing new agricultural methods, fostering little cottage industries, and founding a theater and an orchestra.

The civil and ecclesiastical establishment of New Spain looked down on the lower clergy who staffed the parishes, most of whom were *criollos* (New Spain-born of European ancestry) or *mestizos* (of mixed Indian and Spanish blood), and they kept them from advancement, saving church positions of real power such as bishoprics for their own kind, the European-born

---

3. Bloom, 1:364. Barreiro and Martínez must have had an interesting off-and-on relationship, for in his *Ojeada* (1832) Barreiro had showed great lack of deference to the pastor of Taos: "Father Martínez (a native of this soil) prepared an exposition in which he said that New Mexico had men capable of filling all positions. . . . It created a great sensation, but, one must confess, it was filled with a lot of nonsense—*y en fin, hizo gran ruido; pero es necesario confesar que ella fué disparatada*." Earlier in his book, though, Barreiro had been more kind (though he reversed the Padre's given names): "Since I have been informed that Father Don José Antonio Martínez, the territorial delegate, set forth a statement [*esposicion*] which was approved by the delegation and which was forwarded to the government, I shall refrain from addressing the government more extensively on this subject." *Three New Mexico Chronicles* (Albuquerque: The Quivira Society, 1942), p. xx; pp. 140, 304, 46, and 290. Barreiro left New Mexico in October 1834 not to return, according to Bloom, *NMHR* 3 (1928):74, and the priest soon acquired Barreiro's pioneer printing press and launched his own remarkable career as a publisher.

Marc Simmons refers to Antonio Barreiro's "cultivated and legalistic mind . . . a strong sense of civic responsibility and a respect for social order," phrases that describe Padre Martínez equally exactly; "Antonio Barreiro's 1833 Proclamation on Santa Fe City Government," *El Palacio* 76, no. 3 (Summer 1970), 25.

Josiah Gregg and his partner Joseph Sutton brought the press into New Mexico from Saint Louis in July 1834; see Douglas McMurtrie, "The Beginning of Printing in New Mexico," with "Afterword" by Pamela Smith, *Book Talk* 16, no. 1 (February 1987), 1-6.

gachupines and a few criollos of the finest families. But these clerics of the lower clergy were educated, and when the Hidalgo revolution began many of them turned their talents to revolutionary journalism. And they were able leaders, well-connected with the Indians and *castas* who composed the mass of the people; their pastors knew their sufferings at first hand as few of the lay revolutionists did, and therefore many priests became indispensable leaders during the phase of the Mexican Revolution known as "the insurrection of the clergy."[4]

The Spanish captured, defrocked, and executed Hidalgo within a year of the Grito, but he regained his good reputation after Mexico won its independence in the early 1820s. The New Mexican Diputación de Territorio proposed in March and April 1831 to secure statehood in the Mexican Federation "teniendo la denominacion de Estado de Hidalgo—taking the name State of Hidalgo." But though that plan came to nothing, the name of the revolutionary priest remained in the memories and songs of the New Mexican people.[5]

Rhetorical theory reached high levels during Latin classicism, and in the High Middle Ages it returned as a major force directing the tradition of preaching in western Europe. From here it entered the "textbook tradition" of homiletics in the Tridentine seminaries of the Roman Catholic Church and hence dominated the pulpit from the sixteenth century onward.

Padre Antonio José Martínez's panegyric in honor of Padre Hidalgo,

---

4. Lillian Fisher, *The Background of the Movement for Mexican Independence* (Boston: Christopher Publishing, 1934), p. 256, and especially Karl M. Schmitt, "The Clergy and the Independence of New Spain," *Hispanic American Historical Review* 34 (1954), 289-312, naming Fathers Hidalgo, Morelos, Mier, Torres, Jiménez, Cos, Rayón, Velasco, de Herrera, San Martín, Peredo, and Mina. Schmitt concludes that (despite guesses by some historians that three-quarters to four-fifths of the lower clergy went into rebellion in the 1810–15 period) most of the lower clergy were minimally involved simply because the active rebellion spread into so little of the kingdom.

5. Mexican Archives of New Mexico, reel 13, frames 635 and 638. John Donald Robb Collection, Fine Arts Library, University of New Mexico, no. 523. The first chorus goes:
Viva el nombre de Hidalgo en la tierra
quien proclamó el estandarte
y hacia su patrí le dijo anheloso
¡Libertad, libertad ó morir!

See also the Rubén Cobos Collection, no. 696; tape 51.A.9.f, Colorado College, Colorado Springs.

with its rhetorical flights and its "screaming eagle" nationalism, was a set piece for a solemn, formal, Santa Fe occasion, a sung Mass on a great national holiday which was simultaneously the important feast of Nuestra Señora de los Dolores, in the presence of the assembled community and all its civil and religious leaders when there was as yet no separation of church and state.

The panegyric honoring the supreme national hero stays very close to the classical form of the oration taught in the seminaries during Martínez's day. It begins with the announcement in Latin and Spanish of the text (*thema* or *textus*) from Holy Scripture; then there follow the exordium proper and the statement of the whole subject (the *propositio*, which is like a thesis statement). A prayer for divine help followed by a repetition of the Latin text serves very effectively as a transitional device in the absence of a formal *divisio* or *partitio* of the subject, a feature that might be expected between the *exordium* and the body of the panegyric.[6]

The body of the panegyric is almost entirely an alternation of two "parts" which were often intermingled in practice: *narration* or *history* and *confirmation* or *proof*. The first element, narration or history, tells of the actual occurrences of the past, in this case the events of the Spanish conquest under Cortés and the Mexican Revolution under Hidalgo; the second, confirmation or proof, allows the preacher to follow up his *propositio* by interpreting each event of his narrative and demonstrating that his interpretation is altogether persuasive. Toward the end of the body, Martínez drops in a brief pro-forma *refutatio* (*reprehensio*) to rebut an imaginary adversary's possible objections.[7]

---

6. Louis de la Place, *De Eloquentia Sacra Concionatoris* (Peking: Pei T'ang, 1927), p. 30; Edward P.J. Corbett, *Classical Rhetoric* (New York: Oxford University Press, 1971), p. 303; James J. Murphy, *Rhetoric in the Middle Ages* (Berkeley: University of California Press, 1974), pp. 12-13, 307-8, 321, 325, 346-51. Murphy, p. 225, notes that because the *divisio* was omitted from the *ars dictaminis* (theory of letter-writing) in twelfth-century Bologna, it tended to drop from other rhetorical genres. The divisio could occur after the *narratio-historia* and before the *confirmatio-probatio*.

James L. Kinneavy, *A Theory of Discourse* (New York: Norton, 1980), pp. 266-72, gives a good overview of Aristotle's divisions with helpful references to Cicero and Quintilian.

7. De la Place, pp. 31, 46-48; Corbett, pp. 321, 323; Murphy, pp. 13-14, 348, 351-53. De la Place, p. 37, Corbett, p. 314, and Brian Vickers, *In Defense of Rhetoric* (Oxford: Clarendon Press, 1988), pp. 344-45, all note that the *historia* can just as well take the form of a non-narrative statement of the facts about the subject, so that the word "history" can mean what it means in the phrase "natural history."

The *peroration* or *conclusion* ends the panegyric with a brief *recapitulation*, a highly rhetorical summary of the main points, and an attempt to bring the listeners a few practical resolutions-to-action, the motive power for which stems from some carefully elicited emotions.[8]

The panegyric survives in two copies in the Ritch Papers, Henry E. Huntington Library, San Marino, California. In a ledger, one copy makes up part of the "Biography of Antonio José Martínez" written by Santiago Váldez about 1885, and there is an unsatisfactory English summary by Larkin G. Read; microfilms of the Ritch Papers, no. 2210, reel 8. The preferred version of the Hidalgo panegyric, a step closer to Padre Martínez's final intention, appears in the surviving loose pages of the rough draft (no. 2209, reel 5).

---

8. Bernard Feeney, *Manual of Sacred Rhetoric* (St. Louis: B. Herder, 1901), pp. 284-300; T.J. Potter, *Sacred Eloquence* (New York: Frederick Pustet, 1913), pp. 305-12; Corbett, p. 328; and Murphy, pp. 14, 354.

Panegirica por El Padre Hidalgo

"Contrivit Dominus baculum impiorum, virgam dominantium" (Isaias cap. 14, v. 5)

"Quebró el Señor el vaculo de los impíos, y la vara de los que dominaban."

Aquella mano poderosa, aquel brazo de Omnipotente que en todos los tiempos, en todas las edades, y en todas las naciones, se vé brillar en el misterio de su justicia, de sus juicios incomprehensibles, y de todas sus acciones *ad extra*, pero siempre remunerando constantemente á cada uno, segun el merito ó demerito de sus obras: nos representa en esta vez, en que celebramos el dia, en que se dió principio a la obra maxima de conseguir la libertad, en nuestra America Septentrional los portentos que dispuso practicar para su empresa y consecucion.[9] Nuestra America es libre, y absuelta del pesado yugo, con que por trescientos años, le abrumada la tirania Española, el mago de la Europa, para alcanzar tan grande honor, triunfo tan abultado y ventajoso, usa el Señor de medios, que no dejan de ser comunes, y propios a su providencia en la via ordinaria: el Señor trata de probar a sus queridos, a sus amigos, a sus Ministros fieles, en las adversidades, y contra-tiempos en la mision, a que los destina desempeñen: "Tamcuam aurum in fornace probavit electos suos—asi como el oro en el horno, probó a sus selectos": los hace a veces tocar la muerte, en que les confiere el galardon de felicidades en aquella vida de inmortalidad, pero despues que dejaron demostrado su esfuerza, su constante adhesion al desempeño de su empresa, despues que dejaron por modelo su actividad, su ejemplo, y superados los mas dificiles obstaculos, abrieron los Caminos para que se proceda en rectitud al blanco que les fijó la Providencia.[10] Asi los condecora el Dios de las bondades, y los asemeja a su principal enviado, a su hijo unigenito, a su Cordero, que vino a salvar al mundo de la esclavitud, y dominacion del principe de las tinieblas.[11] Esto hizo con nuestro Hidalgo, con el Parroco de Dolores: lo constituyó pastor de almas en merito de su literatura, y de sus obras, de sus portes finos y arreglados; pero sobre esto

---

9. Actions of the divinity *ad extra*—creating or affecting the external world of spirit or matter—are not performed by one of the divine Persons to the exclusion of the others but by all three as a unity. The sentence also quotes Matthew 16:27 and echoes an often-used Latin prayer that translates "We beseech you, Lord, to direct our actions by your inspiration and carry them forward by your aid, so that every work of ours may always begin from you and through you be brought to completion."

10. There are many scriptural echoes here: Hebrews 12:6, citing Proverbs 3:12 and 13:21; Martínez's own combination of Proverbs 27:21 and Sirach 27:6; and Isaiah 41:1.

11. Martínez sets up a complex analogy like this: Hidalgo is to Christ as his followers are to Christ's followers as the Mexican battlefields ("altars") are to the cross ("an altar") as Spain is to

Panegyric in Praise of Padre Miguel Hidalgo

I. BEGINNING: A. TEXT.

"Contrivit Dominus baculum impiorum, virgam dominantium" (Isaias 14:5)

"The Lord broke the staff of the impious and the rod of those who held dominion."

B. EXORDIUM.

That powerful hand, that arm of the Almighty which in all times, in all ages, and among all nations shines out in the mystery of its justice, of its incomprehensible judgments, and of all its actions upon this our world, always rewarding each man according to the merit or demerit of his works: it reminds us at this time, when we celebrate the day on which He began the great work of achieving liberty in our North America, of the wonders He put into practice through His original impulse and its completion.[9] Our America is free, absolved from the heavy weight under which for three hundred years the tyranny of Spain, that necromancer of Europe, crushed her; to achieve such great honor, a triumph so immense and exalted, the Lord used means which were beyond what would be ordinary and appropriate for His Providence in ordinary life. The Lord resolves to prove His chosen ones, His friends, His faithful disciples, in the adversities and hard times, in the mission which He destined them to accomplish. "Like gold in the furnace He tried His elect"—He tries them, at times even unto death, by which He confers on them the reward of happiness in immortal life, but not before they have left behind a demonstration of their energy, their continual loyalty to the working out of His venture, not before they have provided a model of His activity, His example, and [His] overcoming the most difficult obstacles, opening the pathways along which they might proceed blamelessly to the target which His providence had fixed for them.[10] Thus the God of good gifts adorned them, and He made them resemble this principle, sending them His only-begotten Son, his Lamb, who came to save the world from the slavery and domination of the Prince of Darkness.[11]

Hell and witchcraft. Enrique Florescano, *Memory, Myth, and Time in Mexico* (Austin: University of Texas Press, 1994), pp. 220, 232, notes that many other writers of the era drew the same parallel between Christ and Hidalgo that Martínez does.

Mexican independence led inevitably to a tilt away from Spain and toward the Aztecs. For a fascinating treatment, see John Leddy Phelan, "Neo-Aztecism in the Eighteenth Century and the

lo constituyó el Señor por el heroe Libertador de nuestra America, y al efecto le brindó las ideas filantropicas arbitradoras de nuestra Libertad.

La America se hallaba opresa desde la Conquista de Hernan Cortez, en que quedó dominada por la España; pero en este dia, que Hidalgo da impetuosamente principio a la gran obra de redimirla, de sacudir al yugo de impiedad, y traerla a su primer esplendor, escribe, estampa y autentica en los marmoles irruptibles con letras de oro, la idea exemplar que exitará el entusiasmo para llevarla adelante, a pesar de que entienda, que por esta há de ser sacrificado; no faltarán a este caudillo medios, ni arbitrios, que aunque mortificados por algun tiempo, lleguen a realidad, y a efecto, obra tan importante, que el primer Autor le habia confiado, de sus compañeros que acaudilla, quedaron con los demas medios referidos, dispociciones, que paulatinamente fomentaron aquella, hasta quebrar el baculo de los impíos, romper la vara de los dominantes, y exaltar nuestra America al rango de Nacion libre, independiente, Señora de si misma, y toda habida en felicidad; mientras nuestro gran Hidalgo, despues de sufrir el martirio, que le infieren los tiranos, es colocado en la posesion de recompensa, que el Señor tiene preparada a sus escogidos [1 Corintios 2:9; Isaías 64:4].

Esta será la proposicion que me empeñaré a demostraros, y para lo cual conseguir, me habeis de ayudar a impetrar el divino Auxilio.

"Contrivit Dominus *etc ut supr.*"

El 16 de Septiembre de 1810. En esa epoca memorable, que a esta fecha corren 22 años, amaneció en esta America de los Estados Unidos Mejicanos, el dia triunfante, alegre y lleno de Caridad, que con sus blancos candores, y luminosos radios, comensó a desterrar las mas negras sombras, con que la tirania, se paseaba envolviendo en la ignorancia, en el error, y en la esclavitud a los hijos del Anahuac: en este dia digno de memoria: Hidalgo, este gran hombre, heroe de nuestra felicidad politica y libertad: proclamó en su brillo, el exercicio deste atributo con que la humana naturaleza decora a sus individuos, y de que el mismo Dios, autor de los hombres, nunca los há privado o interrumpido, aun a pesar de que haciendo estos abusos, le violen los fueros de sus preceptos, incurriendo en el pecado.[12]

Estaban los Mejicanos, estaban estos hijos predilectos del Altisimo, en el yugo del servilismo condicion, que le es toda grata al despotismo tiranico de los Reyes para alimentarse, y mantenerse a costa de los miserables oprimidos con sutilesas, con astucias, y con todos aquellos medios desproporcionados, con que la codicia, y ambicion maquinan contumasmente la ruina, y habatimiento [abatimiento] de los pueblos.

Genesis of Mexican Nationalism," *Culture in History*, ed. Stanley Diamond (New York: Columbia University Press, 1960), pp. 760-70; for a judicious contemporary reaction, see Thomas E. Chávez, "Naivete, Cultural Denigration, and Hispanic Bashing: History Comes to Roost in 1992," *La Crónica de Nuevo México*, no. 34 (December 1992), p. 2.

This He did with our Hidalgo, with the Pastor of Dolores: He made him the shepherd of souls in recompense for his literary attainments, his good works, and his exemplary and well-regulated life; but above and beyond this, the Lord fashioned him to be the hero-liberator of our America, and to this effect He endowed him with judicious philanthropic ideas about our liberation.

C. PROPOSITION—ENDING WITH A PRAYER FOR HEAVENLY AID

America found itself oppressed since its conquest by Hernan Cortés during which she remained under Spanish domination. But on that day when Hidalgo gave a powerful impulse to the great work of redeeming her, of shaking off the yoke of impiety and returning her to her original splendor, he writes and attests, on unbreakable marble with letters of gold, the exemplary idea which arouses the enthusiasm to raise her up, to prevail in what he intends; and for that cause he must be sacrificed. That leader lacked neither means nor expedients; although subdued for a time, a work that important would unquestionably be made reality and achieve its effect—a work so important that the original Author had entrusted it to the companions whom he commands to remain with the rest of the appointed means, which would gradually break even the scepter of the impious, break even the rod of those who hold dominion, and exalt our America to the rank of a free and independent nation, her own mistress and possessing complete happiness. Meantime our great Hidalgo, after suffering the martyrdom which the tyrants inflicted upon him, is established in the possession of the reward which the Lord has prepared for his chosen ones [1 Corinthians 2:9; Isaiah 64:4].

This will be the proposition which I will set myself to explicate for you, and for this end you have to help me by imploring the help of God. [Here Martínez probably led the congregation in the Hail Mary.]

D. REPETITION OF TEXT.

"The Lord has broken . . . ," as above.

II. MIDDLE: E. NARRATION AND CONFIRMATION.

The 16th of September, 1810: in that memorable epoch, from which time until now has been twenty-two years, in this America of the United Mexican States dawned the triumphant day, happy and full of love, which with its white freshness and its luminous rays began to banish those black

---

12. Anáhuac is the Nahuatl name for the Valley of Mexico, the region immediately surrounding Tenochtitlán (Mexico City). In the next sentence, Martínez refers to human liberty, which in the Catholic understanding God did not remove from mankind despite original sin. "*Libertad*" was Hidalgo's *grito*.

Si, la ambicion: esta pasion dominante de los testas coronadas, fué la que impulsó a la codiciosa España, a que hiciera sus calculos, tirase sus medidas, y flotarse los inmensos mares, hasta realizar los nuevos descubrimientos, que la habian de enriqueser, y fortificar mas en su trono: llegaronse al fin los tiempos en que lograron saltar en tierra sus navios, en las costas de nuestra America; viose lansar Hernan Cortes sobre los Mexicanos, como un torrente impetuoso que inunda al suelo patria, que desbastará con el tiempo a estos inocentes moradores: observa muy de luego la inquietud y congoja, que causo su arribo a las incolas del nuevo mundo: pulsa los grados del temor que con la sorpresa les produce a aquella insolita, y repentina invasion: compara la distancia de sus conocimientos en el arte de la guerra, sobre la imperfecta ciencia de los Indios para defenderse de choque que les dan; a Monthesuma, que impera este nacion, a este gran principe de sobrapoder y *numen* en sus subditos, pero le falta el valor, la disciplina, y la energia en sus disposiciones.[13]

A consequencia de todo esto, aquellos famosos Pueblos, que cada dia parecian renacer por su vecindad, por sus riquezas, por su inocencia y por todas sus virtudes politicas; se vieron desaparecer como las fantasmas representadas en los sueños; pues validos los Mejicanos en diferentes encuentros: engrosadas la filas del invasor por su astucia; de los incautos Tlaxcaltecas; en vano resistio la Capital, al fin se vió precisada a sucumbir; muere el poseedor del Imperio, de los magnates unos son quemados vivos, otros espiran en el tormento, los Reyes son ahorcados por sentencia de Cortes: y por ultimo con la sangre de cien mil Mejicanos, que se vieron peligrar se tiñeron las aguas de sus rios, y sus campos quedaron cubiertos de cadaveres.[14]

Deste modo constituye la España su trono en el misero Anahuac, y sus habitantes son victima de la sorpresa, yaciendose innumerables en el sepulcro donde descansan mientras por tres siglos quedan sus reliquias en la esclavitud, arrastrando duras y pesadas cadenas, sin poder arbitrar en la practica los medios, que les mejorasen la suerte. Mas cuando ya se llegó el tiempo, cuando ya la providencia del Altisimo, inspiró en su libertador, que destinó heroe, los medios con que habia de restituir a su pueblo a su

---

13. Montezuma, the principal Aztec administrator of Mexico at the time of Cortés's arrival, was more a CEO than a king; Bandelier called him "head war-chief of the confederates"—"Hernando Cortés," *Catholic Encyclopedia* (New York: Robert Appleton, 1908), 4:399. A fortiori, Montezuma was surely not a god. When he was deposed and assassinated, the Aztecs had no particular problem replacing him.
14. The Tlaxcaltecans were colonized enemies of the Aztecs who became the Spaniards' allies. William H. Prescott, working with the best available sources of that time, quoted estimates of the number killed by Cortés during fall of Tenochtitlán at 120,000 to 240,000, adding, "It will be safer to dispense with arithmetic where the data are too loose and slippery to afford a foothold for getting at truth"; *History of the Conquest of Mexico* (Philadelphia: Lippincott, 1873), 3:196-97. The excellent contemporary account by Hugh Thomas, *Conquest: Montezuma, Cortés, and the Fall of Old*

shadows with which tyranny had wrapped the children of Anáhuac in ignorance, error, and slavery. On this most memorable day, Hidalgo, that great man, hero of our political happiness and liberty, proclaimed in his resplendence the exercise of that attribute with which human nature adorns her individuals and which God Himself, Author of mankind, never has removed or interrupted, not even to punish those who abuse and violate the norms of His precepts by falling into sin.[12]

The Mexicans, those chosen children of the Most High, were under the yoke of hard slavery, which is quite acceptable to the tyrannical despotism of the kings who feed and maintain themselves at the expense of those wretched people, oppressed by artifice, by cunning, and by all those disproportionate means with which greed and ambition contrive continually [to further] the ruin and degradation of peoples.

Yes, ambition, that predominant passion of crowned heads, was what impelled greedy Spain to cast up her calculations, risk her means, and sail the immense seas so as to realize new discoveries which must enrich her and fortify her throne more than ever: those times come to pass when the ships successfully land on the coast of our America. Behold, Hernán Cortés throws himself upon the Mexicans like a raging torrent that floods the fatherland, that soon devastates the innocent inhabitants. He observes from a great distance the distress and dismay his arrival causes the people who dwell in the New World, he explores the degrees of fear he produces in them due to surprise and such an unaccustomed and sudden invasion, and he compares his superior knowledge of the arts of war with the imperfect science of the Indians when they try to repel his attack upon them. Montezuma, the ruler of this nation, seems a great prince, a superman, even a deity to his subjects; but his courage, his discipline, his energy in decisions of strategy all fail.[13]

In consequence of all this, those famous peoples who seem because of their neighborhood, their riches, their innocence, and their many political virtues seem to be born anew each day—simply disappear like the fantasies that appear in dreams. Though the Mexicans prevail in various battles, the ranks of the crafty invader grow stronger [by adding] the heedless Tlaxcaltecans; the Capital resisted in vain, finally finding it necessary to surrender; the lord of the empire dies, some of the aristocrats are burned alive, some die under torture, the kings are hanged by Cortés's decree, and finally the rivers are tinged with the blood of a hundred thousand Mexicans, and the countryside lies burdened with cadavers.[14]

Mexico (New York: Simon and Schuster, 1993), pp. 528-29, suggests 100,000 Mexica (Martínez's figure exactly) killed in the fighting, many by the Tlaxcaltecans, and perhaps 40,000 suicides by drowning after the loss.

primer estado, y bajo las regulaciones, que perpetuasen sus felicidades hasta la consumacion de los siglos. Se conmovieron los cielos de nuestra existencia, y impregnandose las nuves de fecundidad, nos llovieron al justo Hidalgo,[15] al que alimentaron nuestros frutos, como al escojido para engrinaldar la deadema [diadema] de inmortalidad en nuestros suelos, plantando el inmarcesible arbol de la livertad; el meditaba dia y noche infatigable los modos en que habia de proceder inflexible hasta vindicar a sus patria querida, como el autor primero lo habia destinado a este rango de patriotismo, comunica sus ideas, y determinaciones al General Allende; lo hayó conforme a sus proyectos; juntan sus brazos amicablemente: dirigen a Dios sus votos, invocando su auxilio, reunen todas las fuerzas, que anticipadamente habian preparado; y a las doce de la noche del 15 de Septiembre de 1810, dijeron "*Libertad*," esta solemne aclamacion: esta voz encantadora de los hombres emanaba de su heroe,[16] se difunde con indecible velocidad; electrisa los aires para propagarla por todos los Angulos de nuestra Republica; luego que resuena este eco de dulsura en los oidos de los oprimidos, estos se levantan erguidos, y como en rapto del amor intenso de la patria se adornan en conspiracion a la importante empresa, que han de llevar a conclusion.

    Me figuro en estos heroes, a los que ocacionaron la historia Sagrada, que se trae en los libros de los Macabeos:[17] a aquellos valerosas campeones que a todo trance se resolvieron a sostener los derechos de su nacion, y deste autenticar su constancia con la sangre de sus venas, peleando esforsadamente por la causa de su patria, de su Templo, y de sus leyes. Así vemos a nuestro Hidalgo, que para realisar sus medidas, ordenadas a la gran empresa, en que ha de salvar a su amada patria, asociado, como hé dicho, con el General Allende: constituyen su exercito: le dan por patrona a Virgen de Guadalupe,[18] los exhortan a que se porten con el valor que les brinda el cielo, segun lo justo de la causa, que controvierten; con todos los demas recuerdos, que exitan naturalmente el inardecimiento a su primer obligacion. Deste modo gerantorisan [garantizaron] sus conatos con el rompimiento de la guerra, procuran en esta economisar la sangre humana;[19]

    15. The Advent and Christmas liturgy applied Isaiah 45:6 to Jesus: "Let the heavens drop dew and the clouds rain down the Just One."

    16. General Ignacio Allende (1769–1811) was an early revolutionary associate of Padre Hidalgo's and his second-in-command. Hugh M. Hamill, *The Hidalgo Revolt* (Gainesville: University of Florida Press, 1966), p. 200, states that later in the revolution Allende was so distressed by Hidalgo's bad instincts as a leader that he plotted to poison him and actually did hold him as a prisoner. More accurately, the *grito* was given at about two in the morning on the sixteenth.

    17. A second-century B.C. family of devout Jewish rebels against the Seleucid Syrian kings who wished to force their cult on the Jews. They symbolize a God-inspired resistance to an unholy colonialism.

    18. Nuestra Señora de Guadalupe became the patroness of the Mexican revolutionaries, and Nuestra Señora de los Remedios became the patroness of the Spanish loyalists. The Olympian deities' involvements in the Trojan War were clear and credible by comparison.

By these means Spain sets up its throne atop the wretched Anáhuac, and its citizens are the victim of surprise, resting in their grave in countless numbers, while for three centuries their offspring remain in slavery, dragging hard and heavy chains, powerless to put into practice the means to ameliorate their lot. But when the time came, the providence of the Most High inspired His liberator, whom He destined as hero, and made available the means to restore His people to their original state, under laws which would perpetuate their happiness until the end of the ages. The skies of our existence moved themselves, and the clouds were heavy with fertility and rained down for us the just Hidalgo,[15] the man who nourished himself on our fruits, as the chosen one to garland the crown of immortality in our land, planting the unfading tree of liberty. Indefatigable, he meditated day and night the means of proceeding directly toward the vindication of his beloved fatherland, [for] the Prime Author had destined him to the first rank of patriotism. He communicated his ideas and plans to General Allende, and he found him amenable to his project. They joined hands in friendship, spoke their vows to God calling upon His aid, joined all those forces which they had prepared in anticipation; and at midnight on the fifteenth of September 1810 cried "Liberty!"—that solemn acclamation, that cry so alluring to mankind issued from the hero.[16] It spread itself with inexpressible speed; it charged the air to propagate itself throughout all the corners of our Republic; this echo of sweetness resounded in the ears of the oppressed. They raised themselves erect, and graced themselves with the rapture of intense love for the fatherland in a united effort for the important project which they were determined to carry through to the end.

These heroes remind me of those others who fill Salvation History, whose deeds fill the Books of the Maccabees,[17] those valorous champions who pledge themselves to sustain through every peril the rights of their country and thereby validate their loyalty with the blood of their veins, strenuously fighting for the cause of their country, their church, and their laws. So we come to our Hidalgo, who (so as to realize his means) ordered everything to the great enterprise through which he must save his beloved country. In union, as I have said, he and General Allende gather their army. They name as patroness the Virgin of Guadalupe,[18] they exhort the soldiers to act courageously as Heaven invites them, in a manner suitable to the justice of the cause they fight for, together with all the rest of the reasons which naturally excite the [tendency] toward their fundamental obligation. By these means they guaranteed their efforts with the outbreak of warfare, contriving thus to avoid wasting human blood,[19] and they saved at

---

19. Martínez here charitably glosses over Hidalgo's unwillingness to commit his army to battle, thereby dithering past various golden opportunities.

y que se salvasen a costa de los comprometidos en la lucha los fueros de la naturaleza, y los preciosos derechos de la sociedad, pero a estas justas pretenciones, la saña impia de la España, todo lo perturba inquieto el espiritu de la paz, y motiva el voras destroso, que cubre los campos de cada seres, enluta la Tumba de de [sic] nuestra America, y exita a formar tristes lamentos, repetidos Ayer, a los padres que quedan sin sus hijos, a estos que les faltaron sus padres, a las esposas que desamparadas quedan por haber peligrado sus maridos, a estos por las miserias de sus consortes, y en una palabra a todos generalmente cuando ven la estrecha necesidad, que la espada cortante ha de decidir la controversa, y empeñarse los Mejicanos hasta morir como lo cumplen.

Sean testigos de todo esto, áquel magestuoso Monte de las Cruces, aquellos anclurosos [sic] campos de Aculco, Guanajuato y Calderon, en cujas sitios se vieron lastimosamente practicar las matansas que exigidos como en Altares se ofrecieron en ellas en holocausto por la livertad,[20] ellos nos recomiendan a la meditacion el valor y gloria de los que pelearon, y que deste modo dieron en aquellos campos de honor, el imitable exemplo, en que habian de continuar despues sus conciudadanos, hasta lograr el triunfo que hoy celebramos, con gran aplauso en accion de gracias al Señor. Seanse los anales de los pueblos, que hacen el Orbe, corranse con el registro las historias de los tiempos pasados, desembuelvanse los faustos de los grandes acontecimientos, y se hallará claramente, que en ningun tiempo, y por ninguna nacion se sostuvo la guerra con mas ardor, ni la causa de la livertad fué defendida y proclamada con mas acierto; pues aquella resolucion en cierto modo sobrenatural,[21] ni fué coactada, ni con interesantes promesas, ni con suplicios practicados, ni con escomuniones fulminadas, ni con todas cuantos arbitrios. Pudo inventar la furia Española, con nada de esto los hacen vanvalear. El justo Hidalgo, nuestro caro libertador, dubla [dobla] cada dia a su empeñoso proposito, y sigue hasta la muerte que le infieren, con el mismo brillo que al principio.

¡O Inmortal Hidalgo! O Glorioso heroe, autor de la libertad en nuestra America! Cuan grandes obras confió a ti la providencia del Altisimo, que siempre designa y acrisola, el destino de sus criaturas, con proporcion a sus justas miras! ¡Cuantas preparaciones, cuantos motivos, revatia aquel tu grandioso espiritu de beneficencia, para salvar a tu amada patria, vindi-

---

20. Monte de las Cruces (30 Oct 1810), Aculco (7 Nov 1810), and Guanajuato (10 September 1810) were sites of fighting between the revolutionists and the loyalists; Puente de Calderón was a disastrous defeat for the Hidalgo rebels on 17 January 1811. The draft version gives "Acapulco," but "Aculco" is correct.

21. The use of this word suggests that Martínez thought that God actively worked on the side of the Mexican revolutionaries in the 1810–20 era in such a manner as to constitute its political

the expense of those involved in the struggle those laws of nature and those precious rights of society. But as to those just claims, the impious passion of Spain perturbs all, disturbs the spirit of peace, and causes a ravenous destruction that covers the fields with cadavers, decks the tomb of our America with mourning cloth, and excites the terrible sad lamentations, repeated yesterday, of parents who have lost their children, children who have lost their parents, of forsaken wives weeping for their endangered husbands, of husbands suffering for the miseries of their wives, and in a word all in general who see the strict necessity of the sharp sword deciding the controversy, embroiling the Mexicans even unto death in the fulfillment of their duty.

Let us cite as witnesses to all this that majestic Monte de las Cruces, those difficult fields of Aculco, Guanajuato, and Calderón, places where those dreadful massacres came about, where lifted up as if on altars a holocaust was offered for liberty.[20] They make us meditate on the courage and glory of those who fought, for in this manner they gave in those fields of honor the example to be imitated which [Hidalgo's] fellow citizens continued until they achieved the triumph which we celebrate today, with great applause and thanksgiving to the Lord. May the annals of the peoples of the world, filled with the history of times gone by, uncover the joys of great events, so that it will be perfectly plain that at no other time and for no other nation was a war fought with more commitment, nor was the cause of liberty defended and proclaimed with greater success. For that resolve was in a certain manner supernatural,[21] not coerced; it was induced neither by seductive promises, nor by the practice of torture, nor by fulminating excommunications, nor by any of the various contrivances which Spanish fury might invent—with none of these can they make them falter. The just Hidalgo, our beloved liberator, continues each day with his bold strategy, continues even unto his inevitable death with the same splendor as at the beginning.

Immortal Hidalgo! O glorious hero, author of liberty in our America! With what great works the providence of the Most High has entrusted you, God who always designates and purifies the destiny of His children in proportion to His just expectations! How much preparation, how many motives and measures your magnanimous spirit of doing good had to un-

---

and military history as part of salvation history properly so-called. The Anglo-American revolutionaries against England in the 1770–80 period even "bent" their deistic theology to enable the God of Natural Reason to intervene on their side; arguing that democracy was what he intended all along, they permitted God to violate the laws of nature a couple of times, then sent him off to behave himself forever after.

candola de las ultrajes del tirano! A ti tributamos los encomios en este dia que celebramos, trayendo a memoria tus [h]asañas, los trofeos, de que se complace el Dios de los alturas, cuyos destinos fielmente le habeis desempeñado! ¡Tu inmortal memoria será propagada de siglo en siglo, y autenticada en el catalogo de los heroes mas famosos, que hán engrandecido su nombre! Si, respetable auditorio, de los mismos hechos se colige que Hidalgo fué de los mas grandes nombres de la tierra.

¿Jusques acaso, que cuando lo comparo a los valerosos Macabeos, trato de elevar su merito, y el de sus Compañeros, acercandolo al de aquellos? Pues ni es este mi intente, sino colocarlo en mas encumbrada Cima: aquellos fueron los testimonias de la Sagrada Escritura, de un valor y merito casi incomparables y protejidas de Dios mismo que Hidalgo invocó; pero lo hicieron comprometidas, dirélo, asi por la dura é indispenable necesidad de defenderse, de repulsar a los agresores de sus suelos patrios que les venian a poner provocacion con fin de arrojarles sus derechos, y explantarlos de la existencia; mas nuestro Hidalgo, puso la expectativa en todo el universo, levantando improvisamente la guerra contra un Gobierno, casi omnipotente, que dominaba nuestra America, bajo el poder que tenia en millones de hombres, que ciegamente le obedecian: que tenia cimentadas sus leyes, y bases de Gobierno, en las mas ingeniosas precoraciones, para atajar a cualesquierá rumor. Aquella lo hacian sobre la suerte indispensable en que se hallaban de, o morir a manos de sus enemigos, o escapar a fuerza de reacer hasta vencerlos. Pero Hidalgo, constituido en livertad, a cerca de hacer la guerra ú omitirla hubo de comprenderla, casi cierto o si me es licito decir, cierto del todo que en ella habia de peligrar. ¡A quien pues lo compararé, para relevar su merito, y que aun le sobra el termino de referencia! ¡Ah! yá lo dije en el exordio! ¡Yá lo anuncié in aquel principio! Lo comparo al libertador al mundo; a J. C. embiado del eterno Padre, a causar la salud espiritual de los pueblos: a este Señor se acemeja en sus hechos, y resoluciones. Jesus vino al mundo, predicó su doctrina, increpó a los malvados, nos dió su exemplo, y por ultimo, murió a persecucion de sus enemigos, y se ofreció al eterno Padre en sacrificio por todos los hombres. Hidalgo siguiendo estas pisadas: amonestó la doctrina de sus determinaciones, atacó a los tiranos, nos dió su ejemplo, y por ultimo murió a espensas de lo mismo por el bien de su patria.

Jesus en su muerte consumio la obra de su Mision, constituyendo los medios en que los hombres habian de ser salvos, pero cuanto a la estencion de las convertidas, solo fué en unos cuantos Pueblos, y estos; no en la totalidad dejando, el complemento de estencion y perfeccion de arreglo a sus Apostoles, y ministros evangelicos, quienes lo cumplen al cabo de muchos

dergo to save your beloved country, avenging for her the outrages of the tyrant! To you we give praise on this day of celebration, recalling your feats, your triumphs, in which the God of Majesty takes delight, He whose designs you have faithfully wrought! Your imperishable memory will be borne onward through the ages, inscribed in the catalogue of those most famous heroes who have glorified God's name! Yes, honored listeners, it is evident from these deeds that "Hidalgo" is one of the greatest names on earth.

F. REFUTATIO.

Perchance you say that when I liken him to the valiant Maccabees, I attempt to inflate his merit and that of his companions, comparing Hidalgo to the Maccabees? But that is not my intention, for I mean to place him on an even more lofty summit: thus the Sacred Scriptures witness to a valor and achievement nearly incomparable and protected by the same God that Hidalgo invoked; but these men were obliged, as it were, by the harsh and unavoidable necessity of defending themselves, of ejecting the invaders from their fatherland, invaders who came to provoke them with the purpose of destroying their rights and eradicating their very existence. But our Hidalgo created hope throughout the whole world, uprising at the moment of war against a nearly omnipotent government that dominated our America under a power that bound millions of persons in blind obedience and that had established its laws, its foundations of government, with the most ingenious care so as to prevent even murmurings against it. This they did, bound by the irreducible dilemma by which they must either die at the hands of their enemies or escape by dint of counterattacking and conquering them. But Hidalgo, conceived in liberty, almost—or if I may say so, surely—understood the dangers of going or not going to war. To whom can I compare him so as to show his merits, so the terms of comparison might be adequate? Ah! I have said it already in the exordium! I have already proclaimed it at the beginning! I compared him to the Savior of the world, to Jesus Christ, sent by the Eternal Father to effect the spiritual salvation of all peoples: Hidalgo resembles the Lord Himself in his deeds and courage. Jesus came into the world, preached His doctrine, reproached the wicked, gave us His example, and at the last He died persecuted by His enemies, offering Himself to the Eternal Father as a sacrifice for all mankind. Following those very footsteps, Hidalgo preached the doctrine of his decisions, attacked the tyrants, gave us his example, finally dying at their hands for the good of his people.

Jesus in His death brought to perfection the work He was sent to do, the creation of the means by which men must be saved, but as to the extent of the converted, He only lived among a few peoples, and those few not

años, aunque esto para el crisol importace mares de Sangre.²² Hidalgo en su muerte, consumó la obra de su destino en los medios, que dejó instituidos, cuales habian de salvar a sus Ciudadanos, y cuyas disposiciones eminentes perseveran en sus dignos compañeros, Apostoles de nuestra libertad: los grandes Morelos, Matamoros, Victorias, Rayones, Brabos, Teranes, Berduscos, y otros muchos . . . con el famoso caudillo de Iguala, quienes al cabo de diez años complementaron la obra, la dieron perfeccion, pusieron en libertad a nuestra America, y deste modo tan honroso el efectivo cumplimiento al juramento de fidelidad prestado a su primer caudillo, al inmortal Hidalgo, aun a pesar de que contaren inmensos sacrificiosos, y de efusion caudalosa de sangre que se causó.²³

Hé aqui los motivos de misteriosa similitud que prestan merito, para compararlo con Jesus en la obra que se confió por el autor Supremo, para salvar al Pueblo Americano, al continente de Anahuac; hé aqui resuelto al paralelo, en los terminos de su glorada [gloriada] contesta, en cuan alto rango de merécimientos, y patriotismo nos colocan al Ilustre heroe, autor de nuestra libertad politica.

¿Por ventura habeis vosotros gustado el dulce nutar, que nos brindan las paginas, que contienen la historia de su vida, y pasos que dió para hacer efectiva esta obra maestra? ¿Habeis acaso alli observado con refleja, que sus instrucciones, sus principios reglamentados con la sana filosofia, disiparon aunque con lenidad la benda, o preocupacion, conque el egoismo Español nos tenia hechisados, y en el letargo de ignorancia, para eternizarnos en la esclavitud, que yaciamos? ¿No es verdad que yá somos libres portales [por tales] medios, y que para regocijar estos gozos, con los conciertos de alegria, que abundan en nuestros corazones, nos habemos reunido el dia de hoy a recompensar el merito de nuestro heroe, con acciones de gracias al Señor, en este aniversario venturoso?

Asi es, venerable auditorio, esto objeto de admiracion, de regocijo, y de contento, se nos há dado a festejar en este dia, en lo que habeis oido referir,

---

22. It is to the work the Father gave him to do that Jesus seems to refer in his "*Consummatum est*—It is completed or perfected" (John 19:30). Martínez repeats the verb *consumó* at the start of the next sentence.

"Complemento de estencion" is a technical latinate phrase from minor logic. The extension of any concept ("calves") is the total set of beings to which it refers (all calves). Any subset of the concept (bull calves) has as its complement all the other beings in the set (heifer calves). Here the set which the concept "totalidad" has as its extension—the whole human race in need of Christ's redemption—would be divided into the subset those-Christ-actually-worked-with and its complement, the subset those-He-left-for-the-Apostles.

23. Many of these revolutionaries are, for some reason known only to Martínez, named in the plural. In the singular, they are as follows:

José María Morelos y Pavón (1765–1815), a priest of poor family who had worked among the poor, became head of a fine organization in southern Mexico. His capture by the Royalists and his trial and execution by the Inquisition was the beginning of the end for the original Hidalgo revolt.

the totality, leaving the complement of extension and its perfection in the hands of the apostles and ministers of His Gospel who completed [the conversion process] after many years, notwithstanding the seas of blood caused thereby.[22] Hidalgo with his death consummated the work he was destined to do through the means that he instituted, means that were meant to liberate his countrymen. His careful arrangement of these means endured in his noble coworkers, the apostles of our liberty: the great Morelos, Matamoros, Victoria, Rayón, Bravo, Terán, Berdusco, and many others, headed by the famous leader of Iguala who at the end of ten years completed the work, brought it to fulfillment, established our America in liberty, and by these means honorably fulfilled the oath of fidelity sworn to their first leader, the immortal Hidalgo, though at the cost of immense sacrifices and the copious shedding of blood which he occasioned.[23]

III. END or PERORATION: G. RECAPITULATION.

Behold here the motives of that mysterious likeness which give merit to a comparison with Jesus in the work the Supreme Author confided to [Hidalgo]: to save the American people, the continent of Anáhuac! Behold here the parallel resolved in terms of his glorious contest: on what a lofty summit of merit and patriotism we place this illustrious hero, author of our political liberty!

Have you, perhaps, tasted the sweet nourishment, offered in the pages which contain the history of his life? Are you not aware of the steps he took to effect his master work? Have you by chance observed there through reflection how his instructions, his well-ordered principles, his healthy philosophy gently dissipated the blindness or distraction by which Spanish egoism held us so bewitched, in such a stupor of ignorance as to keep us perpetually in the slavery in which we lay? Is it not true both that we are now free through his means and that we are glad to rejoice, with the music of happiness

---

Mariano Matamoros y Orive (1770–1814) was a priest and officer.

Guadalupe Victoria, nom de guerre of Felix Fernández de San Salvador (1789–1843), served as Mexican president 1824–29.

Ignacio López Rayón (1773–1832), a criollo lawyer on his honeymoon when he joined the rebellion in Saltillo, continued the rebellion after Hidalgo's death.

Nicolás Bravo (c. 1786–1854) and his father Miguel, members of a wealthy criollo family, joined Hidalgo from the start. Nicolás helped form the government after Iturbide's fall.

Manuel Mier y Terán (1789–1832) served as a general for Morelos in 1814–15.

José Sixto Verdusco (1770–1830) was a chief official in the 1814 congress that set up the revolutionary government.

The *caudillo de Iguala* was Agustín de Iturbide (1783–1824), who finally defeated the Spanish in 1822, named himself emperor of independent Mexico, lost control the next year, and was executed when he returned from exile.

consta que Hidalgo, y sus compañeros lograron con su esfuerzo, con su valor, y su constancia: quebrar el vaculo impio con que nos tiranisaban la España, romper el cetro de los borbones[24] dominantes en nuestra America; constituir la libre, é independiente, exaltarla al rango lustroso en que camina, siendo Señora de si misma; levantarla, en su glorioso concepto, sobre todas las otras naciones, que disputaban este honor.

Estas victorias, estos triunfos referidos a Hidalgo, en el merito de direccion, que les dió: estos, que hacen el jubilo Americano, al verse en salvo los millones, que constituyen sus habitantes, y que le tributan la gratitud, en la perpetuidad de su memoria: el merito en su profesion de fé, que siempre adopto: lo recto de sus obras en la moral evangelica, en todos los demas procederes, dignos de imitacion en la vida social: todas estos, repito, respecto de Dios, de su patria, de los hombres, nos convidan a que lo imitemos, eternicemos sus memorias, y lo contemplemos dichosamente trasportado, en recompensa, a la gloria eterna que os deseo.

---

24. The Bourbon descendants of Louis XIV have ruled Spain intermittently from the War of the Spanish Succession (1701–14) until the present. The passage strongly echoes the initial text from Isaiah.

so abounding in our hearts that we have gathered today to salute the merits of our hero with thanksgiving to the Lord on this happy anniversary?

So it is, worthy listeners, that this object of our admiration, our rejoicing, and our happiness has offered himself to us to celebrate on this day; in what we have heard related, it is clear that Hidalgo and his co-workers triumphed with strength, with bravery, with perseverance—breaking the impious staff by which Spain tyrannized over us, breaking the scepter by which the Bourbons[24] dominated our America, establishing her as free and independent, exalting her to the brilliant rank in which she walks as mistress of herself, raising her up in his glorious plan above all the other nations which claim that honor.

H. RESOLUTION.

These victories, these triumphs belonging to Hidalgo by reason of the merit of guidance he provided, these triumphs bring joy to America; and millions of her inhabitants, seeing themselves saved, offer him the tribute of their gratitude to perpetuate his memory, the merit of the profession of faith he always embraced, the rectitude of his works of living the Gospel, and all his other deeds, worthy of imitation in a life in society: all this, I say again—reverence for God, for his country, for humankind—invite us to imitate him, to immortalize his memory, and to contemplate him happily transported, in recompense, to the eternal glory I wish for you.

—end—

✦

Padre Antonio José Martínez, our orator for the occasion, states the thesis of his panegyric in the Proposition, and its nature is dogmatic theology. Martínez adumbrates his philosophical theology of history—how does God work in human actions?—and he gives his reply in terms of the causal chain that is made up of agents, the means they use, and the effects they achieve.

The *agents* are God and men, especially of course Padre Miguel Hidalgo. The oration refers four times to God as *Primero* or *Supremo Autor* and twice to Hidalgo as *autor de la libertad*. Martínez does not thereby understand God and Hidalgo as equals, nor does he thereby oppose them or their causalities to each other. Instead, he establishes God as the Prime Mover (Universal Efficient Cause) of all the good deeds that humans bring about, and he establishes Hidalgo as a free cooperating secondary agent subordinated *and therefore empowered* to be a co-cause with God.

At one point in the oration, Martínez says that God uses all the Mexican heroes as *means—medios, medidas, modos*—to His end, but he usually presents God and Hidalgo as both using the same means by showing how Hidalgo uses the appropriate means that God has provided. By contrast, the Spaniards use disproportionate means to bring about their tyrannical regime, and they prevent their Mexican subjects from using any means that might better their condition. The mental linkage between Hidalgo's means and the end that he foresees they can bring into being is to be found in the *ideas* which Hidalgo held, ideas which are also referred to as models and exemplars and which Hidalgo both embodied in his very being and integrally imparted to his followers before his death.

The effect (*efecto*) of the combined agency of God and Hidalgo, using appropriate means as instrumental causes, is the realization (the bringing to reality by historical processes) of the ideas of liberty by which Hidalgo thought and lived. As the Father and Christ used appropriate means with a clear sense of purpose and thereby caused the spiritual salvation of the whole human race, so God and Hidalgo used the right means with the correct exemplary ideas and thereby saved the Mexican people politically. Hence the frequent sprinkling of *salvar* (to save) into the text, four times to refer to Hidalgo and six times in reference to Christ.

God, Hidalgo and the other heroes of the Mexican Revolution of 1810–21, the means they used together with the governing ideas that led them to choose those means, and the ultimate effect of liberation are all conjoined into a causal chain which Martínez usually refers to as a work or working (*obra* or *obrar*): God works in human history immediately within the workings of human freedom so as to realize His exemplary ideas which, like the means He employs, are none other than His mysterious purposes in the historical process of becoming.[25]

Like any other traditional hagiography—saint's life—Padre Martínez's panegyric on Padre Hidalgo works to assimilate its subject to a validating pattern to be found in the sacred record of the Judeo-Christian beginning time. Therefore Martínez assimilates Hidalgo to Judas Maccabaeus, but he especially assimilates him to Christ.[26] In so doing, the verbal account of God working wondrous deeds with and through the Christian hero comes into existence as a means by which the saint continues after death to be present and powerful in the world. Hence the saint's life, an *alabanza*, or

---

25. A privately-held devotional document from the same era can plausibly be attributed to Martínez because it makes exactly the same philosophical analysis of divine redemption in exactly the same terms, studying the means (*medidas, medios*) used, distinguishing divinely appointed (*referidos*) from inappropriate (*desproporcionados*) means, and showing how the successful work or working (*obra, obrar*) eventually issues into reality.

26. In a traditional society, archetypalizing meant situating a person in the hierarchically-ordered cosmos which was the only cosmos such a culture knew.

Thomas J. Heffernan, *Sacred Biography* (New York: Oxford University Press, 1988), pp. 63-64 and 78-79, and especially p. 87, "Such a conceptual basis for the depiction of a human personality . . . appears to dismiss *a priori* the belief in a *sui generis* individual, a criterion which is an unquestioned assumption of the modern biographer. However, . . . the idealization of character which resulted from this method was paradoxically not intended by these biographers to diminish the importance of human personality. On the contrary, such a method, they would argue, allowed them to present human personality in its complete fullness, to augment it, by placing the concept of the individual within the larger frame of a collective personality." See Charles F. Altman, "Two Types of Opposition and the Structure of Latin Saints' Lives," *Medievalia et Humanistica* N.S. 6 (1975), 1-11.

Christ as corporate personality is not merely another individual personality competing head-to-head with the human saint; instead, the saint's subordination results in his ontological indestructibility, his noetic authentication, and his pragmatic empowerment.

even a fairly substantial *oración* to the saint should be thought of as an entity in precise parallel to a *santo* or an actual relic: verbal "icon" and verbal "relic" make the saint present in his being, his power, and his intelligibility just as a literal relic or an artistic icon does.[27]

27. Heffernan, *Sacred Biography*, pp. 34-36; on p. 35, Heffernan retells "how a deacon of Autun, suffering from blindness, placed a book containing accounts of the miracles of St. Nicetus over his eyes and was cured at once: 'Immediately the pain and the shadows dissipated, and by the power [*ab virtute*] of this volume he recovered his sight.'"

Fourth of July 1860 Sermon

This patriotic oration is dated 1856 in two hands, neither that of the copyist of the speech itself, but internal evidence—1776 plus 84 years—points clearly to a date of 1860. Consequently, it does not date from the beginning of the falling out between Father Martínez and his rather unbalanced successor Father Dámaso Taladrid but from four years later, two years after Martínez's world had fallen to pieces. Bishop Jean Baptiste Lamy's excommunication, read by Vicar-General Joseph P. Machebeuf on 11 April 1858, was probably not legally valid in canon law, but like many a frontier lynching it was highly effective. The July 1860 date is particularly interesting in that it was at the same time that Lamy made a formal visitation of the parishes of Taos and Arroyo Hondo and entered into the baptismal books the earliest notations of the excommunications of Martínez and his disciple Father Mariano de Jesús Lucero.[1]

This is another patriotic speech, and thus despite its brevity it invites comparison with the Hidalgo panegyric of twenty-eight years earlier. Carlyle and Emerson in particular and the nineteenth century in general tended to focus on great representative individual leaders rather than to think of progress as consisting principally in some broad movement that bears the majority of the people forward from a less satisfactory sociocultural level to a better one: an idea whose time has come. Here "Washistong" replaces Hidalgo as the representative liberating hero.

---

1. Alvarez Papers in the Benjamin Read Collection; item 192 in microfilm reel 2. On the dating of the excommunications, see Steele in E.A. Mares, ed., *Padre Martinez: New Perspectives from Taos* (Taos: Millicent Rogers Museum, 1988), pp. 99-100. On Lamy's visitation in June and July 1860, see Fray Angélico Chávez, *But Time and Chance* (Santa Fe: Sunstone Press, 1981), p. 153, who suggests that Martínez was psychologically out of control—totally in denial—on the topic of Lamy's excommunicating him.

El Cuatro de julio

"Por mi imperan los Principes, y los Poderosos decretan la Justicia"— lib. de los Prov., cap. 8, v. 16.

Este testo del libro de los proverbios, H.T.A., ministra materia para celebrar el aniversario de la gloriosa independencia de los E.U.N.A. que el dia 4 de Julio A.D. 1776, se realisó haciendose independientes de la Gran Bretaña. Pues la sabiduria del altisimo Dios causa universal de todo lo existente :: conservador y Gobernador absoluto, :: inspira, a los legisladores y Gobernantes, lo conveniente para decretar la justicia, para dictar con acierto aquella forma de gobernar, en la que sus criaturas racionales se hán de conducir, a fin de conseguir los honestos fines de la sociedad :: , que son vivir en paz quieta, y tranquilamente; amandose, ayudandose, protegiendose, y llevando uniformemente los pasos por la senda de la justicia; que por ello resulta la felicidad de los Pueblos en general, y de cada uno de los particulares.

Esto fué lo que tubo principio el precitado dia 4 de Julio en el N.A. por el Heroe de la Independencia, el gran Washistong digno de eterna memoria; este Heroe,[2] . . . cuya sabiduria normó . . . publicana, la Simento . . . -ses, que desde entonces ha- . . . alteracion, sino que perm- . . . constitucion uniformem . . . triunfo de libertad fué . . . ficana que a imitacion de los E.U. hizo su independencia desprendiendose de la España, aunque no se halle todavia bien simentada [cimentada], por falta de un genio superior, como el de nuestro Heroe en la America. ¿Pero que digo? No solo fué este triunfo para nuestra Republica y la Mejicana, sino para todas las sociedades del orbe, pues en dondequiera, a ser ejemplo,[3] se sospira [suspira] por esta amada libertad, y por muchas se trata de sacudir el yugo de las monarquias, y algunas lo han sacudido.

Si, H.T. de Distrito y amados conciudadanos: El dia 4 de Julio A.D. de 1776, en esa epoca memorable, que a esta fecha corren 84 años, amaneció, en esta America del Norte, el dia triunfante, alegre, y todo lleno de regosijo a sus habitantes, por haberse oido el orgulloso grito de libertad, de independencia y de union. Sobre este bien deseado y de tanta importancia, pensaron y trataron los Americanos de ordenar y poner en ejecucion los

---

2. The missing passage speaks of the heroic Padre Miguel Hidalgo, who cried the "Grito de Dolores" in 1810 that led ultimately to the liberation of Mexico.

3. The sense that the United States is the sole exemplar and sole hope of liberty and self-government received its classic statement in the Gettysburg Address of the notorious liberal Abraham Lincoln. During the nineteenth century the sentiment was not, as it has become since,

Fourth of July 1860

"By means of me, princes reign and men of power decree justice." Proverbs 8:16.

This text from the Book of Proverbs, my brothers, my fellow Taoseños, my listeners, offers a topic for our celebration of the anniversary of the glorious independence of the United States of North America, for on the Fourth of July in the year of the Lord 1776, they became independent of Great Britain. The exalted wisdom of God, universal cause of all that exists, preserver and absolute ruler, inspires legislators and rulers to do what will be effective in decreeing justice, effective in declaring with certitude the form of government in which his rational creatures may choose for themselves for the purpose of attaining the honorable goals of society. [Those goals] are to live tranquilly in peace and quiet, to love, help, and protect one another, and to walk together some steps along the pathway of justice. From these traits indeed derives the happiness of all people in general and of each people in particular.

This it was that stood as principle on that aforementioned day, the Fourth of July in North America, for the Hero of Independence, the great Washington, a man worthy of eternal remembrance. This hero, whose wisdom serves as a standard . . .[2] which in imitation of the United States achieved her independence, liberating herself from Spain, though she never consolidated herself due to the lack of an outstanding genius like our hero in [North] America. But what am I saying? This triumph was meant not only for our Republic and the Mexican Republic but for all the societies in the world, for wherever they might be, to serve as an example;[3] they long for this beloved liberty, many of them have tried to throw off the yoke of the monarchies, and some successfully have thrown it off.

Yes, my fellow citizens of the District [of Taos] and my beloved fellow-countrymen: the Fourth of July of the Year of the Lord 1776, that remarkable moment, just eighty-four years ago today, there dawned in this America of the North the triumphant, happy day, full of rejoicing for the population because they heard the proud cry of liberty, of independence, and of union. With regard to this benefit, so long desired and of such great im-

---

merely Fourth-of-July political hypocrisy; with all their faults, Norteamericanos of that time sincerely held that if freedom could not survive in this nation, it was forever impossible everywhere and that "government of the *people*, by the *people*, and for the *people*" (Lincoln's emphasis, according to hearers) would indeed perish totally from the earth.

medios capaces, para conseguirlo, porque conocian sus derechos y aspiraban por su libertad, hasta que al fin, pucieron mano a la obra, pues precedidos los medios de insinuacion, y no conseguida por esta via su independencia, aparecieron dos genios superiores al comun de los hombres: el gran Heroe George W[ashistong] . . . Señor Lafayett, los que po- . . . [ho]mbres ilustres y con el . . . -erosamente las medidas, . . . dieron el grito de liber[tad] . . . del ejercito opresor: . . . se ba- . . . guerra por diez años consecutivos tan varonilmente y con tanta eficacia, que tomaron la resolucion de vencer ó morir, antes que quedar dependientes de aquel gobierno monarquico y despotico:[4] asi sostubieron la guerra los Americanos derramando su sangre en los Campos de honor, con tanto empeño y union desisiva en aquella grande empresa, hasta que en el dia precitado 4 de Julio sacudieron el yugo de la monarquia, rompieron las ataduras que los ligaban, quedaron independientes, Señoriandose en sus bastos sueles [suelos] Americanos, conseguida la libertad deseada: la amada libertad, de la cual nosotros los Novo-Mejicanos agraciados por una anexion, somos participantes y llenos de regocijo celebramos el dia de hoy sus faustas y gloriosas memorias.

Aquello conseguido, con una sabiduria Filosofica, organizaron su Gobierno de una tal manera, que desde entonces sus bases constitucionales se llevan y tienen invariables sin sufrir alteracion alguna en las reformas ó aditamentos: resultando de todo los bienes temporal y espiritual. El bien temporal, porque yá se gobernarón por si mismos, y como hasta la presente nos gobernamos, con mejoras sobre mejoras, pues tenemos la libertad de reunirnos quieta y pacificamente para peticionar y deliberar, lo que milite a la mejora de nuestra condicion y [h]ablar el consejo de los prudentes, segun aquello del Prov. que dice: "Mio es el consejo y la equidad, mia es la prudencia, mia es la fortaleza: por mi Reynan los Reys, y los hacedores de las leyes decretan las cosas justas."

De lo mismo resulta tambien el bien espiritual, porque en la constitucion como una de sus bases fundamentales es la que prescribe la libertad de pensar, de hablar, de escribir y comunicar sus conceptos al publico para que las sociedades se instruyesen y adoptasen Religion, segun los dictados de sus conciencias.[5] ¿Se juzgará que este triunfo se estima en poco? pues el

---

4. The mention of Lafayette may be Padre Martínez's magnanimous nod in the direction of the French population of Taos, especially Charles Beaubien and Ceran Saint-Vrain. The consecutive fighting is usually dated from 19 April 1775 (Concord and Lexington) to 19 October 1781 (Cornwallis's surrender at Yorktown). "To conquer or to die rather than remain dependencies" may be an echo of Patrick Henry's "Give me liberty or give me death." And the characterization of Great Britain as a monarchic despotism owes a lot to Jefferson's "Declaration of Independence" of 4 July 1776. Empires throughout history have been despotic to their colonials.

5. Padre Martínez seems to assume here, as did many New Mexican Catholics of various ethnic backgrounds, that a community (town, school district, county, or territory) could commit itself to Catholicism (or any other religion) and shape the public schools in its image. By con-

portance, Americans think and plan how to organize and put into execution the effective means to preserve it, for they know their rights and aspire to their liberty even to the extent . . . they put their hands to the task, . . . two superior geniuses appeared . . . the great hero Washistong and Señor Lafayette. . . . [in the missing part of the page, the orator speaks of the illustrious Washistong and Lafayette choosing the proper means, voicing the cry for liberty, expelling the oppressive army, and waging] war for ten years in a row, bravely and with such good effect because they were determined to conquer or to die rather than remain dependencies of such a monarchical and despotic government.[4] So the Americans continued the war, shedding their blood on the fields of honor, with such commitment and decisive unity in the great enterprise that on the notable day [of] the Fourth of July they threw off the yoke of monarchy, broke the shackles that bound them, became independent, becoming masters of the immense territories of America, achieving the longed-for liberty, liberty so beloved that we New Mexicans are grateful for annexation since we enjoy it ourselves; and filled with rejoicing we celebrate this day, today, their happy and glorious memories.

Having attained liberty, with philosophical wisdom they organized their government in such a manner that, ever since then, their constitutional bases have sustained themselves and stand invariable, without having undergone any alteration by reform or addition, leading to all manner of benefits both temporal and spiritual. Temporal prosperity, since they have always governed themselves, and up to the present we govern ourselves, with improvement after improvement, for we possess the liberty to assemble calmly and peacefully to petition [for redress of grievances], to deliberate on things that will lead to the betterment of our condition, and to speak forth the counsel of the prudent, according to this passage from Proverbs, which says, "Mine are counsel and impartiality, mine is prudence, mine is strength; by me kings rule and lawmakers decree justice."

From the same constitution has come spiritual prosperity, since one of the fundamental bases of the constitution is the acknowledgement of freedom of thought, of speech, of writing, and of communicating one's notions to the public so that communities can study and adopt a religion according to the dictates of their own consciences.[5] Do you suppose this

trast—or more accurately, by comparison—Protestants assumed that New Mexican public schools ought to become like the "generic-Protestant" schools of the East: non-sectarian in not being committed to any one sect, but certainly Protestant in having a tilt away from many Catholic beliefs and practices.

Through much of the nineteenth century, conservatives in the Catholic Church were still unreconciled to individual or communal freedom and to religious pluralism, for they still hankered after the ancien régime in which the state enforced assent to an established church and the church preached loyalty to the state, no matter how despotic or inept: "The King's country, right or wrong."

fué uno de los mas importantes, no solo a nuestra Republica del Norte America, sino tambien a las otras naciones del globo, que deste gobierno han tomado ejemplo, por aqui admitido la tolerancia de cultos, por lo cual han calmado aquellas guerras desastrosas que ocacionaba el fanatismo, y las cuales inundaban de sangre las sociedades y los campos: para causar, mayor horror a la humanidad, en aquellos tiempos obscuros y tenebrosos, se estableció un tribunal llamado de la Santa inquisicion, y unos ejercitos voluntarios nominados de las crusadas, animados del mas cruel y rigoroso fanatismo;[6] pero esta hidra destructora de la humanidad, que sacrifico millones de habitantes en la gran Europa, parte mas ilustrada de mundo, tomando los Gobiernos idea de la liberalidad del nuestro, la hán [h]echa por tierra y le hán pisado la cabeza. Todos estos triunfos, H.A., son conseguidos por la libertad, y la tolerancia: tal idea sin duda la dedució nuestro gran Heroe W. de las sagradas letras,[7] [q]ue predicen la tolerancia de cultos en varios lugares. Citaré por ejemplo al Profeta Jeremias que en el cap. 31 vv.33 y 34 dice "Este será el pacto que haré, Dice el Señor: daré mi ley en las entrañas de ellos y la escribiré en sus corazones: y yo les seré en Dios y ellos me serán en Pueblo. Y no enseñará mas el varon a su projimo y el varon a su hermano diciendo, conoce al Señor, porque todos me conocerán desde el minimo hasta el maximo de ellos." Esto mismo repite el Apostol S. Pablo en su carta a los Hebreos al cap. 8; con ello concuerda lo del Profeta Malaquias en el cap. 1º. reconviniendo a los Sacerdotes intolerantes de Ysrael porque serraban las puertas de Templo diciendolos al v. 11 "Desde el nacimiento del Sol hasta el Ocaso grande es mi nombre entre las gentes, y en todo lugar se sacrifica y ofrece a mi nombre, oblacion limpia, Dice el Señor de los Ejercitos."

Esta maxima politica sobre tolerancia de religiones, H.A., esta maxima politica repito, causó las emigraciones de las naciones estrangeras a poblar los bastos campos que habia desiertos, en tanto numero que con esto y la propagacion de la especie, de tres [trece] estados que habia en la union en aquella epoca, a la fecha se hallan pasando de treinta, muy populosos y varios Territorios:[8] pues el amor a la libertad y a la tolerancia de cultos, que llevan consigo la paz, con mas los otros bienes que les son consiguientes,

---

6. The religious wars of the Middle Ages and the Renaissance, whether between Christians and Muslims or among self-styled Christians, were leading causes of the Enlightenment revulsion against institutional religion and the resultant prohibition against state establishment. It is interesting to find that a century after the Romantic period in Europe began to rehabilitate everything medieval, Martínez still adheres to the neoclassical, eighteenth-century rejection of the crusades.

7. Since like most of the other founding fathers of this nation they were deists and members of Masonic lodges, neither Washington (a Master Mason) nor Jefferson (who wrote the Virginia statute on religious liberty forbidding the establishment of any religion that served as the model for the first article of the Bill of Rights) believed in the divine inspiration of the Bible.

achievement does not amount to much? Indeed, it is of utmost importance not only to our North American republic but also to the other nations of the globe that have followed the example of this government and established tolerance of religions since they have calmed those disastrous wars that fanaticism creates, wars that have drowned societies and battlefields in blood. So as to cause humankind even greater terror, in those dark and shadowy times the tribunal of the Holy Office of the Inquisition arose, along with some volunteer armies called crusaders, incited by the cruelest and most rigid fanaticism.[6] But after this hydra, this destroyer of humanity, had sacrificed millions of inhabitants in the whole of Europe, the most cultured part of the world, their rulers took the idea of liberty [of religion] from us and have established it all over the world, making it the very wellspring [of freedom]. All these triumphs, my brothers of the audience, are the outcomes of liberty and tolerance: and such an idea doubtless our great hero Washington deduced from the sacred scriptures,[7] which preach tolerance of cults in various places, like for instance the Prophet Jeremiah, who in chapter 31, verses 33–34, says, "'This is the pact I will make,' ... says the Lord: 'I will place my law within them and write it on their hearts: and I will be their God, and they will be my people. And a man will no longer teach his neighbor, a man will no longer teach his brother, saying, "Know the Lord," for all will know me, from the least to the greatest of them.'" This same quotation the Apostle St. Paul repeats in his Epistle to the Hebrews in chapter 8. What the Prophet Malachi says in his first chapter agrees with it, when he reproaches the intolerant priests of Israel because they kept closing the doors of the Temple, saying at verse 11, "'From the birth of the sun to its fall, great is my name among the nations, and in all places they offer sacrifice to my name, a clean offering,' says the Lord of the armies."

This supreme policy concerning religious toleration, my brothers in the audience, this supreme policy, I repeat, caused the emigration of foreigners to populate those vast stretches, formerly deserted, in such numbers that with them and the natural population increase, from the thirteen states of the union of the original era, at this date there are upwards of thirty quite populous states as well as several territories.[8] For the love of liberty and religious toleration brings peace with it along with other benefits that logically ensue when they are animated by the philosophical spirit. Industry and the cultivation of the fields through agriculture and other labors, as well as the

---

8. Martínez was so strongly in favor of "toleration of cults" that he was instrumental in making it part of Mexican law.
By late spring 1860, there were thirty-three states and five organized territories: Kansas, Nebraska, New Mexico, Utah, and Washington.

animados de espiritu Filosofico, y de la industria en la labransa de campos por la agricurtura y demas labores, asi como las nuevas invenciones en las artes mecanicas y liberales, dan cada dia nuevos crecimientos a la prosperidad nacional, a su engrandecimiento, y a las riquesas. Ademas.

Por la liberalidad y justicia de nuestro Gobierno fueron quitadas aquellas leyes crueles y tiranicas que se tenian en otros tiempos, y acaso habrá todavia en algunos Gobiernos monarquicos, esto es: que los delitos eran trancendentales [trascendentales]; pero en nuestro Gobierno cayeron en tierra: en estas leyes los delitos de los Padres y las penas infamantes se castigaban hasta en los hijos y otros descendientes;[9] pero nuestro Gobierno, como es justo, los delitos tienen sus autores, y la pena no pasa de la persona que comete el delito. Esto misma se halla en las Sagradas Escrituras, por ejemplo el Profeta Ezequiel en el cap. 18: al v. 20 dice "La anima que pecare, ella misma morirá, el hijo no llevará la iniquidad del Padre, y el Padre no llevará la iniquidad de hijo: la justicia de justo estará sobre el; y la impiedad del impio el la sufrira." Asi lo provisto en nuestro Gobierno y por eso le vienen aquellas palabras de proverbio que cité al principio: por mi imperan los Principes etc.

Esto poco que queda espuesto, H.A., acerca del triunfo de nuestra libertad independencia y union, juego afectara la buena disposicion de esta ilustre concurrencia que solemnisa esta festibidad, y concluyo diciendo; que en la republica del N.A., somos felices sus habitantes por nuestro alto Gobierno justo sabio liberal y bondadoso: felices por sus Jueces y Literatos que llevan los debitos de la justicia en la equidad dando a cada cual lo que le pertenece: felices por la industria en todas clases de arbitrios para vivir en abundante prosperidad: felices por conducirse en la paz armonia y mutua correspondencia en sus contratos y demas relaciones de orden. Por tanto viva nuestro Heroe el inmortal Washintong: viva el alto Gobierno de los Estados Vnidos perpetuando la felicidad de sus Pueblos: y viva Dios recibiendo el homenaje de adoracion de estos habitantes en toda manera decorosa y honesta con que se los tributan.

—*fin*—

---

9. "*Que los delitos eran tracendentales*—that some crimes were all-embracing" and "*penas infamantes*—degrading penalties" serve as a reminder that in more communal societies, certain punishments extended to other family members even though they had not been shown or even suspected of having been accessories, often shaming them by reducing them in social status or even inflicting on them *infamia*, a sort of civil excommunication and social isolation. Martínez goes on to applaud the individualism of United States law. One of Martínez's books, Joachim Escriche, *Diccionario razonado de legislación* (Méjico: Oficina de Galvan, 1837), p. 314, makes it clear that such laws were not part of the code of the Mexican Republic:

> En ningun caso debe ser trascendental a su familia, la cual padece ya demasiado por las consecuencias necesarias del delito de su jefe. . . . Toda pena . . . es precisamente personal del delincuente, y nunca será trascendental a su familia.

new advances in mechanical and liberal arts, give day by day new growth to the prosperity of the nation, to its greatness and its wealth.

The liberality and justice of our government has put an end to the cruel and tyrannical laws which prevailed in former times and are perhaps even now characteristic in certain monarchical governments, laws that decreed that some crimes were all-embracing. But in our system of government, those laws are done away with, laws whereby the crimes of the forebears and degrading penalties punish even the children and other descendants.[9] In our government, by contrast, as is right, [only] the perpetrators are responsible for their crimes, and no penalty descends from the person who commits the crime. The same thing can be found in the sacred scriptures; for example, the Prophet Ezekiel, chapter 18, verse 20, says this: "The soul [the person] that sinned would himself die, the son would not bear the iniquity of the father, nor would the father bear the iniquity of the son. The just man's justice will rest upon him, and the impious man's impiety he himself will suffer." Such is the provision in our country, and that is the reason for those words of the proverb I quoted at the outset, "By means of me, princes and men of power decree justice."

The little I have said, kind listeners, about the triumph of our liberty, independence, and union, will please the good attitude of this illustrious gathering that has celebrated this holiday; and let me conclude by saying that in the republic of North America, we are its happy citizens for having a supreme government that is just, wise, liberal, and generous. We are happy because of its judges and writers, who fulfill the duties of justice fairly, giving to all what is due them; happy because of the industry of all classes of workmen, so that we can live in abundant prosperity; happy because we live in peace, harmony, and mutual cooperation in our contractual obligations and in our other ordered relationships. For all this, long live our hero, the immortal Washintong! [sic] Long live the great government of the United States, sustaining the happiness of its peoples! And long live God, who receives the homage of adoration of these citizens in every appropriate and honorable manner in which they offer it.

—*end*—

PART III

The French Clergy

✜

✣

Because of the celebrated confrontation between Padre Antonio José Martínez on the one side and Father Joseph P. Machebeuf and Bishop Jean Baptiste Lamy on the other, it seems natural to assume that the three men were more or less the same age. But in fact, Machebeuf was one year older and Lamy one year younger than the daughter born to Martínez during his brief marriage.

But the greater change from the New Mexican clergyman to the French clerics is not from one generation to another but from one major cultural period to another. Martínez was a late product of the Renaissance, since from 1817 to 1823 the Tridentine seminary at Durango was the natural home of culture lag, still dominated by the pre-industrial mercantilist economics of a colony. By the mid-1830s, in contrast, the European cutting edge of culture had been exploring Romanticism for seventy-five or eighty years, and the Romantic movement, a reaction to the Industrial Revolution and the new liberal capitalism it engendered, had surely penetrated even the cloistered seminary at Clermont-Ferrand in the Auvergne and affected its young students. By contrast to the clear formal structure of Martínez's orations, Machebeuf's and Lamy's addresses are free form, reading like impromptu effusions rather than planned, executed, and polished pieces. If Martínez's sermons "smell of the lamp," as the saying goes, the Frenchmen's sermons smell of wet ink. Presbyterian minister Sheldon Jackson complained some decades later about "headless" sermons—sermons with neither announced headings (*capita*) nor the consciously chosen structure that goes with them, and when I read his complaint I could only think of Machebeuf.[1]

One inheritance of their religious culture that Lamy and Machebeuf brought from France was Jansenism. In its full form, Jansenism was a strong though subtle current of Calvinism within French Catholicism; it shows

---

1. Sheldon Jackson, "About Sermons," *The Rocky Mountain Presbyterian* 3, no. 41 (14 October 1874), p. 3.

itself in Machebeuf and Lamy not as dogmatic heterodoxy so much as a tilt toward moral Puritanism, a "holier than thou" authoritarianism that flowed from a covert presumption of human depravity.

Joseph P. Machebeuf

Myra Ellen Jenkins liked to quote her mother's description of Bishop Machebeuf: "The ugliest little man I ever saw—with the most heavenly smile." No surviving drawing or photo contradicts the first phrase, for they all show him to have been physically ugly. And no illustration corroborates the latter phrase, so even the smile must have been a function of his living personality in motion. But the Jesuits of the period liked Machebeuf much better than they liked Lamy, and people who got to know Machebeuf well liked him a very great deal.

Lamy and Machebeuf were close friends from seminary days. They had promised each other that they would stay together if possible, they had traveled to the Cincinnati Diocese together, and when Lamy was chosen to begin the new diocese in the Southwest, he invited Machebeuf to come as his Vicar-General. Machebeuf had felt a call to the western frontier due to his reading the "edifying letters" of the great Jesuit missionary Pieter Jan De Smet, so Lamy's request received an immediate positive response.

Machebeuf loved to talk, and his career as a preacher suffered because of his garrulity. In one of his own edifying letters, Machebeuf wrote from Ohio to his sister in a French convent that he delivered two sermons every Sunday, all in bad English; but it mattered little because he was understood. Since he was an extrovert, he kept talking and gradually improved his mastery of any new language.

His maiden Spanish sermon in Santa Fe was memorable, as Salpointe tells it:

> The Reverend gentleman [Machebeuf] was invited by the parish priest of Santa Fe, Rev. Lujan, to sing mass the next Sunday, and tried

to address the congregation.... Nobody understood much of what he said.... Hence it was that a controversy arose among the people on the plaza after mass, as to what religion the stranger might belong to. "He must be a Jew or a Protestant," said some, "because he does not speak as Christians do." "Quien sabe?—Who can tell?" replied others. "Still he said mass in Latin, and like a priest who knows how to do it, and... he sings better than our priests." At last a good woman ... pertinently said, "What reason have you to be perplexed about the religion of this man? Did he not give a good proof that he is a Catholic by the way he made the sign of the cross before giving his sermon?"

But as he improved his skills, Machebeuf spoke more comprehensible Spanish—and got himself into deep trouble when the people of Peña Blanca complained to Rome:

> Whenever he visited [Peña Blanca], all he preached on was the Church's fifth commandment [precept] about paying their tithes; if he turned to other subjects, it was to reveal the secrets of the confessional![2]

A trip to Rome to defend himself against the accusation of breaking the seal of confession cured him of speaking about forbidden matters, but he continued to be too wordy until the end of his long life: "People even then said that he preached too often and preached too long. He always preached at both masses and at vespers, and scarcely ever less than an hour."[3]

Seeing "etc etc etc" in a Machebeuf sermon, the reader now knows to fear the worst for his congregation.

—end—

2. AASF, Horgan Collection, Propaganda Fide, 13 January 1853, no. 1; see also Paul Horgan, *Lamy of Santa Fe: His Life and Times* (New York: Farrar, Straus and Giroux, 1975), p. 191, where in a letter of 15 March 1853 the people of Albuquerque complained of Machebeuf's "boring and annoying preachings; if he began his sermon with the Gospel, he ended up with 'the private lives of the faithful.'"

3. Hugh L. McMenamin, *The Pinnacled Glory of the West* (Denver: Smith-Brooks, 1912), p. 23.

Joseph P. Machebeuf
Sermon on the Passion

Fray Manuel Antonio García del Valle's Deposition sermon of 1821 should already have given the reader some "feel" for the place—the Church of San Francisco de Asís in Santa Fe—and the occasion—Good Friday—where and when Vicar-General Joseph P. Machebeuf preached this sermon in 1856. In the next section, Bishop Lamy will preach once more on this central historical event of Christianity, the death of Jesus.

"El Paso de Santo Entierro—The Scene of the Holy Buried Body," more usually called the deposition from the cross, was an especially dramatic episode of the New Mexican passion play. Its Santa Fe enactment had not changed much from thirty-five years earlier, but it appears from a different perspective when viewed through the eyes of a newcomer to the region. In August 1852, the Baptists' *Home Mission Record* published an excerpt from Reverend Lewis Smith's journal under the title "Superstition Rampant":

> 9th. *Good Friday.*—A great day among the Catholics. They had a theatrical representation of Christ's crucifixion. The cross was planted in the church—an image large as life was suspended upon it. The church was crowded, most of the people were on their knees reading, praying, weeping, and crossing themselves; after permitting us to gaze upon the cross for about half an hour, the image was taken down by two priests. This part of the affair was rather solemn, even to us. The image looked like a corpse—the crown of thorns was upon its head—the nails were in its hands and feet—the head was fallen upon its breast—the face was the picture of intense agony, and blood seemed to be flowing from every wound. It was so constructed that its limbs worked after nature's pattern, and when it was taken from the cross, we could hardly divest our minds of the idea that its was really a human body upon which we were gazing. The women cried aloud, and the church resounded with sorrow. The body was laid in a glass case, covered with artificial flowers, and was to be paraded through the streets. It was followed by some 6 or 8 little children, dressed to represent angels. Then came the ten virgins with their lamps, and such virgins! Most of them were notorious prostitutes. Then came a

crowd of all ages, sizes, and complexions, all with heads uncovered, and all kneeling whenever the procession stopped. After all this balderdash was over, we seated ourselves by a good fire, fully prepared to believe all that we had ever read about the worship of relics, and the baptism of bells and jackasses. May Heaven soon enable us to speak to this people.[1]

The next year, Reverend Smith didn't impress so readily, to judge from his description in "A Burlesque on Christianity":

Last Friday I witnessed the same scenes here which were enacted a year ago. Processions of *saints*, flags, bishop, priests, boys, virgins (?) and people moved through the streets in sun-light and torch-light, while dolorous anthems rose upon the air, and solemnized the hearts of the superstitious crowd. A sermon was delivered in the open air, and afterwards the farce of crucifying the Saviour was enacted in the church, during which the bishop stood before the cross assuring the people that he preached Christ crucified. While listening to him, and almost suffocated by the stench which arose from the dirty blankets around me, a file of men pushed their way towards the altar. Nothing could exceed the vulgar barbarity of their dress and accoutrements. They were the Roman soldiers, and they had come to take the body from the cross. The whole affair, if enacted on a stage, would be condemned as a most miserable burlesque on Christianity; but in a popish sanctuary was considered excusable, if not impressive. I ought to say that there appeared to be far less enthusiasm manifested than I observed a year ago. The women refrained from tears and groans, and the audience seemed to wish the performance to come to a close.[2]

---

1. [Baptist] *Home Mission Record* 3, no. 8 (August 1852), p. 1, journal entry of Good Friday, 9 April 1852. This is the same statue that figured in fray Manuel Antonio García del Valle's sermon from 1821 and that Josiah Gregg described in the 1830s:

Viernes Santo (Good Friday), especially, is observed with great pomp and splendor. An image of Christ large as life, nailed to a huge wooden cross, is paraded through the streets, in the midst of an immense procession, accompanied by a glittering array of carved images, representing the Virgin Mary, Mary Magdalen, and several others (*Commerce of the Prairies* [Dallas: Southwest Press, 1933], p. 169).

And W.W.H. Davis recorded during Machebeuf's era "an image of the Savior" nailed to a large wooden cross and a second time as "the dead body of Christ in an open coffin, on which were a number of small wooden images, with the usual accompaniment of saints" (*El Gringo* [Lincoln: University of Nebraska Press, 1982], pp. 345-46).

2. *Home Mission Record* 4, no. 11 (July 1853), p. 1, from a letter of 28 March 1853, Easter Monday.

As is evident in the sermon that follows to a greater extent than in other sermons, Machebeuf composes his text with the help of innumerable scraps of scripture snipped out of context—"proof texts" as used in the "textbook theology" and controversies of the day, lapidary texts with which to stone one's Christian adversaries. The text is scribbled, seemingly in great haste, with quite a few individual words and brief passages illegible and incapable of yielding up a translation. In the English, I have skipped over these without giving any indication of ellipsis, but all the Spanish is there—transcription, guesses, and ellipses—as best several helpful friends and I could manage.

Viernes Santo

PASION DE N.S.J.CH.
PASO DE SANTO ENTIERRO
INSTRUCCION

Judaei signa peterunt et Graeci sapientiam quaerunt nos autem predicamus Christum crucifixum, Judaeis quidem scandalum, Gentibus autem stultitiam. Ipsis autem vocatis, Judaeis et Graecis Christum Dei virtutem et Dei sapientiam—Los judios por su parte piden milagros, y los griegos, o gentiles por la suya quieren ciencia, sabiduria mas nosotros sencillamente predicamos a Cristo Crucificado, lo cual para judios es motivo de escandalo, y parece una locura a los gentiles: Si bien para los que han sido llamados a la fé, tanto judios como griegos, es cristo la virtud de Dios y la sabiduria de Dios. Ep. 1 ad Corinth. C. 1, V. 22.23.24—

CRISTIANOS, OYENTES MIOS

Si nunca un predicador podia haber verguenza de su ministerio, seria en ese dia, en el cual su deber le manda de publica[r] las humiliaciones del dios que predican los ultrages que recibio, sus languores, sus sufrimientos, su pasion y muerte sin embargo, decia San Pablo contra las ignominias de la Cruz, no me avergonzaré del Evangelio de mi Señor, y la razon que Da de su fe; es que el Evangelio de la cruz es la virtud de Dios. *No erubesco Evangelium*—Virtus est enim Dei [Romanos 1:16]—pues no solamente no se avergonzaba pero se glorificaba de Jesus crucificado—*mihi autem absit gloriari nisi in cruce Domini nostri Jesu Christi* [Gálatas 6:14]. Lejos de darle confusion y verguenza en su ministerio, la cruz era su honor, su gloria, su fuerza Mientras que los Judios piden milagros, y los griegos ciencia, el para confundirlos en su incredulidad les predica a Jesus, y a Jesus Crucifigado y porque? porque la Cruz es la

1. Virtud de Dios *Dei virtutem*, superior a todos los milagros
2. La Cruz es el prodigio de la sabiduria de Dios—*Christum crucifixum Dei sapientiam* que admirable idea, oyentes mios, monstrar [mostrar] la virtud de Dios en las humiliaciones del Dios hombre y la sabiduria de Dios en las aparentes locuras de la Cruz. Adoptaremos la idea de San Pablo vastantes veces

Les hablaron el lenguage de la compuncion y del Dolor, pero Como esos sentimientos tiernos presentan presto, que esenen(?), cuando la razon es convincida; entonces vale tanto recibir el consejo que da el mismo Señor a las mugeres de Jerusalen no llorad sobre mi, mas bien sobre la infiel

Good Friday

THE PASSION OF
OUR LORD JESUS CHRIST
THE SCENE OF THE HOLY BURIAL

Judaei signa peterunt et Graeci sapientiam quaerunt nos autem predicamus Christum crucifixum, Judaeis quidem scandalum, Gentibus autem stultitiam. Ipsis autem vocatis, Judaeis et Graecis Christum Dei virtutem et Dei sapientiam—The Jews want signs and the Greeks seek wisdom, but we preach Christ crucified, scandal to the Jews and absurdity to the gentiles, yet to those who are called, both Jews and Greeks, Christ the power of God and the wisdom of God. 1 Corinthians 1:22–24.

MY DEAR CHRISTIANS:

If a preacher ever need have no fear of being ashamed of his ministry, it would be on this day, when he ought to reveal to the public the humiliations of God which [they] preach, the outrages Christ suffered, his weakness, his torments, his passion and death. Notwithstanding, Saint Paul said of the ignominy of the cross, "I will never be ashamed of the Gospel of my Lord," and the reason he gives for his faith is that the gospel of the cross is the power of God—"*No erubesco Evangelium; virtus est enim Dei* [Romans 1:16]—for not only was he not ashamed, but he gloried in Jesus crucified. *Mihi autem absit gloriari nisi in cruce Domini nostri Jesu Christi*—May I never boast except about the cross of Our Lord Jesus Christ" [Galatians 6:14]. Far from being a source of confusion and embarrassment in his ministry, the cross was his honor, his glory, his power. Meantime the Jews sought miracles and the Greeks sought knowledge; but Paul to confound them in their unbelief preached Jesus, and Jesus crucified. And why? because the cross is

1. The Power of God—*Dei virtutem*—greater than all miracles.
2. The Cross is the prodigy of the Wisdom of God—*Christum crucifixum Dei sapientiam*—what an admirable idea, my listeners, to show the power of God in the humiliations of the God-man and the wisdom of God in the seeming madness of the cross. Let us adopt the concept of Saint Paul so often . . . .

I spoke to them in the languages of remorse and of sorrow, but as those are fond sentiments when reason is convinced, from then on it only helps to accept the advice the Lord himself gives to the women of Jerusalem, "Weep not for me but for this faithless city; ponder my sorrows, study my cross, and learn how to honor it" [Luke 23:28].

Ciudad que meditais mis Dolores, mis Dolores estudian mi Cruz y aprendeis a honrarla [Lucas 23:28].

1° hasta ahora Consideramos quizas la passion y muerte de Cristo, como un mysterio de humillation y de debilidad, y si no diremos mal, les quiero probar que este mysterio de la Cruz, es la virtud de Dios

2° hasta ahora miramos la Cruz como una locura, veremos que es un mysterio de la sabiduria de Dios

1. La Cruz es una virtud de Dios que manifiesta su potencia que Dios haya criado el mundo de una sola palabra que de un solo acto de voluntad; se comprende sino no Señor dios, le faltaria una qualidad esencial, la omnipotencia que Dios hecho hombre por nosotros haya nacido, crecido y manifestado obras maravillosas—no hay que mirar—mas que un dios sufra, muera en los tormentos, el gozando de la inmortalidad eso no estando, y a los angeles, hombres no lo entiendan y con razon podemos decir cual obtupescite cielo—ayer desaparece la Luz de la razon, la luz natural, y en ese consiste nuestra fe—pero tambien en eso nuestra Fe es victoriosa *et haec est victoria quae vincit mundum, fides nostra* [1 Juan 5:4]—es verdad, cristianos, nuestro Señor sufrio y murio sobre la cruz—pero le hablando de sus sufrimientos y de su muerte, y que sendo y eso con el Apostol que J. Ch. sufrio y murio en Dios, eso es, de una manera, de un modo que asi mas podia convenir a Dios.

Digo que J.Ch. a [ha] muerto de un modo que no mas podia convenir a Dios—

1° porque un hombre que muere despues de haber anuntiado preciso y claro las circunstancias de su muerte, 2° que muere haciendo milagros, 3° un hombre que muere pero cuya muerte es un milagro grande 4° un hombre que por la infamia de su muerte penienes la gloria la mas extraordinaria, esepirando en la Cruz destruye la desolasion, la soberbia mundana... sino es un hombre que muere en Dios o es un hombredios—por eso el apostol dicé que Cristo era no el ministro de Dios, pero la virtud misma de Dios, *virtutem Dei*

1. Jesucristo muere despues de haber anunciado su muerte (Rom 2,6) a oir le hablar de su passion, tiempo antes parece ya que esta hablando de un hecho bien cumplido—notando, puntando las menores circumstancias— es verdad que ya habia siglos que los profetas habian predicho su passion y circumstancias pero el mismo viene, precisa el tiempo—vamos a Jerusalem, a donde el hijo del hombre sera bofetado, crucifigado

2. haciendo milagros muere Jesus hace temblar la tierra, se abrieron los se abrieron los sepulcros, se rasgo el velo del templo, se obscureció el sol— las pruebas de esos milagros las hallaron en los libros de los hebreos mismos en las obras de Josef historiano—un solo milagro no quizo hacer, que era

1° Until now, perhaps, we have been considering the passion and death of Christ as a mystery of humiliation and of weakness, and if I do not belie myself, I wish to show them that this mystery of the cross is the strength of God.

2° Until now we have viewed the cross as [if it were] some [kind of] insanity, and now we will realize it is the mystery of the wisdom of God.

1. The cross is the strength of God who manifests his power, for God has created the world by a mere word, by a single act of his will. The omnipotence of God, become man for our sakes, has been born, grown up, and manifested miraculous works—we cannot but observe a God suffering, dying in torment. But nevertheless in that our faith is victorious—"*Et haec est victoria quae vincit mundum, fides nostra*—and this is the victory that conquers the world, our faith" [1 John 5:4]. It is true, my fellow Christians, that our Lord suffered and died on the cross, but in speaking of his sufferings and his death, and with the Apostle that Jesus Christ suffered and died in union with God, that is, in a certain manner, in a fashion that would be able to harmonize with God.

I say that Jesus Christ died in a way that could only harmonize with God.

1. that he was a man who dies after having announced the circumstances of his death precisely and clearly
2. that as he died he performed miracles
3. a man who died but whose death is a great miracle.
4. a man who because of the degradation of his death [attains] the most extraordinary glory, dying on the cross, destroys the desolation [of] worldly pride, but rather he was a man who died in union with God or is a veritable God-man. On this account the Apostle says that Christ was not just the minister of God but the very power of God, *virtutem Dei*

1. Jesus Christ died after having predicted his death (Romans 2:6). In the period beforehand it seemed that he was talking about a deed already accomplished—noting the minutest circumstances. Truly the prophets centuries before had already predicted his passion and the circumstances. But he comes; he specifies the time: let us go up to Jerusalem, where the Son of Man will be stricken and crucified.

2. performing miracles, Jesus dies. He causes the earth to quake; the sepulchers opened, the veil of the temple was torn, the sun was darkened: They found evidence for these miracles in the books of the Jews themselves, in the works of the historian Josephus. Only one miracle he refused to perform, that of saving himself: "If you are the son of God, come down from the cross; save yourself if you are the King of the Jews. He saved others; let him save himself then, if he is the Messiah" [Matthew 27:40]. Why did he suffer such insult and not do so? Since by that miracle the whole mystery of his passion would have been destroyed.

de salvarse—si eres hijo de Dios, abaja de la Cruz, ponte salvo, si eres el rey de los Judios—a otros ha salvado, salvese a si mismo, pues, si es el Cristo [Mateo 27:40]—porque sufrió tantas burlas, y no lo hizo? porque ese milagro, hubiera destruido todo el mysterio de su pasion—

mas diré, en ese momento, Cristo pudiendo salvarse como no hay duda, y no lo haciendo, no queriendo, en su perseverancia a morir por su pueblo que no obrá mas milagros que si se hubiera librado—esa mansedumbre por sus enemigos es esta paz y tranquilida—*agnosce illis, pater mi, nesciunt quid faciunt memor esto, quod mecum eris in paraiso mulier ecce filius tuus, fili, ecce mater tua—pater, in manus tuas commendo spiritum meum*[3]—o prodigio de los milagros—la muerte de Jesus es un milagro constante, y el

3. Su muerte es el milagro unico de los milagros—porque mientras que los otros mueren por debilidad, porque siendo 1º siendo la santidad, era inmortal

2º siendo el sacerdote sumo de la ley nueva y el solo pudiendo ofrecer un sacrificio decente—debia immolarse en eso dice *nemo tollit animam meam a me sed ego pono eam a me ipso* [Juan 10:18]—por eso muere y la señal de su muerte divina es una voz sonora—*et exclamans voce magna, dedit spiritum* [Marcos 15:37]—tuvo, me dicen, las languries, pero hasta en ellas fue milagro

4. por la infamia de su muerte viene la gloria expirando en la Cruz triunfo de la infidelidad del mundo—en el nombre de Jesus crucificado, *omne genu flectatur etc* como fue revelado a San Pablo

Con eso no se entienden los fariseos perseverando en su malicia mas grande es la de tantos que ven al triunfo de la Cruz, y sin embargo una fe

2. *Cristum crucifixum, virtutem Sapientiae Dei* Dios y el hombre siendo tan diferentes, y tan lejos distantes es el Grano de suerte del Sol, no hay tampoco que ser por cuando, si el hombre desvia del derecho camino y tiene pensamientos tan differentes de los de Dios, y que el hombres se a [ha] permitido de critica las obras del Señor. Lo que me tiene atento ami es que el hombre se a escandalizado de la Bondad misma de Dios y de los prodigios de su amor—*unde homo adversus salvatorem scandalum* _____ *unde ei magis debitor esse debuit.*[4] Tanto es que el heresiarca Marcion[5] con el

---

3. These are imprecise recollections of the first (Luke 23:34), second (Luke 23:43), third (John 19:26-27), and last (Luke 23:46) of Jesus's Seven Last Words.

4. There are scriptural echoes, as for instance Acts 4:26-27 and Matthew 18:27-33, but the passage means very little if anything: literally, "Whence a human set against God [is] a scandal ... whence you [singular] are more a debtor, he had better be." Perhaps it means "Christ had better be more of a redeemer."

5. Marcion (c.90-c.160) founded the first major heretical and schismatic Christian church. His Christology was very docetist because he taught that matter (and the whole Old Testament scene) had been created by a lesser, legalistic deity, not by the loving divine Father revealed in the New

Rather, I say, that at that moment Christ, being able to save himself—without a doubt—and not doing so, not wishing to do so, in his perseverance unto death for his people does no miracles other than if he had saved himself. That meekness toward his enemies is this peace and tranquility: *agnosce illis, pater mi, nesciunt quid faciunt—memor esto, quod mecum eris in paraiso—mulier ecce filius tuus, fili, ecce mater tua—pater, in manus tuas commendo spiritum meum.*³ Oh prodigy of miracles—the death of Jesus is a constant miracle.

3. that death is the preeminent miracle of all miracles, for while others [die] from weakness, inasmuch as 1. due to his holiness he was immortal; 2. since he was the high priest of the New Law, he alone was capable of offering a suitable sacrifice; he needed to immolate himself. On this point he said, "*Nemo tollit animam meam a me sed ego pono eam a me ipso*—No one takes my life from me, but I lay it down on my own" [John 10:18]. For this reason he died, and the sign of his divine death was his resounding voice: "*Et exclamans voce magna, dedit spiritum*—And crying out with a loud voice he gave up his spirit" [Mark 15:37]. He had, they tell me, the infirmities, but even in these there was a miracle.

4. through the infamy of his death came the glory: dying on the cross he triumphed over the faithlessness of the world: "at the name of Jesus crucified, *omne genu flectatur* etc.,—let every knee bend," as it was revealed to Saint Paul [Philippians 2:10].

Knowing this, one cannot comprehend the Pharisees persisting in their great malice.

2. Christ crucified, the power of God's wisdom.

God and mankind being so different, and as far apart as a grain of dust is from the sun, there is no least way to compare them. If man strays from the straight path and has thoughts so different from those of God, he allows himself to criticize the works of the Lord. What catches my attention is that man has been scandalized by the very goodness of God and the prodigies of his love—*Unde homo adversus salvatorem scandalum . . . unde es magis debitor esse debuit.*⁴ It is just the same with the heresiarch Marcion.⁵ Under the veil or pretext of giving glory to God, he fought against the cross of Christ—scandalized by his sufferings and his humiliations. The immortal Tertullian defended the cross, making it stand forth in its brilliance like a flower amid thorns. Even so, Christianity, the faith in Christ crucified, also placed in the world, possesses no lack of Marcions, against whom my

Testament, which for him contained only Luke without the infancy chapters and ten Pauline epistles; he also taught a severe morality and created a strong ecclesiastical structure. Hence he may have instigated the Church's own canon of scripture, its development of a heavily Old-Testament and Stoic moral strictness, and its dominant hierarchy.

velo o abajo el pretexto de dar la gloria a Dios, combatió la Cruz de Cristo y se escandalizó de sus sufrimientos y de sus humiliationes—el inmortal Tertuliano fué el defensor de la Cruz, la hizo salir brillante, como una flor entre las espinas—aunque el Cristianismo, la fe in Cristo crucifigado tambien puesta en el mundo, no faltan los Marcion, y contra los cuales mi ministerio me manda delibrar Batalla—pues, hermanos mios, si reparais, encontrareis que la Cruz de Cristo era escandalo a los Judios, mientras que es la señal de la potestad de Dios, *Dei virtutem*—el mysterio de un Dios crucifigado es por los Griegos locura por los mundanos una locura *gentibus stultitiam*, y decimos con San Pablo que por los escogidos y predestinados, el mysterio de la sabiduria de Dios, *Dei Sapientiam*—a ver, quien tiene derecho, el apostol o el mundano a ver, si en este mysterio hay algo que sea contra nuestra razon—porque si la fe es debil, arriba, incima [encima] de nuestra razon no es contra y al mismo tribunal, al pie de la Cruz, les proponga la difficultad entre la razon humana y la sabiduria de Dios—

De que era el negocio ... de dos cosas dice San Leon, egualmente necessarias y difficiles—1° satisfacer a una magestad infinita, ofendida y deshonrada por el peccado 2° reformar la humanidad, el hombre pervertido y corrumpido[6]—tal es el fin, tal es la prenda de la mission de Cristo—pues, les preguntaré, y que me contesten, o me hagan el favor de prestarme atencion, les diré la contestacion.

Dios, en cuanto Dios, tenia a su poder un medio mas eficaz, mas poderoso, mas infalible que la Cruz para satisfacer [y para] reparar? y nosotros, modernos griegos, *stultitiam gentibus*, con toda nuestra ciencia podemos hallar otro mas conveniente y mas sapiente—

Vamos al Calvario, testigos de lo que se passo (Daremos una sentencia legal y justa) estudiemos esta religion aqui esta su altura y su profundidad *sublimitas et profundum* [Efesios 3:18]—

1° no habia medio mas facil y eficaz que la Cruz satisfacer a Dios se debia, y quien lo podia, sino Dios mismo, nadie lo niega—pues que hizo este hombre Dios en que consistio la offensa de Dios—
1° En eso que el hombre habia querido de ser semejante a Dios, *estis sicut Dii* [Génesis 3:5]—y Cristo, para satisfacer a su Padre, se humilla profundamente, *ego sum vermis et non homo ego sum maledictus pro maledictis*[7]

---

6. Pope Saint Leo I, the Great (d. 461), in his Sermon 12, no. 1 (*PL* 54:168), Sermon 21, no. 3 (*PL* 54:192), and various other places, says much about reforming "the old Adam" into the reborn Christian. But the "offended and dishonored majesty of God" and humanity "perverted and corrupt" owe much more to Machebeuf's Jansenism than to the early pontiff's version of Christianity. See for instance Leo's Letter 15, no. 10: "The Catholic faith acknowledges every man to be formed by the maker of the Universe in the substance of his body and soul, and to receive the breath of life within his mother's womb, though that taint of sin and liability to die remains which passed from

ministry obliges me to wage battle. For, my brethren, if you reflect on it, you will find that the Cross of Christ, a scandal to the Jews, is at the same time the manifestation of God's power—*Dei virtutem*. The mystery of a crucified God is for the Greeks madness, for the worldly a madness—*gentibus stultitiam*—and we say with Saint Paul that for the chosen and predestined, it is the mystery of God's wisdom—*Dei sapientiam*. We shall see who has it right, the Apostle or the worldling. We shall see if in this mystery there is any point opposed to our reason—for if faith is filled with doubts more than our reason is, it is not contrary to the same tribunal. At the foot of the cross Christ proposes to them the difficulty between human reason and God's wisdom.

What was the question? It was about two things, Saint Leo says, equally necessary and difficult to comprehend: 1. placating an infinite majesty offended and dishonored by sin; 2. reforming humanity, perverted and corrupt man.[6] Such is the goal, such the gift of Christ's mission; for I will quiz them, and they might answer me, or if they didn't favor me with their attention, I would myself answer this question: Does God, insofar as he is God, have within his power a means more effective, more powerful, more infallible than the cross to satisfy and to make reparation? And we, modern Greeks that we are, *stultitiam gentibus*, with all our science, can we discover another means more appropriate and more wise?

Let us go to Calvary, witnesses of all that transpired there. Let us hand down a legal and just sentence. Let us study this religion of ours; here is "its height and its depth—*sublimitas et profundum*" [Ephesians 3:18].

1° There was no more easy and effective means than the cross to satisfy the debt owed God. And who can do so except God alone, as no one will deny? What did this God-man do? Of what does the offense against God consist? 1. inasmuch as man has desired to be like God: "*Estis sicut Dii*—you will be like gods" [Genesis 3:5]. And Christ to satisfy his Father, profoundly abases himself: "*Ego sum vermis et non homo*—I am a worm and no man"; "*ego sum maledictum pro maledicto*—I am accursed for the sake of the accursed."[7]

---

the first parent into his descendants, until the sacrament of Regeneration comes to succor him, whereby through the Holy Spirit we are reborn the sons of promise, not in the fleshly womb but in the power of baptism."

7. 1 Peter 3:9—Father Machebeuf uses this text in an applied sense (often called a flagrant misquote), for Peter admonishes his readers neither to return evil for evil nor to answer cursing with cursing.

2º Rebelase el hombre contra Dios y Cristo se puso obediente hasta la Cruz—*factus obediens usque ad Crucem, Crucem autem Crucis* [Filipenses 2:8]

3º por una intemperancia criminal, el hombre habia comido del fruto defendido, y Cristo Nuestro Señor se mostro, se hizo _____ de penitencia, hombre de los dolores—*virum Dolorum* [Isaías 53:3] que reparacion mas autentica, mas solemne—

No es sustante en la Cruz Cristo nos enseña y nos da de entender tres cosas, cuya ciencia es necessaria a cada uno de nosotros 1º que quien es Dios 2º lo que es el pecado 3º lo que es la salvacion—pues un mysterio, que me da mas ciencia que todos los filosofos a cerca de la naturaleza divina que me inspira—horror horribilissimo por el pecado, y me enseña apreciar mi salvacion. Como el interes importante, que sera un mysterio de locura o de sabiduria—*stultitiam gentibus, Dei sapientiam*—

2º La cruz de Cristo es el medio el mas eficaz y mas infalible, para conreformar la humanidad, el hombre corrumpido y pervertido—tres son fuentes de vitio, dice San Juan—

concupiscencia de los ojos
concupiscencia de la carne
soberbia de la vida [1 Juan 2:16-17]

a esas tres concupicencias Cristo en su sagrado retrato da esos tres remedios

1º el despojo de todo y la nudidad en que muere, contra el amor de las Riquezas, o concupiscentia de las ojos—

2º sus humiliationes contra lambition [la ambición], orgullo de la Vida

3º sus dolores, sufrimientos contra la sensualidad, concupiscentia de la carne—pero porque Cristo, sin sentir nuestros males, quizo probar en su persona los remedios, por amor, por nosotros *sublimitas et profundum*—para nos facilita la penitencia, etc que sera una locura, o virtud de Dios—*Gentibus stultitiam, et Dei sapientiam*? no, no habia modo mas eficaz, mas infalible que la Cruz para enfrenar a la humanidad. De otro modo, podia adquirir gloria, y aplausos, en la Cruz sola, en las humiliationes y Dolores obligar al mundo—encumrarse—encender en nosotros un grande fuego de amor, mientras vivos, o un fuego terrible de tormentos, mientras muertos, *nunc judicium est Dei*[8]—

Cumplido el sacrificio, dice San Lucas, era ya casi la hora de sexta o mediodia, las tinieblas cubrieron la tierra hasta la hora de nona, el sol se escondió, el velo del temple se rasgó por medio—entonces Jesus clamando con una voz muy grande, dijo—padre mio, en tus manos encomiendo mi

---

8. This passage slightly echoes several verses from different parts of the New Testament: John 3:19, John 12:13, Romans 2:2, and 1 Peter 4:17.

2° Man rebels against God, and so Christ becomes obedient even to the cross—"*factus obediens usque ad mortem, mortem autem crucis*—being made obedient unto death, even to the death of the cross" [Philippians 2:8].

3° Because of a criminal intemperance, man has eaten the forbidden fruit, and Christ our Lord showed himself, made himself [the model] of penitence, the Man of Sorrows—*virum dolorum* [Isaiah 53:3]—what a genuine, what a solemn reparation.

Is it not on the cross that Christ shows us and brings us to an understanding of the three things each one of us has to know: 1) who God is; 2) what sin is; 3) what salvation is. For it is a mystery that gives me more real knowledge than all the philosophers about the divine nature which inspires me, most horrible horror for sin, and it teaches me to appreciate my salvation. As an important consideration, which will be a mystery either of foolishness or of wisdom: "*stultitiam gentibus, Dei sapientiam*—stupidity to the gentiles, the wisdom of God."

2. The cross of Christ is the most effective and most certain means for a reformation of humanity, of corrupt and perverted man. There are three wellsprings of vice, Saint John says:

concupiscence of the eyes,
concupiscence of the flesh,
pride of life [1 John 2:16–17].

For these three temptations, Christ's holy portrait [the crucifix] provides these three remedies: 1) His being stripped of all things, and the nudity in which he died—against the love of riches, concupiscence of the eyes; 2) his humiliations—against ambition, the pride of life; 3) his sufferings, his pains—against sensuality, the concupiscence of the flesh. But since Christ, without personally having committed any sin, desired to experience in his own person the three remedies out of love for us—"*sublimitas et profundum*—the height and the depth" [Ephesians 3:18]; for us he does penance, etc.

And will it be insanity or the power of God? "*gentibus stultitiam, et Dei sapientiam*"? No, there is no more effective means, more likelihood of success, than the cross for controlling humankind. Some other manner could have brought glory and applause; only on the cross, with the humiliation and pain, could he put the world under obligation—raise himself up—kindle in us the great fire of love while we live or a terrible fire of torment when we have died: "*nunc judicium est Dei*—now is the moment of God's judgment."[8]

When the sacrifice was complete, Saint Luke says, it was still about an hour before sixth hour or midday, but darkness covered the earth until the ninth hour, the sun hid itself, and the veil of the temple tore down the middle. Then Jesus cried out in a very loud voice, saying, "My Father, into your hands I commend my spirit! Now all is fulfilled—*consummatum est*."

Espiritu, [Lucas 23:46] ya todo esta cumplido *Consummatum est* [Juan 19:30]: la reprobacion de los malos, que quieren ser siempre malos; la Salvacion de los buenos, que en mi cruz hallan una surabundancia de gracias, para obrar su salvacion y combatir—si cumplió la profetia, y se cumple del viejo Simeon—*hic positus est in runiam et in resurrectione multorum in israel* [Lucas 2:34]—triste nuntio, triste memoria, terrible verdad que nos ha de espantar, de un santo y fervoroso temor, dando nos golpes de pecho, como aquel concurso de los que se hallaban presentes a este espectaculo—publicando con el centurion, al mirar tantas maravillas y cosas extraordinarias, verdaderamente que este hombre era hijo de Dios [Marcos 15:39]—aquellos fieles discipulos de Jesus, que esperaban el Reino de Dios, y entre los cuales mas conocido José de Arimatea, fueron a Pilato y le pidieron el cuerpo de Jesus—y le habiendo descolgado de la Cruz le envolvió en una sabana y le colocó en un sepulcro abierto en peña viva, en donde ninguno hasta entonces habia sido sepultado; y las mugeres, Maria Magdalena aquella penitente, y otra Maria hicieron prevencion de aromas y Balsamos y le pusieron al sepulcro—

Mas numerosos, segun lo que se dice, los fieles de Cristo, presentan colocado, en un sepulcro nuevo, es el cuerpo del mismo Señor aun en el velo de sacramento, esta pidiendo sepulcro, y este sepulcro, que quiere, es su Corazon, Cristianos, *praebe fili mi cor tuum mihi* [Proverbios 23:26]— *Desiderio desideravi hoc pascha manducare vobiscum* [Lucas 22:15]—y que desolacion, que dolor—

No mas unas mugeres, y un hombre conocido se presenta, lo demas va huyendo con el concurso, dandose golpes, como pecadores vaya, pero sin engañarse

—*fin*—

The reprobation of evil persons who desire to be evil forever; the salvation of the good who find in my cross a superabundance of graces to work their salvation and to combat. Yes, I have fulfilled the prophecies, and that of old Simeon is fulfilled: "*Hic positus est in ruinam et in resurrectionem multorum in Israel*—This child is made present for the ruin and restoration of many in Israel" [Luke 2:34]. Sad message, sad memory, terrible truth which shocks us with a holy and fervent fear, making us beat our breasts like the crowd that found itself present at this spectacle, voicing with the centurion, who has seen so many miracles and remarkable events, "Truly this man is a son of God" [Mark 15:39]. Some faithful disciples of Jesus, who awaited the Kingdom of God, best known among them Joseph of Arimathea, went to Pilate and requested the body of Jesus. They took him down from the cross, wrapped him in a shroud, and placed him in a tomb hewn out of the living rock where no one before had been buried. And the women, Mary Magdalen the penitent and the other Mary, had arrived with a supply of perfumes and spices and placed him in the tomb.

More numerous, according to what is said, are the Christian faithful who place in a new sepulcher the body of that very Lord now under the sacramental veil. He is asking for a tomb, and the tomb that he desires is your heart, O Christians: "*Praebe fili mi cor tuum mihi*—My child, offer me your heart" [Proverbs 23:26]. "*Desiderio desideravi hoc pascha manducare vobiscum*—with how great a desire have I desired to eat this passover meal with you" [Luke 22:15]. And what desolation, what sorrow!

Only a few women and one well-known man remain. The others disperse with the crowd of people who beat their breasts like sinners; but mark well, without fooling yourselves.

—End—

Machebeuf Sermon on the Priesthood

This talk echoes a memorable scene in James Joyce's *Portrait of the Artist as a Young Man*, when a Jesuit invites Stephen Dedalus to join the Society of Jesus, tempting him in terms of power. Of course one could see the priesthood as the ultimate magic—having power over God's power. Unless the priest perceived himself as a mere instrument of the Church, of Christ's humanity, and of God's will, he might easily develop exaggerated ideas of his own importance. If on the other hand he preserved a clear sense of his call to be of service to others rather than to be served by them, he was apt to overemphasize the clerical esprit-de-corps and lapse into elitism. The fraternal spirit among clerics in moderation alleviated the disasters the Church had suffered in the previous several decades.[1]

It is hard to guess the audience for whom this sermon was written. It sounds like a talk preached to priests at a retreat, except perhaps for the "O Christians" at start of the third paragraph. Whoever the audience was, we should hope that they did not take too literally all the hyperboles of Father Machebeuf's devotional language.

---

1. James Joyce, *A Portrait of the Artist as a Young Man* (New York: Viking Press, 1964), pp. 157-62; note all the imagery of power in general and militarism in particular. For French clerical elitism among the Sulpicians and their seminary students, see Christopher Kauffman, *Tradition and Transformation in Catholic Culture* (New York: Macmillan, 1988).

Engraving. Joseph P. Machebeuf.

El Sacerdocio

San Vicente de Ferrier, que nos dice: hallandose enfrente de un Angel y de un sacerdote,—1° besaria las pisadas de los pies del ministro de cristo— 2° ofreceria sus homenages al delegado del cielo[2]

No me extraño ahora de ver al maestro del mundo, el imperador Constantino, en el Concilio Niceno, no querer sentarse a delante de los padres del Concilio, hasta lograr su licentia—no me extraño de ver a San Martin Obispo, a la mesa del [de] un imperador Romano, Maximiano, después de haber Bebido, ofrecer la copa a su capellano, de preferencia al imperador.[3] porque es inexplicable la ventaja de los sacerdotes sobre los reyes—consiste pues esta potestad soberana de cada una de las ordenes a la Consagracion de este hombre que hace a Dios el obispo, que al punto que dandole la materia de cada orden, le dice las palabras de la forma con la gracia que al alma le confiere, le imprime en el alma el caracter por el cual esta dignidad es eterna[4]—las mas sublimes dignidades del mundo, las mas durables, son de por vida, y la muerte desnuda a los reyes, depone a los emperadores, y aun antes cuantos se han visto caerse de las manos el cetro— pero de la dignidad sacerdotal ni hay fuerza, ni en el cielo, ni en la tierra, su caracter es en el alma, endeleble, y han de brillar en el cielo como unas estrellas—oh! dignidad Sacerdotal! oh mis amados sacerdotes! de cuanta veneracion no sois dignos—los angeles, si fueran capaces de envidia, les enviarían [envidiarían], pero os reverencian, las potestades os veneran, y los principales, y la corte celestial asisten humillados a vuestro excelso ministerio—

Oh Cristianos! con que veneracion, con que respeto no deberemos acatar nosotros a estos encargados de Dios, a estos dioses visibles que nos representan al Dios invisible, a estos dioses de la tierra que hacen las veces del Dios del cielo—

---

2. The little tale that Machebeuf attributes to Vincent Ferrer is usually told of Francis of Assisi; see Franz Spirago, *The Catechism Explained* (New York: Benziger Brothers, 1899), pp. 644-45.

3. García del Valle used the same legend about Constantine in his sermon on the occasion of Father Rafael Ortiz's first mass; see Eusebius, *Life of Constantine* 3:10, and Theodoret, *Ecclesiastical History* 1:6. The story of Bishop Martin of Tours appears in Alban Butler, *Lives of the Saints* (New York: P.J. Kenedy and Sons, 1895), 4:439, and in Franz Spirago, *Anecdotes and Examples Illustrating the Catholic Catechism* (New York: Benziger Brothers, 1904), pp. 327-28.

4. Thomas J. Steele, S.J., and Rowena A. Rivera, *Penitente Self-Government* (Santa Fe: Ancient City Press, 1985), p. 191:

> The matter-and-form analysis of each of the sacraments arose gradually in the Church's theological reflection. It is perhaps latent in Ephesians 5:25-26, "Christ loved the Church and gave himself up on behalf of it to sanctify it, cleansing it with a washing of water by the word" (see also James 5:14-15). For the neo-Platonist Saint Augustine (d. 430), the "wash-

The Priesthood

Saint Vincent Ferrer said to us that if he encountered an angel and a priest, he would first kiss the footsteps of the minister of Christ and only then offer his homage to the heavenly messenger.²

I do not think it strange to consider that the ruler of the world, the Emperor Constantine, at the Council of Nicaea, did not wish to sit down before the fathers of the council sat, and until he obtained their permission. I do not think it strange to consider that Saint Martin the Bishop, at table with the Roman Emperor Maximian, after having drunk, offered the cup to his chaplain rather than to the Emperor.³ For the superiority of priests to kings cannot be explained away. This sovereign power is found among each one of the orders of consecration in any man whom the bishop consecrates to God. At the moment the bishop applies the matter of each order and pronounces over him the words of the form with the accompanying grace it confers upon his soul, it imprints upon his soul the character by which this dignity is made eternal.⁴ The most sublime and enduring dignities of the world are lifelong, and death strips kings, deposes emperors, and makes their hands slip from the scepter. But there is no power in heaven or on earth to compare with priestly dignity. Its character lies in the soul, indelible, and it must shine in heaven like the stars. Oh, priestly dignity! Oh, my beloved priests! Of what veneration are you not worthy! The angels, if they were capable of envy, would envy you, but they revere you, the powers venerate you, and the principalities and the whole heavenly court wait humbly upon your exalted ministry.

Oh Christians! with what veneration, with what respect should we not heed those charged by God, to those visible deities who represent for us the invisible God, to those gods on earth who act in the place of the God of Heaven.

---

ing of water" became the "element"; he kept the scriptural term "word." For the Aristotelian Thomas Aquinas (d. 1274), "element" became "matter" and "word" became "form." From Thomism the terminology entered the official church teaching of the Councils of Florence (1438-45) and Trent (1545-63), then passed into popular Catholicism through the *Catechism of the Council of Trent*.

The *matter* of a sacrament is either a static item (bread and wine for the Eucharist), an item in action (water being poured on the forehead for Baptism), or a mere action (imposition of hands for Holy Orders). The *form* of a sacrament is an audible formula of words spoken over the item or recited in tandem with the action.

The *character* of a sacrament also appears in García del Valle's 1823 sermon for Rafael Ortiz's first mass. According to Catholic doctrine, the sacraments of Baptism, Confirmation, and Holy Orders leave a permanent trace on the recipient and hence need never and can never be validly repeated.

Pero los sacerdotes no solo son dignos de nuestra veneracion, por su caracter sagrado y encumbrada dignidad, sino tambien por la multitud y grandeza de Bienes que nos dispensan—

Pués el sacerdote es el Bienhechor de la humanidad, del genero humano por sus oraciones, sus instructiones y su caridad—

Un sacerdote, solo para estar señalado con este sagrado caracter, se halla encargado de los intereses del pueblo, y viene a ser uno de aquellos angeles, que Jacob vió en sueños, subiendo y Bajando una escala cuyo pié estaba sobre la tierra, y su remate tocaba en el cielo—Baja el sacerdote, por cumplimiento de su ministerio de mediador, a encargarse de las necesidades y peticiones del pueblo y sabe por medio de la oracion propia a su ministerio a presantarles hasta los pies del trono divino de J. Ch.—para alcanzar por los meritos de este divino salvador la misericordia[5]—no nos engañemos, la pobre humanidad, luego seria victima de los infiernos, de las insidias de sus oficiales, si no tuvieran un mediator, rogando siempre a Dios—Como hubieran sido vincidos [sic] los judios en sus combates con abimelech,[6] si Moyses en el monte no hubiera rogado por su pueblo—Si el mundo la tierra, llena de maldades, mil veces hubiera merecido de sentir el peso de la justicia divina, pero no, en todo el mundo, hasta en los rincones los mas escondidos, hay un hombre, mediator entre el cielo y la tierra, establecido por j. Ch. en favor de los hombres acerca de Dios, este hombre, el sacerdote, ruega por oficio, ruega no en su nombre mas bien en el nombre de Jesucristo, en el nombre de toda su iglesia, y que no concedera Dios a los ruegos de un sacerdote que presenta las supplicas de toda la iglesia? Cada dia, unos millones de sacerdotes, ofrecen la victima pura a los altares, y en poder de su Dios hacen fuerza a la justicia y Dios hace misericordia al mundo—pero si, un sacerdote, aunque no tuviera otro destino que orar como ministro publico, siempre contribuian poderosamente al bien estar y felicidad temporal de los fieles (*Catecismo expl.* 391)[7]

2° Pero no solo ofrece cada dia sus oraciones al Señor, y ofrece diariamente la victima de propiciacion, pero tambien es el cooperador directo de J. Ch. en la salvacion de las almas, ya por los sacramentos que les administra, ya por la explicacion y predicacion de la divina palabra—*euntes discete omnes gentes—predicate evangelium omni creaturae* [Mateo 28:19]—fiel al mandamiento de su Dios, miren esta tropa de obrarios [obreros], que se marchan valientes armados de una cruz y de su breviario, se dividen el

---

5. Genesis 28:10-22; Malachi 2:7, noted by Spirago, *Catechism Explained*, p. 644.

6. Machebeuf gets the name of the pagan king wrong. It was really Amalek, as reported in Exodus 17:8-16 and Numbers 24:20.

7. Machebeuf refers here to some edition of the Spanish translation of Antonio Claret's

But priests are worthy of our veneration not only because of their sacred character and lofty dignity but also for the number and greatness of the good things they convey to us.

For the priest is a benefactor of humankind, of the whole human species, because of his prayers, his teachings, and his charity.

A priest, simply because he is marked with this sacred character, finds himself charged with the needs of the people, and he becomes like one of the angels whom Jacob saw in his dream, ascending and descending a ladder whose foot stood on the earth and whose top rung touched heaven. The priest condescends to fulfill his ministry as mediator, to charge himself with the needs and prayers of the people, and by means of the prayer proper to his ministry he knows how to carry them clear to the foot of the divine throne of Jesus Christ, in order to achieve mercy through the merits of this Divine Savior.[5] Let us not deceive ourselves. Poor suffering humanity would fall victim to hell, of the snares of its agents, if they could find no mediator who always prayed to God.

How the Jews would have been conquered in their battles with Abimelech,[6] if Moses had not been praying on the mountain for his people. Indeed, the world, the earth, full of iniquity as it is, would have deserved to feel a thousand times the weight of divine justice. But no, throughout the whole world, even unto the most out-of-the-way corners, there is a man who is a mediator between heaven and earth, established by Jesus Christ for the sake of men before God. This man, the priest, prays as a duty, prays not in his own name but in the name of Jesus Christ, in the name of Christ's whole church. And what will God not grant through the prayers of a priest who presents the petitions of the whole church? Each day, millions of priests offer the pure Victim at the altar, in the power of their God they strengthen righteousness, and God then shows mercy to the world. But if a priest had no other destiny than to pray as a public servant, they (sic) always contribute mightily to the well being and temporal happiness of the faithful (*Cat. Expl.* 391).[7]

2° But he not only offers his prayers to the Lord each day and offers daily the propitiatory victim, but he is also the direct cooperator with Christ Jesus in the salvation of souls. Through the sacraments he administers to them as well through explication and preaching of the divine word: "*Euntes discete omnes gentes*—go out and teach all peoples . . . *Predicate evangelium*

Catechismo de la Doctrina Cristiana Explicado; in another edition (Barcelona: Los Herederos de la V. Pla., 1848), p. 369, we read, "que los sacerdotes, aun cuando no tuviesen otro destino que el de orar, su utilidad para el bien público no podia ser mas manifiesta—even when priests have no vocation other than prayer, their usefulness for the public good could not be more manifest."

mundo, para instruir a los hombres y les enseñan el camino del cielo—unos libros se necessitarian para decir aqui y los trabajos y las maravillas de los primeros sacerdotes, los apostoles—unos libros, no menos grandes se necessitan, para anunciar y publicar los trabajos, los sacrificios diarios que hacen los successores de los apostoles, para alumbrar los pueblos que duermen todavía en las tinieblas del error, confundir los impios, convencer a los peccadores, conmover las conciencias, sostener y confortalecer a los justos—oh! estan el echo [hecho] de esta voz grande y poderosa que gritaba en el desierto, *ego vox clamantis* en el desierto, *parate viam Domini* [Isaías 40:3]; ay te penitentiam—se hallan unos herodes, y mas unas herodiadas, que no pueden sufrir y aguantar de oir siempre: no es licito de vivir asi,[8] y si lo pudieran, para no oir mas una voz tan importuna, acabarian con el de una vez—pero el Sacerdote, poco atonito, persigue su camino y segun el consejo de su divino Amo, predica siempre, ruega y obsecra, ameneza y consuela; y aunque el sacerdote predicator, sea un pesar grande por los malos, es verdad y necesario de confessar, que el sacerdote ha de ser una luz para illuminar el mundo, un capitan para exhortar sus soldados en el combate, un padre de familia enseguardo [enseguido?] a defender y cuidar los intereses de casa—si el mundo a [ha] progresido [progresado?], si las Bibliotecas son llenas de Libros, si la mayor parte del mundo es civilizada, a quien lo debe la humanidad, a los sacerdotes, a esos hombres cargados de Dios a predicar el evangelio, que es la Verdadera Luz.

3° el sacerdote es el bienhechor de la humanidad en sus oraciones, y instrucciones es tambien por su caridad—si recibe el secreto de las conciencias, cuantos pecadores no saca de la muerte del peccado a la vida de la gracia? Cuantas ignorancias no destierra? cuantos desordenes no precave? cuantos males no evita? en aquel tribunal del cielo,[9] colocado en la tierra, cuantos odios no extingue? cuantos matrimonios no pacifica? De este tribunal hace reynar la paz y la felicidad en las familias—pero un hombre ha caido, gimiendo y llorando en una cama de Dolor; no solamente padece de los Dolores del Cuerpo, pero mas bien siente las cadenas de su pobre alma—quien vendra le presta la mano, visitarle a su casa, participar a sus dolores, el sacerdote sentado a su cama—el prisionero—el condenado—

Y si a citar obras de misericordia y de abnegacion, yo considero el sacerdote como hombre de la sociedad, lo veo agregado a todas las congregaciones y tomando empeño en todas las obras quien ha dado a la humanidad tantos monumentos dedicados a la enfermedad—estos son los

---

8. Mark 6:18 tells the tale of King Herod, Herodias, Salome, and John the Baptist's head.
9. The confessional, where the priest administered the Sacrament of Penance (Reconciliation).

omni creaturae—Preach the good news to all creatures" [Matthew 28:19]. Faithful to the command of their God, behold the throng of laborers who march out valiantly, armed with the cross and their breviaries, they divide up the world so as to instruct men and teach them the way to heaven—many books would be needed to state here both the works and the miracles of those first priests, the apostles. Many books at least as large would be needed to proclaim and publish the works, the daily sacrifices made by the successors of the apostles to enlighten those peoples who still sleep in the darkness of error, to confound the impious, to dissuade sinners, to move consciences, to sustain and comfort the just. Oh, they are the echo of that strong and powerful voice that cried out in the desert, "*Ego vox clamantis*—I am a voice crying in the desert—*parate viam Domini*—prepare the Lord's way" [Isaiah 40:3]. We find some Herods, and some Herodiases that cannot suffer, cannot bear to hear continually "It is not allowed to live thus."[8] And if they could silence that importunate voice, they would destroy it at once—but the priest, undaunted, follows his path and, according to the counsel of his Divine Master, preaches always, prays and supplicates, warns and counsels; and although the priest-preacher may be a great nuisance for evil men, it is true and necessary to confess that the priest must be a light to illuminate the world, a captain to encourage his soldiers in the combat, the father of a family charged with defending and securing the interests of the household. If the world has made progress, if libraries are filled with books, if the greater part of the world is civilized, to whom is the world indebted for such successes? To the priests, to those men charged by God to preach the gospel, which is the true light.

3° The priest is a benefactor of the human race because of his prayers, his instructions, and his charity. Since he receives the secrets of consciences, how many sinners does he not bring from the death of sin to the life of grace? How much ignorance does he not dispel? How much riotousness does he not prevent? How many evils does he not prevent? In that heavenly tribunal[9] placed here on earth, how many hatreds does he not extinguish? How many marriages does he not pacify? This tribunal makes peace and happiness reign within families. But if a man has fallen, moaning and weeping upon his bed of suffering, not only does he suffer the pains of his body, he also especially feels the chains of his soul. But who will come to lend a helping hand, to visit his home, to partake of his sorrows? The priest seated by the bed—of the prisoner—the condemned man.

sacerdotes (a fuero, lejos el pensar que se hallan algunos que no corresponden a su estado—en tan lamentable estado) debemos compadecernos de su extravío y venerar su Dignidad), porque esta siempre es la misma)—

O Dignidad venerable de los Sacerdotes, oh puedo ahora comprender estas palabras de Jesucristo a sus apostoles—*qui vos audit, me audit, qui vos spernit, me spernit* [Lucas 10:16]—pero es possible quizas, que se hallan algunos que faltan a la veneracion tan justa que deben a los encargados? se hallaron unos farizeos, que Blasfemaron contra el Señor, etc.—y si el maestro ha sido calumniado, como no lo han de ser etc.

—*fin*—

And as for naming works of mercy and of self-denial, I consider the priest as a man of the social order. I see him joined to all communities, taking an active part in all works, a man who has given humanity so many monuments dedicated to healing illness. These are the priests (by [canon] law, perish the thought that there are some who do not live up to their calling—in a deplorable state) whose straying we ought to pity and whose dignity we ought to venerate, for that remains always the same.

Oh venerable dignity of priests! Oh, I now comprehend these words of Jesus Christ to his apostles, "*Qui vos audit, me audit, qui vos spernit, me spernit*—Whoever hears you hears me, whoever rejects you rejects me" [Luke 10:16]. But is it perhaps possible that there are some who fail to reverence as appropriately as they should these agents [of God]? There were Pharisees who blasphemed against the Lord, etc. And if the master has been slandered, how will they not be, etc.

—end—

*5. Soledad. San Felipe Neri Church.
Albuquerque, New Mexico.*

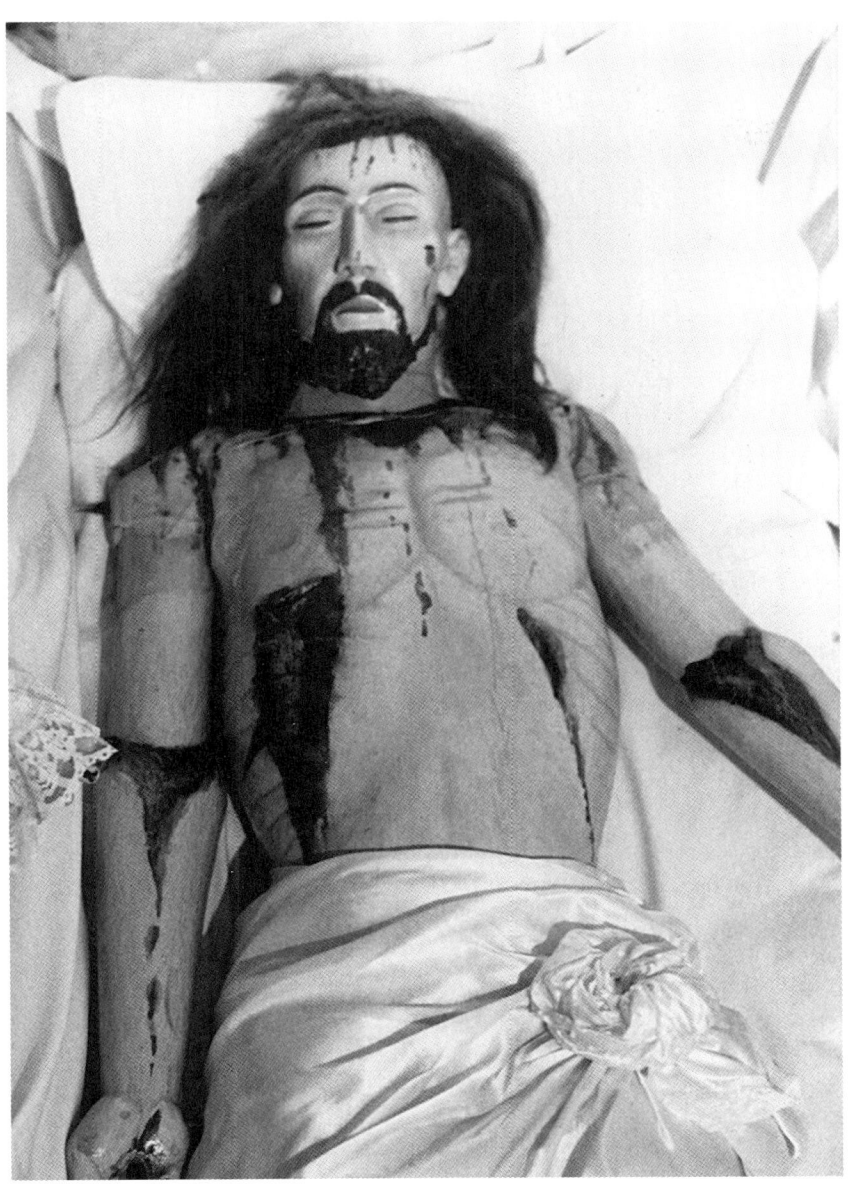

*6. Santo. San Felipe Neri Church.
Albuquerque, New Mexico.
Author photograph.*

Jean Baptiste Lamy

Jean Baptiste Lamy was born on 11 October 1814 in Lempdes, Auvergne, and he died in Santa Fe on 13 February 1888. Lamy and Machebeuf became friends while studying together in the Clermont Seminary, and they were recruited together for the Cincinnati Diocese shortly after ordination. Lamy served as pastor of Danville, Ohio, and several other growing towns in the surrounding region, and of Covington, Kentucky, just across the Ohio River from the diocesan see. When he was chosen and consecrated as bishop for New Mexico after the United States conquest, Lamy asked Machebeuf to join him as his vicar. They traveled separately by way of New Orleans and Galveston, where Lamy suffered shipwreck. The two met in San Antonio, and continued through El Paso, arriving in Santa Fe on 9 August 1851.

As quickly as he could, Lamy recruited French priests (suspending native New Mexican clergymen whom he thought unsuitable) and United States nuns and brothers to foster education. He stopped preaching in Spanish about 1876, probably recognizing the commercial and cultural revolution represented by the approaching railroad, which he strongly supported (hence the name "Lamy Junction"). He successfully accomplished what he and most others expected him to attempt; it is only in more recent years, conscious of the cultural insularity and human limitations of nineteenth-century mainstream society, that we take exception both to some of the means by which he accomplished his task and to the nearly-universal acclaim accorded him during his lifetime and into the early twentieth century. We are also more aware of a Jansenism that Lamy possessed. Like Machebeuf's, Lamy's Jansenist beliefs were less dogmatic than ethical: "holier than thou."

A warning about Archbishop LaTour's personality in Willa Cather's novel *Death Comes for the Archbishop*: it is Cather's *own* personality, not the historical Lamy's personality in the least. But there is hearsay evidence that the real Lamy was a good preacher besides the corroborating evidence of the sermons themselves: brief, plain, and at times quite effective in their expression of fresh insights into religious truth.[1]

---

1. William Howlett, *Life of Bishop Machebeuf* (Denver: Regis College, 1987 [orig. 1908]); Paul Horgan, *Lamy of Santa Fe* (New York: Farrar, Straus and Giroux, 1975), especially pp. 422-25; Thomas J. Steele, S.J., "The Poet, the Archbishop, and the Heavenly Jerusalem: Romanticizing Lamy's 1851 Arrival in Santa Fe," pp. 104-20 in *Folk and Church in Nineteenth-Century New Mexico* (Colorado Springs: The Colorado College, 1993).

*7. Archbishop Jean B. Lamy.
Courtesy of the Museum of New Mexico,
negative number 9969.*

Lamy's 1860 Instruction

Bishop Lamy wrote the following short talk in his typically difficult handwriting on both sides of a single piece of blue paper neatly torn at one edge.

Bishop Jean Baptiste Lamy had a close relationship with many religious women. His own sister had been an Ursuline nun; she died in the Ursuline convent in New Orleans where Lamy had left her and his niece Marie while en route to his new Vicariate-Apostolic of New Mexico. Lamy recruited the first group of Sisters of Loretto from Nerinx, Kentucky, and traveled over the Santa Fe Trail with them in 1852. Five years later he brought Marie west to attend the nuns' new school in Santa Fe and saw her enter the convent upon graduation. She was therefore in the chapel when the bishop delivered this little talk on 30 March 1860, after a short retreat preached by Vicar General Father Machebeuf. On that occasion two sisters pronounced their first vows after two years of postulancy and novitiate and three novices were invested in nuns' habit with the white veils of novices.[1] It is hard to avoid the thought that the uncle was very conscious of his niece both when he composed and when he delivered this sermon.

Lamy also introduced the Christian Brothers (1859), the Sisters of Charity of Cincinnati (1865), and the Jesuits (1867), thereby providing a large number of educational and charitable institutions for his fledgling diocese.

---

1. "Annals of the Convent of Our Lady of Light," pages 8-12, microfilm reel 1, New Mexico State Records Center and Archives: "The Vicar General gave a retreat to the Novices during Lent, it began on Passion Sunday & ended on Passion Friday March 30th. On this day, two Novices, Sisters Beatriz [Dolores Maes-Torres] & Teresa [Petra Alire], pronounced their first vows & Misses Cesaria Ribera, Refugio & Teresa Chaves received the holy habit. His Lordship, assisted by the Vicar General, presided over the ceremony & preached." See also Sister Richard Marie Barber, S.L., *Light in Yucca Land* (Santa Fe: Loretto Academy of Our Lady of Light, 1952), pp. 34, 152.

Profesión Religiosa

Por una profesión religiosa

Consagrarse a Dios por los tres votos de castidad, de pobreza y de obediencia, y sujetarse a vivir en comunidad bajo una regla es lo que constituye la vida religiosa. En el principio las personas que abrasaban la vida relig. No tenian otra intencion sino de servir a Dios con mas perfeccion que en el mundo y de santificarse por la oracion, el silencio, el trabajo manual, y los ejercisios de una caridad mutual; pero ahora la mayor parte de las comunidades religiosas se consagran al servicio del publico, sea en cuidar los pobres y infermos, sea en enseñar la Juventud. Las comunidades religiosas son asilos sagrados para la virtud en donde los buenos ejemplos sostienen esta misma virtud. Los votos que se hacen despues de un noviciado o prueba bastante larga son para fijar la inconstancia de nuestra pobre naturaleza, y para dar al mismo tiempo mas merito a nuestras buenas obras. Estos votos no se hacen, ni la Yglesia permite que se hagan sino despues de mucha deliberacion y con plena libertad, y de haber pasado un tiempo regular para probar su vocacion, y de haber pedido a Dios las luces y gracias necesarias antes de dar un paso tan importante; pues abrasar la vida religiosa con temeridad y sin haber hecho las debida reflexiones seria la desgracia la mas grande.

La vida religiosa nos hace semejantes a los angeles[,] desposa nuestras almas con N.S. Jesu C. pero para cumplir con las obligaciones de perfeccion que ella nos impone, hemos de revestirnos de N.S. Jesu Cristo. La ceremonia de este dia no consiste solamente con un cambio de ropa o de traje; pero es una ceremonia sagrada, santificada por la palabra de Dios; asi como dejan un traje que el mundo se esfuerza de hacer honorable por el lujo y la vanidad para tomar otro que saca todo su adorno de la modestia y del pudor; pues del mismo modo han de pensar de despojarse hoy del hombre viejo segun el cual habeis vivido, y de sus apetitos viciosos, para vestiros del hombre nuevo (Efes. 4.24) (que es Jesu C. segun la voluntad de Dios). Ahora nos revestimos de N.S. Jesu C., cuando tomamos los mismos sentimientos, la misma disposicion que tenía nuestro Salvador. *Hoc sentite in vobis quod et in Christo Jesu* (Filip. 2.5). Procurando tener las mismas disposiciones, haciendo por El lo que El ha hecho por nosotros, tomando por modelo y regla en su Sto. Servicio lo que El ha hecho por nuestra Salvacion. *Induimini Dominum Jesum Christum* (Rom. 13.14). De este modo debemos revestirnos de N.S. Jesu C. imitando su caridad. El siendo igual a Dios, y Dios mismo se anonadó tomando la forma de Siervo[2] por nuestro amor, para procurarnos la verdadera libertad, la libertad de los hijos de Dios; y nosotros, sus indignas criaturas, no podriamos sujetarnos en Su servicio?

---

2. This is further material from Philippians 2:5-11.

Religious Profession

For a Religious Profession

Consecrating oneself to God through the three vows of chastity, poverty, and obedience and subjugating oneself to a life in community under a rule are what constitute religious life. During the early years of the Church, the persons who embraced a life in a religious order intended only to serve God with greater perfection than they could in the world and to sanctify themselves by means of prayer, silence, manual labor, and the exercise of mutual charity; but today the majority of religious communities dedicate themselves to the service of people at large, whether it be in caring for the poor and the sick or in teaching young persons. Religious communities are sacred refuges of virtue in which good example sustains that same virtue.

The vows which one makes after the novitiate or some considerably longer probation are meant to fix the inconstancy of our weak human nature and at the same time to gain more merit for our good works. These vows are not made, nor does the Church allow them to be made, except following upon lengthy deliberation and in complete freedom, after the required time for proving one's vocation has passed, and after beseeching God for the illumination and grace necessary before taking such an important step ; for embracing religious life rashly and without having entered into serious reflection would be a truly great blunder.

Religious life makes us like the very angels and weds our souls to Our Lord Jesus Christ; but in order to fulfil the obligations of perfection imposed by that life, we must dress ourselves anew in Our Lord Jesus Christ. Today's ceremony does not consist only in a change of clothing or of uniform, but it is rather a sacred ceremony, made sacred by the word of God, as if they are leaving one mode of dress that the world tries to make seem honorable because of its luxury and vanity, to adopt instead another which derives all its attractiveness from modesty and reserve. For in the same manner they plan to forsake today "the old man," according to which you have formerly lived, and to abandon your unworthy desires so as to clothe yourselves in "the new man" which is Christ Jesus, according to the will of God (Ephesians 4:24). Today we clothe ourselves anew in Our Lord Jesus Christ when we adopt the same sentiments, the same attitudes which Our Savior held—"*Hoc [enim] sentite in vobis quod et in Christo Jesu*" (Philippians 2:5), assuming the same dispositions, doing in that regard what He has done for us, taking as a model and norm in His holy service what He has done for our salvation: "*Induimini Dominum Jesum Christum*" (Romans 13:14). In this manner we should clothe ourselves anew in Our Lord Jesus Christ, imitating his love.

Being equal to God [the Father] and being Himself God, He humbled Himself, taking the form of a slave[2] out of love for us in order to gain true

Tengan bien presentes que la perfeccion de la vida cristiana no consiste en entrar en religion, mas bien consiste en hacer en todo la voluntad de Dios que os ha llamado a ser sus dignas esposas. Han de decir como N. Señor: mi alimento es de hacer la voluntad de mi Padre que me ha enviado (Juan 4.34), de mi Dios que me ha llamado a una vocacion tan sublime.

El velo santificado por la bendicion de la yglesia, este velo que toman en esta solemne ocacion, significa el velo espiritual de la modestia y de la simplicidad. Habiendo renunciado con toda generosidad a las pompas y vanidades del siglo, tomen el mayor empeño para adornar vuestras almas de las virtudes que agradan al divino Esposo que no faltará de recompensarlas en esta vida por la paz de su conciencia y en el cielo con su eterna felicidad.

—*fin*—

liberty, the liberty of the children of God; and we, His unworthy creatures, can we not subject ourselves in His service?

Bear in mind that the perfection of Christian life does not consist of entering a religious community; rather it consists of performing every act as the will of God Who has called you to be His worthy spouses. Be able to say with Our Lord, "My food is to do the will of my Father Who has sent me" (Saint John 4:34)—of my God Who has called me to so sublime a vocation.

The veil sanctified by the blessing of the Church, this veil you receive on this solemn occasion, signifies the spiritual veil of modesty and simplicity. Having renounced with complete generosity the pomps and vanities of the age, you take a larger pledge to adorn your souls with the virtues that please your divine Bridegroom Who will not fail to recompense those virtues both in this life with the peace of your conscience and in heaven with His everlasting happiness.

—*end*—

Lamy's Christmas Sermon

Both the English and the Spanish versions of this sermon are Lamy's own. Christmas was a special occasion in Santa Fe, as elsewhere, and so a large number of the Anglo population of Santa Fe, few of whom were Catholic, would visit the nearest church at hand to celebrate the feast. Since the Bishop expected Protestants as well as the regular parishioners to be present, he drafted his homily in two languages.

I cannot say whether his Spanish is a translation of his English, or vice versa, or whether he still thought and wrote in French and translated both versions from a French original that no longer survives.

I detect here a sort of "Grinch Theology" because more than half of the sermon is about sin. The topic may have recommended itself to Lamy's Jansenist tendencies every day of the year, but the circumstances might excuse him: Christmas was and is a pastor's sole annual opportunity to speak to some of members of his congregation—and some complete strangers—about matters he considers to be of ultimate importance.

8. *"Interior of Cathedral" [La Parroquia].*
Santa Fe, New Mexico, ca. 1880.
From Harper's New Monthly Magazine.
Courtesy of the Museum of New Mexico,
negative number 76952.

Navidad 1865

Natividad de N. S. Jesu C.

    Queriendo El Apostol San Pablo expresar el mysterio de la encarnacion de Verbo divino nos dice "Filip. 2.6" que Jesu C. teniendo la naturaleza de Dios, y siendo igual a Dios . . . no obstante de anonado a si mismo, tomando la Forma de Siervo, hecho Semejante a los hombres y reducido a la condicion del hombre; y eso de tal modo que en este misterio adorable, toda la virtud del hijo de Dios esta traendo en debilidad, enfermedad y flaqueza pero El Señor Jesu Cristo se sujetó a tantas humillaciones y trabajos no para conseguir una gloria esteril, Sino que este Dios de misericordia Se hizo hombre paraque el hombre Se hiciese Dios. Asi tambien lo declara San Juan el Evangelista, cuando refiriendo este mismo misterio de la Generacion eterna y de la Encarnacion temporal, el nos explica los soberanos fines, que tuvó en esta la Divina Sabiduria, y nos dice "cap. 1º" vino Dios al mundo; y a aquellos que le recibieron les dio potestad para hacerse hijos de Dios a los que creen en su nombre . . . que nacen de Dios . . . *id est* . . . que quieren corresponder a su gracia, conformandose en todo a su Santa Voluntad, llevando una vida digna de Dios. *Et verbum caro Factum est*—El verbo se hizo carne, y habito en medio de nosotros; y el Apostol nos dice el motivo por el cual el se hizo carne, habito entre nosotros[.] La gracia de Dios Nuestro Salvador "Tito 2" Se manifestó a todos los hombres, enseñandonos para que renunciando a la impiedad y a los deseos mundanos, vivamos en este siglo con templanzas con justicia y con piedad, aguardando la bienaventuranza esperanza y la venida de la gloria del gran Dios y nuestro Salvador Jesu Cristo. Para lograr pues el beneficio de la Encarnacion de Nuestro Señor que es La gloria de Dios y nuestra Salvacion es preciso de Seguir la enseñanza que nos manifiesta la gracia de Dios, evitar los desordenes que son un obstaculo a Nuestra Santificacion y practicar las virtudes que deben adornar el alma de un cristiano, de un hijo de Dios. Estos obstaculos, Segun el Apostol son la impiedad y los deseos mundanal[es], o en otras palabras la Falta de religion. La falta de Fé, la soberbia, la codicia, el amor desordenado a los placeres carnales. Estos son los obstaculos que debemos evitar; y luego empeñarnos de buena gana y con una voluntad Fuerte a vivir una vida digna de un hombre racional, "hablo a personas que tiene Fé,["] digna de un hijo de Dios. Practicando las virtudes de Sobriedad, de Justicia y de piedad: de Sobriedad por lo que respecta a nosotros mismos, de Justicia por lo con el projimo, tratandole como deseamos Ser tratados nosotros mismos, y de piedad por lo que respecta a Dios dandole a este Dios la obediencia que le debemos, un culto no especulativo, pero bien practico, no de la clase de estos, segun el mismo

Christmas 1865

"Today is born to you a Saviour" [Luke 2:11]

An observation on the Feast of this day—

Wishing to express the great mystery of the Yncarnation of the divine Word St. Paul tells us (Filip. 2.6) that "Christ Jesus being in the Form of God thought it not robbery to be himself equal to God: but debased himself, taking the form of a Servant, being made to the likeness of men, and in Shape found as a man"; and this took place in such a way that in this adorable mystery all the Strength, all the virtue of the Son of God was changed into debility, infirmity and weakness. And if our Divine Saviour Submitted himself to all those humiliations and labours, it was not to acquire a steril[e], vain glory; but being a God of mercy, he became man, that man might become like God. This is what St. John the Evangelist declares, when speaking of this same mystery of the Yncarnation he explains to us the great object the Divine Wisdom had in view; *et Verbum caro Factum est et habitavit in nobis*, the Word was made Flesh, and dwelt in our midst[,] and to those who received him, he gave them power to become the Sons of God, to those who believe in his name ... are born of God, that is who wish to correspond with his divine graces, conforming themselves in all things to his holy will. The great Apostle will tell us (Titus 2) that same great object for which the Word of God was made Flesh and dwelt in our midst: the grace of God our Saviour, he says, has appeared to all men, teaching us that renouncing impiety and worldly desires, we should live in this world soberly, justly and piously with the hope to obtain the glory of God. To put to profit the graces our Saviour Jesus Christ offers to us in his incarnation, we have to follow the teaching of the Apostle. We have to shun the disorders, the ofences[,] which are an obstacle to our Sanctification and endeavor to practice the virtues that should adorn the Soul of a Christian, of a Son of God. The obstacles we should shun, according to the same Apostle, are impiety and worldly desires, or in other words the want of religion, the want of faith, pride, avarice, the disorderly love of carnal pleasures. We must not only avoid evil in every shape and in every form, but also we should make every effort to live a virtuous life, a life worthy of a rational being, "What do I say, I hope I address Christians," a life worthy of Sons of God. These virtues are Sobriety, Justice and piety[.] Sobriety for what concerns our own selves personally in our private life; Justice towards our neighbors doing to others as we wish to be done by; piety giving to Almighty God the practical obedience we owe him; and not like those (Tit. 1.16) who profess to know God, but renounce him, deny him by their

Apostol "Tito 1.16" que profesan conocer a Dios, mas le niegan con las obras: "Siendo como son abominables y rebeldes y negados para toda obra buena."¹ No permita Dios que Seamos de esta clase de gente, ni tampoco como aquellas infelices habitantes de Belen que no quisieron dar la posada a Nuestro Señor Jesu Cristo. pues refiere el Evangelio que no hubó lugar en el meson para la madre Santisima de Salvador del mundo. En obediencia al edicto del Emperador que ordenaba que cada cual fuese a la ciudad de su estirpe para el [censo], La Sagrada Familia se marcho para la ciudad de David; aunque muy pobres hubieran tenido conque pagar un pobre rincon, pues lo buscaban para al [alojarse]; pero por el gran concurso de gente se reservan los alojamientos para huespedes mas ricos asi se vieron obligados a retirarse en un establo. Tal Fué el palacio en el cual nacio el hijo de Dios. El Divino Salvador ha bajado de Cielo en la tierra para levantarnos hasta al cielo; aprovechandonos de sus gracias, conseguiremos la Salvacion de Nuestras almas y la gloria eterna que les deseo a todos—

—*fin*—

1. At this point, Lamy's Spanish text has some material that does not appear in the English. It may contain a reference to the age-old Hispanic custom of *las posadas*, a religious folk drama by which parishioners enact Joseph and Mary's search for lodging. It translates as follows:
May God keep us from being part of that class of people, from being at all like those unhappy inhabitants of Bethlehem who chose not to give Our Lord Jesus Christ shelter. The gospel tells us that there was no room in the inn for the Most Holy Mother of the Savior of the World. In obedience to an imperial edict that required every man to go to his ancestral city for a census, the Holy Family traveled to the City of David.

work, being abominable and rebels or incredulous, and reprobate for every good work.[1] if we are men of good will the grace of God will keep us from those disorders, from those excesses and we will have a share then in that divine peace announced by the angels on that occasion to the good Shepherds, and by corresponding faithfully to the grace of God, we will secure to ourselves the blessing of a happy eternity which I wish you from my heart.

—end—

Though they were quite poor, they had brought along enough money to pay for some poor corner, for they wished to obtain lodging; but because of the great press of people, all the spaces were reserved for wealthier guests, so they found that they had to retire to a stable. Such was the palace in which was born the Son of God. The Divine Savior has come down from Heaven to the Earth to lift us up to Heaven. By corresponding with his graces, let us pursue the salvation of our souls, seeking the eternal happiness I wish for all of you.

Lamy's Instruction on the Passion

Lamy delivered this instruction to the Sisters of Loretto as one of fifteen or so talks he gave during their annual retreat. It goes with two other presentations of the Lord's Passion and Death—those of García del Valle and Machebeuf.

Lamy here neglects the late-medieval Franciscanism that might have appealed more to his Hispanic listeners and adopts instead an approach that most Protestants and some Catholics might describe as semi-Pelagian: thinking that Christ did what he did during his earthly career not to save us but principally to teach us how to behave so we could be our own saviors. As Lamy phrases it, "Let us earnestly imitate the virtues [Christ] demonstrated in the various circumstances of his passion." Not only Calvin and Jansenius but even Paul and Augustine must have rolled over in their reliquaries.

9. Statue of Jean B. Lamy,
outside cathedral.
Santa Fe, New Mexico.
Author photograph.

Instrucción sobre la Pasión

11ª Instruccion—Pasión

Como hijas de Maria Santisima al pie de la cruz[1] deben tener una devocion particular a la pasion, a los padecimientos de N.S.J.C. sera entonces muy conforme al espiritu de su santo instituto hablarles en esta instruccion de la pasion de Nuestro Divino Redentor. En la vigilia de su muerte entre otras que dijo Nuestro Señor a sus Apostoles en su discurso de la ultima cena, hallamos estas palabras: ya no hablaré mucho con vosotros porque viene el principe de este mundo, aunque no hay en mi cosa que le pertenesca; mas para que conosca el mundo que yo amo al padre y que cumplo con lo que me ha mandado; levantemos y vamos de aqui. Juan 14.31. Si reflejamos algo veremos la generosidad [d]el animo de Nuestro Señor, cuando el sabia muy bien lo que le preparaban. Pero eso era para enseñarnos que en lugar de evitar las ocasiones de padecer de sufrir alguna humiliacion, deberiamos mas bien hallarnos prontos a encontrarlas con animo y determinacion. Sino, miren que verguenza, despues de haber hecho profesion de imitar de Jesu Cristo mas perfectamente que los cristianos que viven en el mundo, nos hallamos cobardes y muchas veces mas impacientes que ellos y que luego perdemos animo. Esto no es en conformidad con nuestra vocacion, antes bien opuesto a ella. Si ahora reconociendo nuestra inconsistencia, le pedimos humildemente a Nuestro Salvador de darnos su gracia para meditar sobre su pasion de tal modo que eso nos ayude para amar la cruz[,] los padecimientos, tener un mas grande arrepentimiento por nuestras ofensas y ser mas resignadas a la voluntad de Dios en todo[,] entonces esta instruccion no les será inutil[.] cuando llamamos a nuestra memoria las principales circumstancias de la pasion y muerte de Nuestro Señor Jesu Cristo[,] como el fué traicionado y entregado por Judas, desemparado [desamparado] de sus discipulos, cargado de cadenas por los soldados, arrastrado del tribunal de Caifas al de Pilatos, de alli a Herodes, y despues delante del gobernador que le Hizo azotar cruelmente, burlado por la guardia que le habian dado hasta poner en su sagrado cabeza una corona de espinas, en fin cargado de su cruz y llevado al calvario, en donde el se murió en medio de los mas grandes tormentos; acordandonos de estas varias circumstancias de la pasion y muerte de Nuestro Señor Jesu Cristo le damos verdaderamente una prueba de nuestra gratitud, como tambien de nuestra voluntad para compadecer

---

1. The formal name of the Loretto Sisters was and is "The Sisters of Loretto at the Foot of the Cross."

In left margin of the first page, Lamy penciled the Latin of Galatians 2:20, "*Dilexit me et tradidit semetipsum pro me*—He loved me and handed himself over for my sake."

Instruction on the Passion

11th Instruction—Passion

As daughters of Mary Most Holy at the Foot of the Cross,[1] you should have a special devotion to the passion, to the sufferings of Our Lord Jesus Christ. It will therefore be very much in keeping with the spirit of your holy institute if I speak to you in this instruction about the passion of Our Divine Savior. On the evening before he died, among the other things he said to his apostles in the discourse at the Last Supper, we find these words: "I will not say much to you now, for the prince of this world is coming, although there is nothing in me that belongs to him; but so that the world may know that I love the Father and that I obey whatever command he gives me. Let us rise and go from here" (John 14:30–31).

If we reflect a bit, we will see the generosity of the soul of Our Lord, even when he knew very well what lay in store for him. But this was to teach us that instead of avoiding occasions of suffering some humiliation or other, we should rather go forward to meet them with energy and determination. Otherwise, look what shame it would be, after having made our profession to imitate Christ Jesus more perfectly than the Christians who live in the secular world, for us to show ourselves cowards, less willing to suffer than the laity, and for us to show that we have given up. This is not in conformity with our vocation, but rather quite contrary to it. If we now recall such inconsistency on our part, we humbly ask Our Savior to give us his grace to meditate upon the passion in such a manner that it will aid us to love the cross, the sufferings, to feel a great repentance for our offenses, and to be more resigned to the will of God in all things—and then this instruction will not have been fruitless.

We call to mind the principal circumstances of the passion and death of Our Lord Jesus Christ: how Judas betrayed and handed him over, how his disciples abandoned him, how the soldiers loaded him down with chains and dragged him from the tribunal of Caiphas to that of Pilate, then to Herod, and then back to the governor who had him cruelly scourged and mocked by the guard who went so far as to place on his sacred head a crown of thorns, how finally they placed the cross on his shoulders and led him to Calvary where he died in the midst of the greatest torments possible. Calling to mind these various circumstances of the passion and death

con El, ayudarle a llevar su cruz resignarnos a las que nos manda su divina providencia. ¿Que diremos de aquella tristeza mortal que padecio el hijo de Dios, cuando el dijo a sus Apostoles[:] mi alma esta [está] triste hasta la muerte? [Marcos 14:34]. De su agonia que le hizo sudar sangre ahora Hermanas carisimas en Dios, contemplemos lo que el padece en sus bienes exteriores: Pues en su libertad, se la arrebatan de la manera la mas injusta, la mas violenta, la mas ignominiosa. Se Apoderan de su divina persona en medio de sus discipulos[.] Le cargan de cadenas, como un vil malhechor. Le arrastran por las calles de aquella misma ciudad por en medio de aquel mismo pueblo que habia sido testigo tantas veces de su predicaciones y de sus milagros ... y cuando lo sueltan es para clavarle a la cruz adonde el ha de espirar [expirar.] ¿Que padece Nuestro Señor en su reputacion? por el espacio de tres años no hablaban de otra cosa sino de su sabiduria[,] de su poder divino; ahora en su pasion no le miran mas que como un impostor que ha engañado el Pueblo, y que con todo su poder de hacer milagros no puede libertarse de las manos de sus enemigos. Lo que padece Nuestro Señor en su honor, no hay ni una clase de insultos que no padesca, le dan bofetadas, le velan los ojos, lo visten de una tunica blanca por derision, como un insensato; un insigne ladron le es preferido, poniendole en la cabeza una corona de espinas, y una especie de ceptro en la mano, por burla[r]se arrodillan delante de el y le dicen Dios te salve, rey de los Judios.[2] Lo que padece en su cuerpo, su flagelacion, su crucifixion, todo su cuerpo lacerado de golpes, no ofrece mas a la vista que una sola llaga sangrienta. Lo hemos visto, dice el profeta Isaias, 53–3. Y no lo hemos conocido ... un hombre de dolor, y como uno que Dios ha herido, y humillado[.] Ahora si nos preguntamos a nosotros mismos porque todos estos padecimientos del Hombre Dios? El mismo profeta nos responde *id.* que El ha sido herido por razon de nuestras iniquidades; El ha sido molido por Nuestros crimenes[.] La contemplacion de estos padecimientos debe escitar [excitar] en nuestras almas una contricion viva por nuestras culpas[,] tan viva que en lo venidero no tengamos la desgracia de renovar esta pasion del Señor por nuestras culpas. Antes bien esforzamos de imitar las virtudes que el ha practicado en estas varias circumstancias de su pasion. Para enseriarnos una resignacion perfecta a la voluntad de su padre el no quiere libertarse ni por un milagro, lo que le hubiera sido muy facil; mas bien el se entrega [entrega] libremente al poder de sus enemigos sabiendo bien como lo tratarian. Pero lo que le fué mas sensible, fué de verse desamparado de sus

---

2. Matthew 27:29 and Mark 15:18 give "Hail, King of the Jews" or some equivalent translation, but Lamy's use of "Dios te salve—may God save you," one of the commonest poetic formulas of Marian devotional poetry in Spanish, is delightful and insightful and wonderfully ironic.

of Our Lord Jesus Christ, we truly give him proof of our gratitude and of our willingness as well to suffer along with him, to help him carry his cross, to resign ourselves to whatever Divine Providence asks of us.

What shall we say about that mortal sadness the Son of God suffered, when he said to his apostles, "My soul is sorrowful even unto death" [Mark 14:34]? or about the agony that made him sweat blood? Now my dear Sisters in the Lord, let us consider all that he suffered in his exterior well being. For by his free will they ravished his free will in a completely unjust, violent, and ignominious manner; they took his divine person captive in the midst of his own disciples. They loaded him down with fetters like a terrible criminal. They dragged him through the streets of the very city and through the midst of the very people who had witnessed so often his preaching and his miracles—and they only loosened him in order to nail him to the cross where he would have to die.

What did Our Lord suffer in his reputation? For a period of three years they hardly talked of anything but his wisdom and his divine power, but now in his passion they concern themselves only with the way this imposter has fooled the people, and how with all his power to perform miracles he cannot liberate himself from the hands of his enemies.

[Now let us think for a moment of] what Our Lord suffered in his sacred honor. There is no sort of insult he did not suffer. They struck him with their hands, they blindfolded his eyes, they clothed him in a white robe in derision, as if he were a moron, they favored a notable robber over him, and placing a crown of thorns on his head and a sort of scepter in his hand to mock him, they knelt before him and addressed him, "God save you, King of the Jews."[2]

And now for Christ's bodily sufferings. After his flagellation, his crucifixion, his whole body torn with blows, he did not look like anything except a single bloody wound. "We have seen him," said the prophet Isaiah (53:2–5), "and we did not know him. . . . a man of sorrows, like one whom God has wounded and humiliated."

And now if we ask ourselves why the God-Man had to suffer all of this, the prophet answers in the same passage that he was wounded for our offenses, he was beaten for our crimes. The contemplation of these sufferings ought to arouse in our souls a lively sorrow for our faults, so lively that hereafter we will not have the misfortune of renewing the Lord's passion by our faults. Quite the reverse, let us earnestly imitate the virtues he has

amigos; y en lugar de quejarse el vela sobre ellos y obliga sus enemigos de dejarlos libres y sanos. Pedro lo niega, y el divino maestro no le hace ni una reprehension, mas bien por una mirada llena de bondad conviete al Apostol[.] Con respecto a Judas el no desecha [deshecha] su beso perfido todavia[.] El lo trata de amigo; y si le dice Judas, con un beso entregas al hijo del hombre, es mas bien para convertirle que para reprenderle ¿Que caridad tan grande? Que ejemplos tan sublimes? Ahora si son verdaderamente las hijas de Maria Santisima al pie de la cruz, y si han recibido de Dios tantas favores especiales deben darle prueba de su gratitud por su amor[,] por su fervor, tener gusto de poderle ofrecer algunos sacrificios, padecimientos.

Muchos presenciaron la passion de N.S.J.C.[,] unos por pura curiosidad, otros con odio a su divina doctrina; pero tambien unos pocos con compasion y amor, y con estos ultimos hemos de asistir en espiritu al Calvario. Y el centurion dice San Lucas 23:50. Mirandolo que se pasaba glorifica a Dios, diciendo: en verdad este hombre era justo, verdadero hijo de Dios [Marcos 15:39, Lucas 23:47]; y toda la multitud de los que eran presentes a lo que sucedio se volvieron dandose golpes al pecho. Pues ¿que vieron? La conversion del ladron, la tierra cubierta de tinieblas por tres horas, el velo del templo rasgado en dos; que oieron a Nuestro Señor Jesu Cristo esclamarse, no con una voz debil como un no con una voz debil como un moribundo, pero con una voz fuerte, *voce magna*: padre en tus manos encomiendo mi espiritu. Pidamos por la intercession de Maria Santisima una compasion grande a la pasion de Nuestro Señor Jesu Cristo y pidamos los mismos sentimientos que animaban al buen ladron, al centurion y a los muchos que se convirtieron entonces; para tener una parte abundante en los meritos de su muerte en esta vida y en la otra.

—*fin*—

demonstrated in the various circumstances of his passion. Since he was serious about having perfect resignation to the will of his Father, Christ did not wish to free himself, even by some miracle, as would have been quite easy for him; instead, he voluntarily handed himself over to the power of his enemies knowing full well how they would treat him. But the most painful thing of all was to find himself abandoned by his friends; and yet instead of complaining, he protects them and commands his enemies to let them go free and unharmed. Peter denies him, and the Divine Master does not reproach him at all, merely turning on him a glance filled with kindness which will transform him into an apostle. In regard to Judas, Christ does not reject his traitorous kiss but treats him simply as a friend; and if he says to Judas, "Do you betray the Son of Man with a kiss?" it is to convert him rather than to reproach him. What great love we see here! What a sublime example! Today you are truly the daughters of Mary Most Holy at the Foot of the Cross if God has given you these special favors. You ought to give him proof of your gratitude with your love, with your fervor; be glad to offer him some of your sacrifices, some of your sufferings.

Many people were present at the passion of Our Lord Jesus Christ, some out of simple curiosity, some out of hatred of his divine doctrine, but a few others out of compassion and love; and with these last we wish to be present in spirit at Calvary. And the centurion, Saint Luke tells us (23:47), "saw what happened and glorified God, saying, 'Truly this was a just man, a true son of God'" [Mark 15:39, Luke 23:47]; and the whole multitude that was present returned beating their breasts. For what did they see? The conversion of the thief, the earth wrapped in shadows for three hours, the veil of the temple torn in two; and they heard Our Lord Jesus Christ cry out, not with the weak voice of a dying man but "with a loud voice—*voce magna*—'Father, into your hands I commend my spirit!'" Let us ask through the intercession of Mary Most Holy a profound compassion with the passion of Our Lord Jesus Christ, and let us pray to have the same sentiments that animated the good thief, the centurion, and the many people who were then converted to gain an abundant share in the merits of Christ's death both in this world and in the next.

—*end*—

PART IV

*Addresses at
Religious Schools*

✢

✣

Here we have a peculiar genre of oratory. Each of the following addresses was delivered at a religious school—both, as it happens, Roman Catholic—to a mainly adult audience. The second was delivered at the beginning of a school year in celebration of the new school building that still stands just north of San Felipe Church in Old Town Albuquerque, the first at the end of the school year as part of an awards day which a Jesuit educational document describes thus:

> Then on the appointed day, with as much eclat and before as large a gathering of people as possible, the names of the winners should be publicly announced. The winners should come before the whole assemblage and each receive his award with due honor.[1]

Such speeches as these were printed by one or another of the weekly newspapers in the Territory, and by doing so the papers probably went a long way toward establishing the religious academic address as a literary genre. Moreover, the newspapers may well be the best clue to the oratorical tone. At the time, secular newspapers were so openly and stridently adversarial along party lines that an average reader did not need to read two paragraphs before he knew which party's paper he had in his hands. And religious newspapers were equally biased and just as open about their confessional commitments.

The schools also tended to have some of the same combative character as the newspapers of the time. Catholic private schools were aggressively Catholic, Presbyterian schools were the Presbyterian equivalent, Congregational or Methodist or Baptist schools ditto. And if the Catholics in an area got control of the local public school system, the public schools—

---

1. Allan P. Farrell, S.J., *The Jesuit "Ratio Studiorum" of 1599* (Washington: Conference of Major Superiors of Jesuits, 1970), p. 61. Father J. B. Ralliére, pastor of the Tomé parish from 1858 to 1913, wrote a great deal of religious music, including one song to preface the ceremony of the distribution of prizes in schools and another to conclude it; see most editions of his *Cánticos Espirituales*, nos. 267 and 278.

taught by Jesuits or Sisters of Charity or laity handpicked for their Catholic loyalty—were indistinguishable from Catholic private school and often enough literally identical with them, at least until the sad day when the county ran out of money and the public school was suddenly privatized. And if on the other hand the Protestants gained control, the public schools in New Mexico became like the public schools in most of the rest of the United States at the time, where Protestant ministers often taught school to eke out a living for themselves and their families.[2] The public schools were non-sectarian in being hospitable enough to children who belonged to any Protestant sect or denomination—but at the same time they were quite anti-Catholic in a "generic Protestant" sort of way. There was reading from the King James Bible, and a Protestant spin marked the teaching of many of the subjects from one end of the school-day to the other.

In the Spanish, French, and Italian worlds, though there was nearly always an effective distinction, there was no separation between church and state. In Catholic New Mexico (and for that matter in Catholic Europe until the Second Vatican Council in the 1960s), there was no comprehension of Thomas Jefferson's separation doctrine. In the early territorial period, Hispanic Catholic civil authorities changed parish boundaries, certified pastors, and fined persons for engaging in religious arguments, and just after the Civil War the Federal Government itself indulged in the highly confessional "Grant Peace Policy" experiment of parceling out the different Indian reservations to different Christian denominations. Small wonder that the Hispanic settlers, French diocesans, and Italian Jesuits were chronically confused about what public schools were supposed to be.

For all these various reasons, the invited orators at Catholic school functions made use of the oratory of praise and blame with and earnestness and rancor otherwise inexplicable. In other addresses of the sort, Carlos Blanchard praises the Loretto Sisters and attacks the author of an article in *Apóstol Evangelico* in particular and the "godless-school" crowd in general. Severino Trujillo blames the anti-Catholic press and praises the Christian Brothers in Mora. Leandro Sánchez extols Father J.B. Guerin and attacks the press. Only Father Guerin has an irenic and ecumenical word for anyone, though the most memorable passage in his address is a charming self-ironic reminiscence of his and his companions' first view of a New Mexican plaza:

---

2. Mark Banker, *Presbyterian Missions and Cultural Interaction in the Far Southwest* (Urbana: University of Illinois Press, 1993), pp. 51-52.

Upon seeing what then was the little plaza of Las Vegas, we all asked our beloved prelate [Lamy] in total honesty if the plaza was entirely under construction, for it looked to us as if none of the houses had roofs. It was the first time we had ever seen roofs of adobe. What a difference today! What ever became of the little plaza that existed in 1854?[3]

---

3. Jean Baptiste Guerin, *Revista Católica* 8 (1882), 394-95. Paul Horgan, *Lamy of Santa Fe* (New York: Farrar, Straus and Giroux, 1975), pp. 205-8, offers further information on the trip: with Lamy was a total party of twenty-eight including Fathers Etienne Avel, Pierre Eguillon, Jean Baptiste Guerin, Antoine Juillard, Eugene Paulet, and Dámaso Taladrid and seminarian Sébastien Vaur, who died immediately after their 18 November 1854 arrival in Santa Fe. Horgan mentions ten canvas-topped wagons, whereas Guerin recalls "eighteen vehicles, counting wagons and carriages."

Rafael Romero Speech at Colegio de Las Vegas

In the nineteenth century when the prevailing economic system was still agricultural, the school year normally began in November and concluded in August so that the children could then help with the labor-intensive work of the harvest. Hence the Jesuit College of Las Vegas (Colegio de Las Vegas)—still in existence today as Regis University and Regis Jesuit High School in Denver—concluded its first academic year at 8 a.m. on 16 August 1878 with a public examination and distribution of prizes in the borrowed *sala* of the huge Romualdo Baca home in Las Vegas.[1]

The big news of the academic year had been the attempt by the Jesuits to get a bill through the Territorial legislature establishing them as a tax-exempt entity and empowering them to grant diplomas and degrees, a bill copied word for word from an 1874 incorporation of the Sisters of Loretto. But Abraham Rencher had been governor then, and in 1878 Territorial Governor Samuel B. Axtell vetoed the bill and communicated his action to the legislature in a letter gratuitously insulting to the Catholic Church in general, Jesuit priests in particular, and Father Donato Gasparri by name. When both houses of the legislature immediately and resoundingly passed the bill over his veto, Axtell went to Washington and, aided by Delegate Trinidad Romero, convinced Congress, which oversaw all territorial legislation, to annul it.[2]

So the Jesuits availed themselves of the cold comfort of inviting don Rafael Romero (1850–1919), a friendly legislator from La Cueva in Mora County, to speak at their first commencement. Romero was later described as "one of the most finely educated citizens of Latin-American ancestry in the State of New Mexico," for he had attended a private prep school in Pennsylvania and later Princeton University. Born of a wealthy family in the Rio Grande Valley, he was active as politician, county superintendent of schools, and rancher (raising Shorthorns and Clydesdales). He died as a result of a fire in a Roy hotel.[3]

1. *Revista Católica*, 4, no. 32 (10 August 1878), 373; 4, no. 34 (24 August 1878), 397-98, with a full program. Gabino Rendon, the recipient of a Reward of Merit, remembered the event clearly in his autobiography *Hand on My Shoulder* (New York: Board of National Missions, 1953), pp. 33-35: "Archbishop Lamy, the great church dignitary for Santa Fé, was present with his vicario, whose name I have forgotten [Pierre Eguillon]. It was the vicario who pinned the medal on my soldier coat, in the midst of great applause. I felt a glow more satisfying than any I had ever felt."

2. Trinidad Romero to Samuel Beach Axtell, 3 and 25 February 1878, Ritch Papers, no. 1748 and 1750, reel 5; "An Act to Incorporate the Academy of the Sisters of Loretto [sic] in New Mexico," New Mexico State Records and Archives, Sisters of Loretto microfilm, reel 1, and "An Act to Incorporate the Society of the Jesuit Fathers in New Mexico," *Acts of the Legislative Assembly of the Territory of New Mexico, Twenty-Third Session* (Santa Fe: Manderfield and Tucker, 1878), pp. 73-74; Arie Poldervaart, *Black-Robed Justice* (Santa Fe: Historical Society of New Mexico, 1948), pp. 121-25; Calvin Horn, *New Mexico's Troubled Years* (Albuquerque: Horn and Wallace, 1963), pp. 192-97; Porter A. Stratton, *The Territorial Press of New Mexico* (Albuquerque: University of New Mexico Press, 1969), pp. 136-39; Philip J. Rasch, "The People of the Territory vs. the Santa Fe Ring," *New Mexico Historical Review* 47 (1972): 185-202; Edwin Verdieck, "No Strangers to Adversity: Those Stalwart Jesuits of the New Mexico-Colorado Mission," unpublished paper, 1979, pp. 10-18.

When Axtell was finally forced into resignation after Washington had sent an investigator to look into his Lincoln County and Colfax County dealings, the Jesuits could not resist nailing his hide to the barn door of their newspaper for all to see; "La Caida de Gobernador Axtell," *Revista Católica* 4, no. 44 (2 November 1878), 524-26. Less restrained was William McGuiness of the Albuquerque *Review*, "F-a-a-ar-well," 3, no. 19 (14 September 1878), p. 2, and "Axtell's Lament," 3, no. 20 (21 September 1878), p. 1, a parody of Jeremiah reprinted from the Cimarron *News and Press*.

3. Ralph E. Twitchell, *Leading Facts of New Mexico History* (Cedar Rapids: Torch Press, 1915), 2:494n407; Charles F. Coan, *A History of New Mexico* (Chicago: American Historical Society, 1925), 2:223-24.

Distribucion de Premios de Colegio de Las Vegas

Señoras y Caballeros:

He sido honrado con una súplica de hacer algunas observaciones sobre la presente ocasion. —Reconozco y aprecio el grande honor que se me confiere al hacerme semejante invitacion en ocasion tan fausta.

En varios paises existe una costumbre agradable de celebrar la cosecha de las mieses del año. Entre gentes de habla inglesa se apellida esta funcion el *Harvest Home*. Los ancianos y los jóvenes se reunen en vestido de gala; se pasan en revista los trabajos del año, contando los incidentes de la siembra, del cultivo y demás quehaceres campestres; se tributa una fervorosa accion de gracias al Dador de todo bien, y luego se participa en una fiesta de general regocijo. —Siendo esta la primera cosecha del Colegio de Las Vegas, los directores de esta institucion se han esmerado en regalarnos con una fiesta parecida a un banquete de manjares ambrosíacos: fiesta de la razon y alborozo del alma, para cuya conclusion me parece muy oportuno y propio decir algo acerca de los designios de este instituto y de los que a él se han dedicado.

No hay tarea mas noble ni ocupacion mas esencial que la educacion. En un sentido, el hombre se está educando hasta que respira su último aliento. Pero, la educacion de la escuela tiene de suyo un carácter importantísimo. Educar es cultivar, desarrollar y pulir todas las facultades; físicas, intelectuales, morales y religiosas; y dar a la naturaleza del niño su complemento y perfeccion para que sea lo que ha de ser y haga lo que ha de hacer; para formar de él un hombre y prepararlo a ejercer sus deberes en la vida, hácia [hacia] aquellos que lo rodean, hácia su país y hácia sí mismo, de modo que perfeccionando su vida presente se prepare para la vida que ha de venir. Este es el deber que los padres y las madres tienen con sus hijos, y este el deber que los maestros de una escuela como esta, toman sobre sí para aquellos que les han sido confiados.

Y con respecto a los niños que hoy concluyen sus trabajos escolares, lo que acabo de decir debe enseñarles que hay un intento y un propósito en la obra que hoy suspenden, espero yo, por un corto intérvalo. Y este intento es procurarles lo que brevemente he expresado. Este trabajo es para Vds. Los padres de familia y los maestros de la escuela deben hacer su parte en educarlos, pero Vds. deben quererlo. No son Vds. pedazos de mármol que se les pueda dar figura con un escoplo; ni tampoco son retazos de tela sobre los cuales un pintor pueda poner colores y borrarlos a su antojo. No; son seres vivos, dotados de una voluntad libre; y Vds. pueden estimularse a sí mismos y dominarse, si lo quieren, y ya sea que Vds. lo piensen, o no,

Distribution of Prizes, College Of Las Vegas

LADIES AND GENTLEMEN:

I have been honored by being asked to offer some remarks on the present occasion. I am aware of and appreciate the great honor conferred upon me by such an invitation on such a propitious occasion.

In various lands there is a pleasant custom of celebrating the grain harvest of the year. Among English-speaking peoples, this festival is called "Harvest Home." Old and young gather in holiday clothing and recall the labors of the year; recounting the incidents of the spring sowing, the cultivation, and the other chores of the field, they fervently give thanks to the Giver of all good things, and finally they partake in a banquet of general rejoicing. Now since this is the first harvest of the College of Las Vegas, the directors of the institution have been careful to regale us with a feast that resembles a banquet of ambrosial morsels: a feast for the rational mind and a celebration of the soul, at the conclusion of which it seems opportune and appropriate for me to say a few words about the purposes of this institution and about those who have committed themselves to its existence.

There is no labor more noble, no occupation more essential than education. In one sense, man undergoes education till he draws his last breath. But formal education in the schoolroom has in and of itself a most important character. To educate is to cultivate, to develop, to polish the physical, intellectual, moral, and religious faculties, and to give completion and perfection to the lad's nature so that he will be what he should be and do what he should do. In this way, he will become a man ready to fulfill his duties in life toward those around him, toward his country, and toward himself in such a manner that as he improves in this life he also prepares himself for the life to come. This is the duty parents have toward their children, and this is the duty the teachers in a school of this sort take upon themselves on behalf of those who entrust it to them.

And with regard to the boys who are finishing their scholarly labors, what I said at the beginning should put them on notice that there is a purpose and a design in the work they suspend today—for only a brief interval, I hope. This work you yourselves should do. The parents and the schoolmasters must do their part toward your education, but you have got to want it. You are not blocks of marble to be given a shape with a chisel, nor are you pieces of canvas upon which a painter can place colors, changing them according to his whim. No, you are living beings, endowed with free will, and you can inspire yourselves and take charge of yourselves if you wish, and it may be that you might decide to grow forever and change

siempre están creciendo y alterándose, ya sea de bien en mejor, ya de mal en peor. De manera que un padre o un maestro no tiene buen éxito con un díscipulo [sic] a menos que *él* desee educarse. Admitiendo, pues, y deseando que a ninguno entre Vds. le falten estos requisitos, pasaré a la consideracion de los fundadores y promovedores de esta institucion.

Un gran parte de los que aquí están presentes son los descendientes de aquellos valientes y arriesgados de la altiva sangre de España, los pobladores mas antiguos de los Estados Unidos. Nuestras poblaciones, no muy lejanas de esta, son de las mas viejas entre aquellas sobre las que flota la gran bandera Americana.[1] Nuestros antepasados penetraron en estas regiones desiertas y fragosas, muchos años antes que el "May Flower" danzara sobre las olas que bañan la Roca de Plymouth. Cuando ellos llegaron aquí brillando en las nobles y ricas vestiduras de los Hidalgos Españoles del siglo 16°, soldados de la Corona; tambien vinieron con ellos ciertos personajes simplemente vestidos, pero nobles e intrépidos soldados de la Cruz, cuyos colegas mas recientes han dado a Vds. hoy una prueba de sus desvelos y afanes en la formacion de nuestra juventud. Los emigrantes que desembarcaron sobre la Roca de Plymouth vinieron bajo la bandera Inglesa. Nuestros antepasados vinieron bajo el gallardete real de la heróica España. La nueva Inglaterra fué colonizada por hombres de *espíritu* osado, valerosa, enérgico, inflexible, pero quienes, a imitacion del falso "porta-estandarte de la luz," pecaron por orgullo, y fueron maldecidos con la pérdida de su fé. La nueva España, o lo que ahora llamamos el Nuevo Méjico, fué poblado por hombres igualmente atrevidos y esforzados; que juntaban la altivez con mas fina cortesía; nobles, amistosos, leales; pero, dotados al mismo tiempo de una concepcion mas alta del Criador, y poseidos de un amor mas acendrado del hombre se deleitaron en reconocer la autoridad suprema de Dios *(Aplausos)*. Nuevo Méjico fué poblado por Católicos; llenos de respeto por toda asociacion dedicada a la cultura e incremento de la fé y doctrina Católica *(Aplausos)*. Y es el galardon mas lisonjero de los verdaderos descendientes de los antiguos exploradores de Nuevo Méjico, que a despecho de todas las vicisitudes y mudanzas de este mundo, aun conservan la fé y las doctrinas de sus antepasados, teniéndolo todo en la mas alta reverencia, y considerándolo el objeto de su mas íntimo y obsequioso rendimiento. Despues de las doctrinas de la fé Católica, ellos, hablando de hombres, honran a los comentadores de estas sublimes enseñanzas, por medio de las cuales el

---

1. In the 1870s, the city fathers of Santa Fe decided unilaterally that the City Different had been founded in 1550. The operative reasons were so that it could be older than St. Augustine, Florida, and so that they could declare a Tercio-Millennial Exposition in 1883. They left a lot of people and a lot of historical accounts confused for quite a long time.

forever, going either from good to better or from bad to worse. Thus it is that a parent or a teacher can have no good result with a student unless the student *himself* wants an education. Let us suppose, then, let us hope that not a one among you fails in this regard, and I will proceed to the consideration of the founders and supporters of this institution.

A great number of those who are here present are the descendants of those valiant and daring men of the proud blood of Spain, the oldest settlers of United States. Our settlements not very far from here are the most ancient over which the grand American flag flies.[1] Our ancestors penetrated into these deserted and dangerous regions many years before the Mayflower floated over the dancing waves that washed Plymouth Rock. Some of the settlers came here resplendent in the gorgeous rich clothing of sixteenth-century *hidalgos*, soldiers of the crown, while certain other persons arrived quite simply dressed. [They were] the noble and intrepid [Franciscan] soldiers of the Cross, whose more recent colleagues [the Jesuit fathers] give us in our own day proof of their commitment to and solicitude for the education of youth. The emigrants who disembarked at Plymouth Rock came under the flag of England. Our forebears arrived under the royal pennon of heroic Spain. New England was colonized by men of a daring, valiant, energetic, unbending spirit—but in imitation of the false "standard-bearer of enlightenment," they committed the sin of pride and were cursed with the loss of their faith. New Spain, or what we call today New Mexico, was settled by equally fearless and forceful men who joined their pride to a wonderful courtliness. They were noble, friendly, and loyal, but they were at the same time endowed with a loftier concept of the Creator and possessed of a more refined love of their fellow men, and they rejoiced to acknowledge the supreme authority of God *(Applause)*. Catholics settled New Mexico, people filled with respect for any group concerned with the culture and growth of Catholic faith and doctrine *(Applause)*. And it is the most pleasant recompense for being true descendants of the ancient explorers of New Mexico that in the midst of all the troubles and changes of this world they have preserved the faith and doctrines of their ancestors, holding them all in the greatest reverence and considering them the object of their most sincere and obsequious submission. Besides the doctrines of the Catholic faith and on a human level, they honor the teachers of these sublime lessons by means of which man comes to disdain

hombre desprecia los deleites terrestres, y aspira a los glorias eternas. Y entre los expositores de estas doctrinas, Vds. no lo ignoran, no ocupan el último lugar los Padres Jesuitas; [some material omitted by the *Revista Católica* editors][2] .... Desde los salones clásicos de Coimbra, hasta las remotas regiones cruzadas por el Oregon, ignorante, hasta nuestros dias, "de todo sonido excepto el de sus olas"; desde las llanuras del Thibet, hasta las montañas del Perú,[3] los hijos del sayo negro, de Loyola, han llevado la cruz del Redentor, y han encendido la única luz que conduce al hombre de la tierra al Cielo. En sus luchas con tribus bárbaras e inhumanas, así como en su guerra contra las pasiones y vicios de los pueblos mas cultos, han encontrado lo que aguardaban, a saber los recelos, la enemistad, la oposicion, la opresion. Era el cumplimiento del voto de su ilustre fundador, Ignacio, una vez gallardo soldado español, conociendo la naturaleza del hombre con una inteligencia sobrehumana, rogó por sus hijos para que nunca y en ninguna parte les faltase la persecucion, verdadero manantial de vigor, de firmeza, de desprendimiento del mundo, y adhesion al Cielo. Aquí en nuestro viejo país de Nuevo Méjico, Vds. saben cómo se han cumplido estos ruegos de San Ignacio.

El Salvador Divino fué atormentado por un Gobernador provincial, y no ha faltado aquí un Gobernador que desempeñase aun peor parte que la de Poncio Pilato. *(Aplausos)*. El antiguo Pilato hízose culpable por falta de proteccion al inocente. Nuestro Pilato se lanza a perseguir. *(Fragorosos Aplausos)*. ¿Porqué, pues, he de poner una mordaza a mis labios? ¿Porqué, he de dejar de proferir la verdad? ¿No soy yo dueño en mi casa? ¿Y no estoy yo, por decirlo así, en mi propia casa? ¿No soy yo un ciudadano Católico del país Católico, de Nuevo Méjico? ¿Y no he sido yo, como Católico de Nuevo Méjico, groseramente insultado por un miserable Oficial Público? ¿Qué significa esto que un hombre enviado de Gobernador, a un país Católico, en un mensaje oficial dirigido a nuestros legisladores Católicos, y por tanto a nuestro Pueblo Católico, acumula insulto sobre insulto contra una Orden Religiosa de la Iglesia Católica?[4] ¿Hará él esto y no estigmatizaré yo su

---

2. In their introduction to the address, the editors of *Revista Católica* stated that they declined "to repeat out of boastful vanity the friendly words the orator chose to offer in praise of the Society of Jesus we are honored to belong to; on the contrary, these are the only words of the speech we have taken the liberty of deleting, retaining only enough not to interrupt the thread of ideas."

3. These are all places associated with the Jesuits: Coimbra in Portugal was an early center of Jesuit training, and the Oregon River is now called the Columbia.

4. The whole episode and nearly all its parts exemplify the lack of understanding of the separation of church and state that prevailed in New Mexico during the late nineteenth century. Mason and deist Thomas Jefferson must have rolled over in his grave many a time.

A sampler of Axtell's insults:

> It is difficult to decide whether the man who seeks to establish this society or the society which he seeks to establish [the Jesuit Fathers] is worse. Both are so bad you cannot decide

the delights of this earth and aspire to the glories of heaven. And among the expositors of these doctrines, as you are surely aware, the Jesuit Fathers do not occupy the last place [some material was cut by the *Revista Católica* editors].[2] From the classical classrooms of Coimbra to the remote regions through which the Oregon River flows, ignorant till our own days "of all sound except that of its own waves"; from the Tibetan plains to the mountains of Peru,[3] the black-robed sons of Loyola have raised the cross of the Redeemer, have kindled the only light that conducts man from earth to heaven. In their efforts with barbaric and inhuman tribes as well as in their battles against the passions and vices of the overly sophisticated, they have met with what they anticipated—suspicion, enmity, opposition, and oppression. Those adversities have fulfilled the prayer of their illustrious founder Ignatius, at one time a gallant Spanish soldier. He knew human nature with a superhuman intelligence, and he prayed that his sons would never lack persecution, the genuine wellspring of steadfastness, of indifference to the world, and of reliance on heaven. Here in our ancient land of New Mexico, you know how this prayer of Saint Ignatius has been fulfilled.

The Savior God was tormented by a provincial governor, and we are not without a governor who has been playing a worse part even than Pilate *(Applause)*. The Pilate of old failed by not protecting the innocent; our new one devotes himself to persecution *(Thunderous Applause)*. And should I then put a muzzle over my mouth? Why should I fail to speak the truth? Am I not the master of my own home? And am I not so to speak in my own home? Am I not a Catholic citizen of a Catholic land, New Mexico? And have I not, as a New Mexican Catholic, been grossly insulted by a pathetic public official? What does it mean when a man sent to be the governor of a Catholic land, in an official message directed to Catholic legislators and to our Catholic people, piles insult upon insult against a religious order of the Catholic Church?[4] That man does this, and am I supposed to refrain from stigmatizing his language, on an appropriate occasion, attacking it as it deserves? Does he supposed that the sons of Spanish *hidalgos* need lec-

---

between them. This Neapolitan adventurer Gasparri teaches publicly that his dogmas and assertions are superior to the statutes of the United States and the Laws of the territory. No doctrine or teaching can be more dangerous to good government than this, especially in New Mexico, where the masses of the people are ignorant. He also by his writings and harangues endeavors to excite animosities and to stimulate the people to acts of violence towards those lawfully exercising civil authority over them. He comes here while the Legislative Assembly is in session and lobbies in the most brazen and shameless manner to defeat needed and most wholesome laws and to force through bills antagonistic to the Laws of the United States. . . .

The society which he seeks to establish in New Mexico is worthy of such a leader. It has been denounced time and again by the head of the Catholic church and justly expelled from the most enlightened countries of Europe.

Journal of the House of Representatives, pp. 165-66 (TANM microfilms, reel 5, frames 529-30).

lenguaje, en la ocasion oportuna, reprobándolo como merece? ¿Acaso cree él, que los hijos de los Hidalgos Españoles necesitan lecciones de moralidad de esos que se llaman "ex-Obispos Mormones," y oficiales vagos de ["]Reserva del Poniente"?[5] Nada me importa de las vociferaciones de la patrulla cuyo interlocutor es nuestro presente Pilato, ni deseo responderles. Lo que deseo es mostrar a nuestros hermanos de afuera que no olvidamos quienes somos, y que mientras velamos al enemigo, nos reimos de sus asaltos *(Aplausos).*

Es principio cardinal y bello de nuestras creencias que distingamos siempre entre individuo y sus hechos. Podemos reprobar y enteramente execrar los hechos malos de un hombre y tal vez nunca podamos decir que el hombre mismo es malo. Suenan siempre en mis oidos aquellas terribles palabras: "No juzgueis y no sereis juzgados." Denuncio, pues, los hechos malos, pero, en cuanto al hombre mismo le extiendo el manto de la caridad, y le aplico aquella frase consoladora del Divino Maestro: "Perdonadle, Padre, pues no sabe lo que hace" *(Prolongados Aplausos).*

Este desviado Gobernador es solamente la boquilla de un elemento descaminado, de una porcion del pueblo de los Estados Unidos. Y tal vez crea él que obra bien. Por caridad lo admitiremos. Pero, replico a estos evangelios de "razon." ¿Porqué no escucharais las enseñanzas de vuestro Dios; las amonestaciones de la razon sola; la razon clara y sencilla? Se dice que los Gobiernos se deben sostener. ¿Cómo podeis sostenerlos, a menos que enseñeis a la juventud de la nacion que Dios gobierna este pequeño mundo nuestro, el cual EL en cierta ocasion se dignó sacar de la nada? ¿En qué manera se podrá inculcar esto eficazmente en los niños, si no se hace diariamente allí donde se cultiva, y se desarrolla su mente? Si excluís la religion de las escuelas donde se instruye la juventud, ¿no os muestra la razon que estos niños no tendrán instruccion religiosa? Los hombres proceden de los niños;[6] son pues, lo que han sido en su infancia y adolescencia. Las escuelas sin religion necesariamente producen hombres irreligiosos. Los hombres irreligiosos obedecen a las leyes mientras estas les agradan, o se pueden ejecutar con suficiente fuerza física. Hombres sin religion son los que llegan a ser bandoleros, desesperados, comunistas, destructores del órden social, rebeldes contra toda autoridad política. Las escuelas seglares producen hombres seglares los que roban los bancos, y

---

5. Axtell, a graduate of Western Reserve, had written some silly letters to a Salt Lake City newspaper signing himself "El Obispo—The Bishop," the ordinary title of a Mormon minister.

6. *Los hombres proceden de los niños*: despite the translation, this is not a verbal echo of Wordsworth so much as an echo of the developmental worldview that was nearly universal among educated persons during the nineteenth century.

tures on morality from those who style themselves "ex-Mormon bishops" and official vagabonds from "Western Reserve" [University]?[5] I care nothing about the vociferations of the gang whose mouthpiece our present Pilate is, nor would I care to reply to them. All that I want is to let our foreign brethren [the Jesuits] know that we do not forget who we are and that as long as we keep our eyes on the enemy, we laugh at their attacks *(Applause)*.

It is a beautiful cardinal principle of our creed that we distinguish between the individual and his deeds. We can reprove and totally execrate a man's bad deeds without asserting that the man himself is bad. In my ears always echo those terrible words "Judge not lest you be judged." So I denounce the evil deeds, but to the man himself I extend the cloak of charity and apply to him the consoling prayer of the Divine Master, "Father forgive him, for he knows not what he does" *(Prolonged Applause)*.

The misguided governor is merely the mouthpiece of a deviant element of a small minority of the people of the United States. And perhaps he believes he is doing right. Out of charity let us say that he does. But I reply to those evangelists of "reason": why not listen to the teachings of our God, the warnings of plain logic, of reason clear and simple? They say that governments ought to see to their own continuation. How can you enable them to survive unless you teach the youth of the nation that God is Lord of this little planet of ours, which He on a certain occasion deigned to fetch out of nothingness? How can you inculcate this effectively in children if you do not do so daily in the place where they are taught, where their minds grow? If you exclude religion from the schools where the youth are instructed, does not common sense tell us that those children will have no religious instruction? The child is father to the man;[6] they will become what they were in their infancy and adolescence. Schools without religion produce irreligious adults. They will obey laws as long as it pleases them or so long as the laws are enforced with sufficient physical force. Men without religion become bandits, desperadoes, communists, destroyers of the social order, rebels against all political power. Secular schools produce secular men who rob banks and cut throats if they think they can do so while getting something and getting away with it. And why not? By virtue of their theory, they would be stupid if they did not.

cortan la garganta a otros, si creen poderlo hacer sin ser castigados, y ganando alguna cosa. ¿Y porqué no? En virtud de su propia teoría, tontos son si no lo hacen.

¿Y es esta la especie de sociedad que deseais? Esta es la que tendreis, si abolís la enseñanza religiosa. El more de nuestro presente Poncio Pilato y sus secuaces es: "Abajo la enseñanza religiosa." El mote de los Padres Jesuitas es: "la Religion y la Ciencia."

Conciudadanos: Escoged entre los dos. Para hablar breve y claramente, el primero os conducirá a la perdicion, el segundo a la bienaventuranza. Escoged, pues; sois libres; pero ejerced antes vuestro juicio sobre el objeto de vuestra eleccion.

Si he habaldo con énfasis, es porque los tiempos lo requieren. Los que juegan con el fuego deben esperar quemarse. Pensad bien lo que haceis. No es lijera responsabilidad encargarse de educar a un alma inmortal.

Los dignos directores de este instituto son hombres que han sacrificado sus vidas a la educacion de la juventud. La mejor escuela es por cierto el hogar doméstico, cuando los padres son competentes para guiar y dirigir a sus hijos, y poseen las comodidades para hacerlo satisfactoriamente; pero, si es preciso confiar a otros el cuidado de vuestro hijos, como lo es para la mayoría, enviadlos a los Jesuitas siempre que podais. Hacen que vuestros hijos se sometan a la autoridad. Reprimid en ellos toda insubordinacion y un dia tendreis razon de gloriaros de los jóvenes vástagos de vuestro antiguo linaje. Desearia añadir algo mas, pero temo que ya me he extendido demasiado.

Regocijémonos, pues, de la primera celebracion de este Colegio Católico de Las Vegas, y sea el preludo de celebraciones sin número, parecidas en carácteres superiores tan solo en interés.

—*fin*—

Is that the sort of society you want? That is what you will have if you abolish religious instruction. The motto of our new Pontius Pilate and his followers is "Down with religious education." The motto of the Jesuit Fathers is "Religion and Knowledge."

Fellow citizens, choose between the two. To make it short and simple, the first will lead you to perdition, the second to happiness. Choose, then; you are free men and women; but first use your judgment about the matter about which you are choosing.

If I have spoken with emphasis, I have done so because the times require it. Those who play with fire should expect to be burned. Think well about what you are doing. It is no trifling responsibility to be charged with the education of an immortal soul.

The worthy directors of this institution are men who have sacrificed their lives to the education of youth. The best school is surely the home, so long as the parents are capable of guiding and directing their children and have the leisure to do so satisfactorily. But should it be necessary to entrust to others the care of your sons, as it is in the majority of cases, send them to the Jesuits whenever you can. They will see to it that your sons submit to authority. Reprimand in them all insubordination, and one day you will have reason to be gratified in the young offspring of your ancient lineage. —I might wish to add a bit more, but I fear I have already gone on too long.

Rejoice, then, at the first celebration of this Catholic College of Las Vegas, and may it be the prelude to innumerable celebrations, similar in kind and only superior in interest.

—*end*—

Vito Tromby, S.J.

Vito Tromby was born in Nicastro, Calabria, toward the toe of the Italian boot, on 18 October 1837. He joined the Jesuits in 1856, and four years later when the Jesuits backed the inept and unpopular Bourbon King of Naples during Garibaldi's reunification of Italy, Tromby endured exile, going to Spain to study and teach. The onset of epilepsy nearly prevented his ordination to the priesthood, but he persevered and arrived in New Mexico in 1872 as a young priest. He taught the boys of the Albuquerque parish from that year until ill health forced his retirement, but he continued his writing until his death on 9 December 1904. He is buried in the Jesuit plot in Santa Bárbara Cemetery.

During 1870 and 1871, Jesuit Father Alessandro Leone's small school operated intermittently in the Fathers' "Cerco House" about a hundred yards southeast of the Plaza. In 1872, the Territorial Legislature authorized a four-member school board for each county and allocated to the public schools of the various voting precincts a quarter of general tax revenues, the whole of the poll tax, and a share of any county surplus above $500. With that encouragement, Father Tromby's school began in December of that year in the Ambrosio Armijo hacienda on the east side of the plaza, moving the next month to the Cerco House.

During the summer of 1877, the Fathers successfully lobbied the Bernalillo County commissioners for permission to enclose most of the remnant of the original town plaza that lay north of the church and rectory. In the fall, the two-classroom school Tromby describes in his talk began to rise along Romero Street. The area to the east became a playground, with a public road (Church Street) lying to the north.[1] Though school resumed the day after Tromby's talk, classes did not move to the new building until a few days before Christmas 1878.

*10. Our Lady of the Angels School.
Old Albuquerque.
Photo by John Collier, 1943.
Courtesy of the Albuquerque Museum.*

1. Draft of Latin obituary, Vitus Tromby, 1904, Regis Jesuit History Library; Thomas J. Steele, S.J., *Works and Days: A History of San Felipe Neri Church, 1867-1895* (Albuquerque: Albuquerque Museum, 1983), pp. 27, 50, 96-98, and 101; pp. 121-34 present a translation of Tromby's 1872 Latin "History of the New Mexico Mission."
   See also *Laws of the Territory of New Mexico Enacted by the Territorial Assembly of 1871–72* (Santa Fe: A.P. Sullivan, 1872), pp. 34-37, 42-43; H.H. Bancroft, *History of Arizona and New Mexico* (1889, reprint Albuquerque: Horn and Wallace, 1962), p. 711; C.E. Hodgin, "The Early School Laws of New Mexico," *Bulletin of the University of New Mexico*, no. 41 (1906), pp. 28-33; Byron A. Johnson and Robert K. Dauner, *Old Town, Albuquerque, New Mexico* (Albuquerque: Albuquerque Museum, 1980), pp. 78-81; Charles D. Biebel, "Cultural Change on the Southwest Frontier," *New Mexico Historical Review* 55 (1980), 212-13. The Sisters of Charity of Cincinnati took over the school in 1881, after the railroad was built through Albuquerque.

La Escuela Nueva de San Felipe Neri

Honorables Señores: La ocasion de estar ya acabado el nuevo edificio para las Escuelas Públicas de este precinto nos ha parecido la mas oportuna para dirigiros la palabra, espresaros nuestros sentimientos y hablaros sobre algunos puntos tocante a la pública instruccion y educacion de los niños.

Y en este primer lugar no es sino mucho gozo de nuestro corazon que os podemos presentar esta nueva obra que por mucho tiempo se habia hecho desear. Porque si bien es verdad que ella no ha sido hecha sino con grande esfuerzo y sacrificio nuestro; sin embargo tenemos la consolacion de pensar que este lugar deberá servir para el fin mas noble y excelente de una sociedad, cual es la educacion de los niños en las letras y buenas costumbres. Y no somos solo nosotros, sino toda la plaza la que se alegra de un tal suceso; y varias veces personas distinguidas nos han felicitado con grande entusiasmo por haber finalmente quitado las escuelas públicas del estado precario y de las impropias condiciones en que se hallaban. Y para que se conozca cuanto esto es verdad, voy a daros una breve cuenta de lo que se ha hecho para estas escuelas. Como veis se han levantado estas dos grandes y hermosas aulas, muy bien condicionadas, con dos tabiques de madera que forman en medio un salon de entrada el cual tiene cuatro puertas; dos de ellas que dan entrada a las escuelas y otras dos mas grandes[,] una de las cuales sirve de entrada al edificio y la otra para pasar al corral, grandes las dos y de órden perfecto.[1] Los tabiques se han hecho movedizos para poderlos quitar en muy poco tiempo en ocasion de grandes concurrencias, como por ejemplo en tiempo de ensayos públicos, en cuyo caso de las tres piezas se hace una sola. A las aulas sigue por el lado de oriente una plazuela, en la que los niños pueden en medio de las ocupaciones escolásticas exhilararse algun tiempo, para volver despues con mas brios al estudio. El lugar escogido para este edificio es el mas central y cómodo para los niños de toda la plaza y al mismo tiempo es el mas decoroso por estar, para decir así, bajo el amparo del templo de Dios: de aquel Dios, del cual (aunque blasfemen los impíos) únicamente desciende la verdadera sabiduría. En fin me parece que no puede negarse que lo que hasta ahora se ha hecho ha sido pensado con acierto y ejecutado hábilmente por inteligentes artistas.[2]

---

1. There was a strong neo-classical influence in the "territorial style" architecture of nineteenth-century New Mexico, and the "perfect order" that Father Tromby speaks of here is the Corinthian order, the most elaborate of the three Greek architectural orders. The building even today shows many survivals of Brother Michael Cofano's "Carpenter Corinthian." See Susan Dewitt, *Historic Albuquerque Today* (Albuquerque: Historic Landmarks Survey, 1978), p. 30; Vivian Holmes,

The New School Building at San Felipe Neri

Honorable Gentlemen: Our completion of the new building for the public school of this precinct seems a most opportune occasion of saying a few words to express to you our feelings and to treat certain points having to do with public instruction and the education of boys.

First of all, we cannot present this work without great joy in our hearts so deeply desired for such a long time. Although it is quite true that it has not been accomplished without great effort and sacrifice on our part, we nevertheless have the consolation of thinking that this place is designed to serve the noblest and finest goal of any society, that is to say, the education of children in letters and virtues. And we are not alone, for the whole plaza will rejoice at this successful outcome, and at various times, distinguished persons have congratulated us with great enthusiasm for having finally rescued the public school from the unsettled state and the unsatisfactory circumstances in which it formerly found itself. And in order that you can see how true it is, I intend to give you a brief account of what we have done in building these classrooms. As you see, there are two large and lovely halls, very well appointed, with two wooden partitions that form a central entrance hall with four doors: two that provide access into the classrooms and the other two, somewhat larger, one for access into the building and the other to go into the schoolyard. These are large and of perfect [architectural] order.[1] The partitions have been made moveable so we can remove them in a very short time on the occasion of great assemblies, as for instance at times of public exhibitions, in which case the three rooms become one. Beyond the classrooms there is a plazuela to the east where the boys can take their recess in the midst of their scholastic occupations and return shortly with greater eagerness for study. The site chosen for this edifice is the most central and convenient for all the boys in town, and at the same time it is the most suitable since it is, if I may put it thus, under the protection of the temple of God—of that God from whom alone, despite what the blasphemers say, true wisdom derives. Finally, it seems to me that I cannot fail to state that what has been done thus far was wisely planned and ably executed by capable artisans.[2]

"Architectural Woodwork of Colonial and Territorial New Mexico," (Ph.D. diss., University of New Mexico, 1979), pp. 83–94.

2. Mason Mick McGuire raised the adobe walls; carpenter Mr. Willey and a helper built the interior moveable partitions; Jesuit Brother Michael Cofano, a skilled cabinetmaker, constructed the doors and windows; and carpenter Pedro Lobato installed the roof and the floors.

Pero aunque mucho es lo que hasta ahora se ha hecho, sin embargo no es todo lo que se necesita para dejar estas escuelas en estado satisfactorio y perfecto. Falta en ellas, Hon. Señores, casi todo el material escolástico. Falta una buena provision de bancos, porque los que hay de presente son ya casi inútiles por estar viejos y carcomidos; falta una coleccion de buenos mapas, pues los presentes, que han sido hechos por privada industria, pueden suplir a la pura necesidad, pero no sirven para el adorno de la escuela; deberia hacerse un techo mejor y mas seguro para poner las escuelas al abrigo de las intemperies: de otra manera cada año tendrán que perderse varios dias en arreglos y reparaciones. Otras cosas podrian aquí añadirse muchas y menudas, algunas de las cuales son necesarias, y otras servirian para el adorno de las escuelas. Y aquí no puedo dejar de manifestaros una idea que estoy seguro aceptareis favorablemente. Podrian ponerse en estas aulas unos armarios en los cuales se haria, con lo que ofrece de mas notable el Territorio, una hermosa colleccion de mineralogía, zoología, e insectos. La cual coleccion al mismo tiempo que manifestaria las riquezas de esta país, serviria tambien para que los niños se acostumbren a ver tales objetos y los reconozcan por sus nombres: lo cual despues cuando ellos sean mas grandes les ayudará para la lectura e inteligencia de buenos libros y buenos periódicos. Pero aunque esto sea útil, lo que mas importa por ahora son, como os decia hace poco, una buena provision de bancos, una coleccion de buenos y grandes mapas y un conveniente arreglo del techo de las escuelas. Si alguno de vosotros, Hon. Señores, quisiese con corazon generoso y liberal ayudarnos en una obra tan digna, haciendo algun beneficio a estas escuelas, se haria acreedor al eterno agradecimiento nuestro, de estos buenos niños y de toda la plaza.

Todo lo que acabo de decir, Hon. Señores, pertenece a la parte material de una buena escuela. Vamos ahora a lo mas importante, que es la enseñanza y educacion de los niños: hablemos brevemente de la material, órden y extension que entendemos dar a la instruccion, y a la parte que nosotros de un lado y vosotros de otro debemos tener en la educacion de estos niños.

Hé aquí, pues, el sistema de educacion que hemos adoptado y que vamos a seguir.[3] Despues de haber ejercitado a los niños en leer y escribir (lo cual es el objeto de la escuela elemental) pasan ellos a la superior. En ella en primer lugar se perfeccionan en la escritura y se acostumbran al dictado,

---

3. Father Tromby's "system of education" was the *Ratio Studiorum*, a sixteenth-century Jesuit document still very influential in nineteenth-century Jesuit pedagogical thinking. Its most prominent features were (1) a uniform pedagogical method; (2) a subordination of method to teacher; (3) a wide range of subjects implying a positive, anti-Calvinist view of human nature and intellect; (4) emphasis on drama and (5) public speaking; (6) supervision rather than compulsion or corporal

But although much has done, it is nevertheless not all that is needed if we are to leave this school in a satisfactory and completed condition. It lacks, honorable gentlemen, nearly all instructional materials. It lacks a good set of benches, for those now here are nearly useless due to age and their rickety condition. It lacks a collection of good maps, for the present ones are the result of private efforts, and while they meet the need, they do nothing for the adornment of the school. It needs a better and more secure roof in order to keep the classrooms sheltered from bad weather, for otherwise we are apt to lose several days every year in adjustments and repairs. Other things great and small could be added here, some truly needed, others serving for the decoration of the schoolrooms. And here I cannot refrain from revealing an idea I am sure you will like: building some display cases in the classrooms to show a beautiful collection of mineral, animal, and insect specimens from among the more notable offerings of the Territory. Such a collection, at the same time that it would manifest the riches of this land, would serve also to accustom the lads to recognize the objects and learn their names, which would help them when they get older to read and understand worthy books and periodicals. But although this would be useful, more important for the present are, as I have said a few minutes ago, a good set of benches, a collection of nice big maps, and an appropriate repair of the school roof. If any of you, honorable gentlemen, should wish with generous and liberal heart to help us in such a worthy effort, doing a good turn to this school, it would be worthy of our eternal gratitude, that of these fine boys, and that of the whole plaza.

Everything that I have just said, honorable gentlemen, pertains to the material part of a good school. Let us go on now to what is more important, the teaching and education of the boys. Let us talk briefly of the matter, sequence, and scope that we mean to give to the instruction and of the part that we from our side and you from yours ought to play in the education of these lads.

First, the system of education that we have adopted and that we intend to follow.[3] After we have drilled the students in reading and writing (the goal of the elementary school), they pass to the advanced grades. They first of all perfect themselves in writing and grow accustomed to taking dictation, striving to correct and forget the innumerable faults of orthog-

---

punishment; (7) early promotion for better students; and (8) a sacramental and liturgical life to support the religious and moral formation. Allan P. Farrell, S.J., trans., ed., *The Jesuit "Ratio Studiorum" of 1599* (Washington: Jesuit Conference, 1970), p. iii, citing Robert R. Rusk, *Doctrines of the Great Educators* (New York: Macmillan, 1969), pp. 83-87.

procurando corregir y olvidar la innumerables faltas de ortografía que suelen cometer los niños del país, y que tal vez son una consecuencia de la viciada ortografía de los tiempos pasados ya por desgracia demasiado arraigada. Y aquí entiendo hablar solamente de la ortografía; porque por lo que toca a la sustancia de la lengua me parece que en general se puede decir que todavía se conserva en su pureza.

Cuando los niños han llegado a escribir correctamente al dictado, se les insinúa poco a poco y suavemente algunos de los géneros mas fáciles de escribir, como seria una pequeña descripcion y sobre todo algunas cartas familiares de las mas sencillas; y de esta manera podrá cada uno escribir en su lengua natural las cosas mas necesarias que le pueden ocurrir, sin necesidad de manifestar a otros los secretos de su casa.

Junto con el ejercicio de la lengua patria se acompañará el estudio de la lengua inglesa, la cual mas tarde deberá ser para cada uno muy útil y muchas veces tambien necesaria. Por esta necesidad y por el interés que, segun vemos, va creciendo cada dia mas hácia este idioma, nosotros procuramos en estas escuelas darle en cada año mas realce y animar siempre mas los niños a su estudio. Esto empero deberá entenderse de tal manera que por el estudio del idioma inglés no se descuide y olvide la lengua patria, el hermosísimo y riquísimo idioma español, que en este territorio es la lengua natural, la lengua de la familia, la lengua social.[4]

Contemporaneamente al estudio de ambos idiomas procederá tambien el de la geografía y de la aritmética, dos ramos de los mas importantes de los conocimientos humanos, procurando entre tanto en las explicaciones de enlazar otros conocimientos análogos a las dichas materias y provechosos, para que esas inteligencias ahora tan tiernas, un dia cuando hayan crecido en los años no queden mudos espectadores de la naturaleza, sino que sepan darse cuenta a lo menos de las cosas de mas importancia que pasan a su alrededor.

Se podrá tambien (como se ha hecho en este curso pasado) enseñar un muy breve y elemental curso de historia; pero esto se hará solo cuando haya unos cuantos niños mas adelantados e inteligentes.

Finalmente en todas las varias clases arriba dichas, no deberá faltar nunca la enseñanza del catecismo de memoria, acompañado de una buena explicacion, una o dos veces la semana, sobre la religion y los deberes de un buen cristiano.[5]

4. Father Tromby was quite clear about the practical need of teaching the boys English. While discussing the appearance in Albuquerque of a Protestant ex-priest schoolmaster, he remarks:
> When this Mac-El-Roy had opened his school as we have said, many boys—not only Protestant but Catholics as well—attended out of what I would call a sheer necessity of learning English, for in these parts its use is to necessary for trade with the Americans of the United States that the Spanish people make great and protracted sacrifices to send their boys to schools where it is taught (*Lettere Edificanti* 1 [1874-75], 43-44).

raphy that the children of this land tend to commit, mistakes which are the result of the corrupt spelling of times past and already, to our great misfortune, firmly rooted here. And here I mean to speak only of spelling, for as to the substance of the language, it seems to me that in general it can be said that it has endured in all its purity.

When the boys have learned to write correctly from dictation, we introduce little by little and quite gently some of the easier genres of writing such as short descriptions and above all some familiar letters of the simplest sort, and in this manner every one of them is able to write the more necessary things that can come up in his native tongue, without needing to reveal his family secrets to others .

Together with the exercise of the mother tongue comes the study of the English language, which later ought to be extremely useful for each person, and quite often necessary as well. Because this need and the interest in this language, as far as we can see, continue to grow every day, we will try in this school to achieve greater excellence every year and to encourage the boys further in their study of it. But this ought to be understood in such a manner that in the study of English the ancestral tongue is not discarded or forgotten. [We refer to] the rich and beautiful Spanish language which in this Territory is the native tongue, the language of the family, the speech of the social world.[4]

Side by side with the study of these two languages proceeds that of geography and arithmetic, two very important branches of human knowledge, endeavoring at the same time to convey in the lessons some knowledge of matters related to [geography and arithmetic—that is to say, the natural sciences—] and useful as well. These tender minds, when some day they have grown in years, will no longer remain mute spectators of nature but at least will know how to account for the more important occurrences that take place around them.

It might even be possible, as was the case during the past school year, to try a brief and elementary course in history, but this will be the case only when a fair number of boys are more advanced and intelligent.

Finally, memorized catechism will always be taught in all the classes mentioned above, accompanied by a thorough instruction once or twice a week touching on religion and the duties of a good Christian.[5]

And for this reason, Father Camilo Capilupi had been teaching some English in the Albuquerque school since early 1877.

On the other side of the American coin, Richard Rodríguez, *The Hunger of Memory* (Boston: D.R. Godine, 1981), presents his memoir from a century later of the twin language-worlds of English and Spanish for an acculturating Hispanic: English the language of school, business, and standard of living, Spanish the language of family, religious and cultural heritage, and quality of life.

5. The reader should recall at this point that Father Tromby was describing a public school.

Para formarse en estos conocimientos, de que acabamos de hablar, bastarian, segun creo, unos cuatro años, pero se necesitaria para esto una condicion indispensable y es que los niños no faltasen a la asistencia debida. Es necesario que los padres de familia hagan un sacrificio y se priven por cierto tiempo del módico provecho que podrian sacar de sus niños, estando seguros que tal privacion les dará en los años venideros un abundante fruto así a sus hijos, como tambien a ellos. Aunque, si tengo que decir la verdad, en algunos padres de familia no es la necesidad la que los detiene para enviar a sus niños a la escuela, sino es una muy culpable frialdad e indolencia [por la cual prefieren (lo diré con mucho sentimiento mío de todos los Padres) prefieren, digo, la ignorancia y embrutecimiento de sus hijos]. Esta queja, que otras veces ha sido expuesta en público, de nuevo os repito a vosotros, Hon. Señores, para que con vuestra influencia animeis a esos tales a que se aprovechen de la ocasion favorable, y no desperdicien el tiempo mas bello y precioso cual es el de la niñez.

Este es el plan de instruccion que seguiremos en estas escuelas, y que, en cuanto nos ha sido posible, hemos seguido en lo pasado. Y aquí permitidme, Hon. Señores, que os haga una reflexion. Estas escuelas, tales como de presente están constituidas en general por todo el territorio, no exigian de por sí tal desarrollo, sino que hubiera bastado para ellas la parte elemental solamente. Pero lo que hubiera sido suficiente para el cumplimiento de nuestro deber, no lo ha sido por cierto para hartar los deseos que tenemos de hacer a esta plaza y a todo el territorio todo el bien que nos sea posible. Por esto hemos procurado dar a dichas escuelas mas extension y realce, para que vosotros y todos los demás entendais cuanto os apreciamos, y cuanto queremos a vuestros hijos, a vuestras mas dulces esperanzas. Sí, vuestros hijos son tambien hijos nuestros y nosotros los amamos de todo nuestro corazon y en su cultura y educacion estimamos bien empleado todo nuestro cuidado y esmero: antes nos gloriamos de haber dejado lugares mas civilizados y cómodos para venir en busca de ellos y ayudarlos y encaminarlos en la senda de la civilizacion. ¡Felices nosotros si un dia podamos ver el fruto de nuestro sudores, y si esos niños lleguen al grado de cultura que les conviene! Estad, pues, seguros que de nuestra parte no faltaremos en lo mas mínimo a un deber tan sagrado como es la educacion de vuestros hijos, porque conocemos muy bien cuan precioso es el depósito que nos ha confiado la divina Providencia y cuán grande es el bien que de ellos se espera.

Pero, Hon. Señores, ¿qué efecto producirian nuestros cuidados y desvelos si vosotros no nos ayudáseis de vuestra parte? o, lo que es peor, ¿si hallásemos oposicion en alguno de aquellos que deben apoyarnos en una obra tan santo? o a lo menos si mirasen las cosas de la pública instruccion con frialdad e

For a good formation in the bodies of knowledge that I have named above there about four years are needed, I believe, and this can be accomplished only given one indispensable condition, that the boys not fail to attend school regularly. It is necessary for parents to make a sacrifice, deprive themselves for a certain period of the modicum of help their boys could have provided them, resting secure that such a deprivation will afford abundant recompense in years to come both to their boys and to themselves. To tell the truth for some fathers of families it is not necessity that prevents them from sending their sons to school but an altogether culpable carelessness and indolence because of which they prefer (I will say this with great pain on my part and on that of all the Jesuit Fathers)—they prefer, as I say, that their children be as ignorant as brute animals. This complaint, which I have voiced in public many a time, I repeat anew for you, honorable gentlemen, so that with your influence you might animate such men as these to make use of the favorable opportunity, not to waste a time so beautiful and precious as is that of childhood.

This is the plan of instruction that we follow in this school, and which as far as possible we have followed in the past. And here allow me, honorable gentlemen, to offer you a reflection. Schools such as are now in existence throughout the entire Territory have no need of such development, since merely the elementary years would be enough for them. But what would suffice for the fulfillment of our duty would surely not be enough to satisfy the desires we Jesuits have of conferring upon this plaza and the entire territory all the benefit we can. Therefore we have managed to give this school as much scope and excellence as we can, so that you and all others may understand how much we esteem you and how much affection we hold for your sons, your fondest hopes. Yes, your sons are our sons as well, and we love them with all our hearts; and we think all our efforts and care to be well employed in introducing them to education and culture. We rather boast of having left places more civilized and comfortable in order to come here in search of them, guiding and directing them on the path of civilization. We are content if some day we might see the results of our sweat, if these sons attain the level of cultivation that is suitable for them! Rest assured, then, that on our part we will not fail in the least particular of a duty so sacred as that of the education of your children, for we know very well how precious is the treasure Divine Providence has entrusted us with and how great is the good that is hoped from them.

But, honorable gentlemen, what result will our concern and watchfulness produce if you on your part do not help us? or, what is worse, if we meet opposition from any individual among those who ought to support us in such a holy work? or if you even look on the matter of public education

indiferencia? Esto no me es lícito ni aun sospecharlo de vosotros, sea porque conozco muy bien vuestros sentimientos en esta parte; sea tambien porque muchos de vosotros para tener una educacion esmerada han hecho grandes sacrificios, privándose por muchos años de las dulzuras del hogar doméstico. ¿Cómo se podria, pues, sin injuria suponer en tales personas poco interés por la cultura y civilizacion de su patria? ¿Cómo podria caber en ellas tanto anhelo por la cultura personal y ninguno o escaso por la de su país? Yo por mí estoy seguro que vosotros al mismo tiempo que teneis una justa idea de la alta importancia de la educacion, teneis tambien celo bastante para favorecerla y llevarla adelante. Y esto tanto mas lo creo así porque estoy cierto que vosotros muy bien conoceis los tiempos en que andamos y la necesidad que hay de actividad y vigilancia. Estamos en un terreno movedizo en que por un lado se nos presentan las grandes mudanzas que tendrán que efectuarse a su tiempo en el territorio; y por otro, hay entre nosotros hombres muy impíos y poco ilustrados, los cuales han tentado y tientan echar por tierra todo lo bueno. No hace mucho que habeis oido el necio grito de las escuelas no sectarias, (entendiendo con esto las escuelas sin ninguna religion y sin Dios) emitido por aquellos mismos que debian protegerlas y favorecerlas. Pero esos tales han quedado aplastados bajo el peso de la indignacion pública, la cual les ha hecho conocer que el Nuevo Méjico es un pueblo eminentemente religioso y Católico y que su fé es su vigor, su unidad, su dignidad.

Hon. Señores, esto es lo que se pide tambien de vosotros, es decir que mantengais con valor vuestra religion y que procureis favorecer aquella instruccion que con ella se armoniza y que sobre ella se funda: estando seguros que de esta manera huireis de la degradacion de muchas naciones, y marchareis por la senda derecha del verdadero progreso y de la verdadera gloria.

Concluiré con las palabras de un sabio e ilustre protestante. "La unidad es la fuerza de una nacion y esta unidad no se puede hallar en otro elemento que en la religion, la cual sola da la unidad de las creencias, la unidad de afectos y sentimientos, la unidad del fin al cual todas las naciones se enderezan."[6] He dicho.

—*fin*—

---

6. I cannot discover the author of these words.

with a lack of concern, with indifference? It is not permissible for me even to suspect [such thoughts] of you, for I know quite well your sentiments in this regard. I know that many of you, to get a thorough education, have made great sacrifices, depriving yourselves for many years of the enjoyments of the family home. Then how could I, without slander, suppose that such persons lack interest in the culture and civilization of their homeland? How could they entertain such a deep longing for personal culture and such a disdain for that of their own land? I for my part am positive that all of you, as soon as you attain an adequate notion of the high importance of education, also attain an appropriate zeal for assisting it and carrying it forward. And I am even more firm in my belief because I am certain that you are very familiar with the times in which we live and the necessity for energy and watchfulness. We live in an unstable region where on the one hand loom great changes, which will occur at their own pace in this territory of ours, and on the other there are men among us who are very irreligious and minimally enlightened and who have tried and are still trying to bring down everything that is good. Recently you have been hearing the ignorant call for non-sectarian schools (understand by this phrase schools with no religion and no God) uttered by the very persons who ought to protect and favor education. But such as these have been crushed beneath the weight of public indignation, which has put them on notice that New Mexicans are an eminently religious and Catholic people and that their faith is their energy, their unity, their dignity.

Honorable gentlemen, here is what I ask of you, that you valiantly maintain your religion and that you try to favor that instruction which is in harmony with religion and which is based on it. Be assured that in this manner you will escape the degradation of so many nations and march instead along the straight path of true progress and true honor.

Let me conclude with the words of a wise and famous Protestant: "Unity is the strength of any nation, and this unity cannot be found in any element other than religion, which alone gives the oneness of beliefs, the oneness of affections and feelings, the oneness of purpose toward which all nations strive."[6] I am finished.

—end—

PART V

Presbyterian Christianity on the Western Frontier

✜

✣

From the still-medieval Franciscans whose sermons open this book to the late nineteenth-century Presbyterians whom we meet at this juncture seems a great distance in the theological world. It must be remembered, though, that the great Franciscan theologian was the Augustinian-Platonist Bonaventure and that Calvinist tradition itself was equally Augustinian-Platonist, however different it was in most other ways. Although the Scottish Puritanism of John Knox subtracted church authority and the church's sacramental activity, John Calvin's fervent desire for the truly divine, for that which was so purely God and of God that it was nearly unmixed with anything of God's creation, was no more or less passionate than that of the Poverello of Assisi. To the Franciscan tradition as well as to the Calvinist, perhaps, Augustinian Platonism seemed to safeguard God's ability to transform sinners by the graces of faith, hope, and love without the need for sinners to subject themselves to external, earthly means. Aristotle might be all well and good for the peripheral machinery of perception that we humans share with the brute animals, but Plato offers us a far more religious world view.[1]

Pragmatic Americans drew away from the "wire-drawn metaphysics" of dogmatic theology, but even on the western frontier—perhaps especially on the frontier—the living tradition of Presbyterianism endured into the last years of the nineteenth century. Because it was Protestant, Presbyterianism protested so continually against Roman shortcomings that one southern Colorado evangelist complained that he seemed to spend more time preaching against the local Catholicism than he did preaching on Christ's behalf.[2] Because it was also Calvinist, it insisted on a pure and rigid morality to counter innate human depravity, found even among the redeemed. And because it was Presbyterian, it attempted rule by church elders, but such a grass-roots church polity rarely worked out in practice as long as New Mexico was fundamentally a mission field.

1. Perry Miller, *The New England Mind: The Seventeenth Century* (Cambridge: Harvard University Press, 1954), pp. 4, 269, 300, 312.
2. Quoted in Mark Banker, *Presbyterian Missions and Cultural Interaction in the Far Southwest, 1850–1950* (Urbana: University of Illinois Press, 1993), p. 111.

The missionaries were in the Territory of New Mexico, above all, to preach the word of God. "*Sola Scriptura*—Scripture alone" was a Protestant byword, and the Presbyterians were scandalized by Roman Catholic opposition to the King James bibles in Spanish translation. That opposition Bishop Lamy had put into writing early in 1854, giving his reasons:

> A version of the Holy Bible in the Spanish language that has been circulating in this Territory for a few years . . . is falsified in many verses and in many editions lacks entire books of Scripture. You should not request or accept any version of Scripture without knowing beforehand if it is the correct one approved by our Church, and no family should keep one in their home without having first shown it to their pastor to be assured of its authenticity. . . .
>
> [Saint Peter] tells us that in the epistles of Saint Paul "there are certain things hard to understand which the unlearned and unstable distort, just as they do the rest of Scripture, unto their own destruction (2 Peter 3:16)."[3]

Lamy continued his message by encouraging the reading of a Catholic-Church-authorized edition of the Bible.

The good effect of the Bible and the effects of their preaching, the Presbyterians would have said, had little or nothing to do with the eloquence of any printed translation or spoken oratory and everything to do with God's almighty will predestining one person or another to eternal life. And so the reader will probably find the following sermons noticeably less ornate, less adorned with patristic allusions or scraps of church history, and totally untroubled by the Latin phrases that were a constant feature of the Catholic pulpit.

---

3. Bishop Jean Baptiste Lamy, Epiphany Pastoral, 6 January 1854, pp. 5-6.

José Vicente Ferrer Romero

José Vicente Ferrer Romero was born in August 1844, the youngest child of Teodora Romero and, by Vicente's own account, of Padre Antonio José Martínez of Taos. He married in about 1864, doubtless with his father officiating. In August 1874 he met Rev. J. M. Roberts, a Presbyterian minister (who knew him as Vicente Martínez), and by November he had become one of the first two elders of the local Spanish Presbyterian Church. He subsequently founded the El Prado congregation and was licensed as a preaching evangelist in 1877. Though he hoped in 1891 to be ordained a minister, he was refused for his lack of knowledge of the Latin, Greek, Hebrew, and arts and sciences of a formal seminary education, but he remained active in the ministry into the twentieth century.[1]

Mind and Heart

The present brief sermon pretty much explains itself, though it also verifies Perry Miller's hypothesis about the strong influence of Romanticism on mainstream American Protestantism, especially where Miller comments that the mid-nineteenth-century preachers "instinctively realized [that the older] conception of the heart was entirely of the eighteenth century, and that what they meant was the infinitely more palpitating organ being currently celebrated in romances and gift-book fiction."[2] Romero's sermon was published on 27 September 1884 in the paper run by Reverend J.J. Gilchrist, *El Anciano* 3, no. 17. It was founded in La Junta, Colo-

---

1. Fray Angélico Chávez, *But Time and Chance* (Santa Fe: Sunstone Press, 1981), pp. 39-40. While still in his teens, Romero was running his father's printing press, publishing (among other items) broadsides that joined battle in various religious controversies of the period; pp. 144-58. J.M. Roberts, "Taos, New Mexico," *Rocky Mountain Presbyterian* 3, no. 43 (28 October 1874), p. 1; Lela Weatherby, "A Study of the Early Years of the Presbyterian Work with the Spanish-Speaking People of New Mexico and Colorado and Its Development from 1850–1920," (master's thesis, Presbyterian College of Christian Education, 1942), p. 68; R. Douglas Brackenridge and Francisco O. García-Treto, *Iglesia Presbyteriana: A History of Presbyterians and Mexican Americans in the Southwest* (San Antonio: Trinity University Press, 1987), p. 58; W.C. Buell, "The Taos Field: A Sketch," *La Aurora* 4, no. 8 (26 March 1903), 1, 3-4.

Gabino Rendon, *Hand on My Shoulder* (New York: Board of National Missions, 1953), pp. 54-55, writes:

rado, and then moved with its editor to Las Vegas, to Mora, and back to Las Vegas. In 1884 it was still in La Junta. The name of the paper is Spanish for "the elder," which would be rendered into Greek as "ho presbyteros," from which we have "presbyterian": a church ruled by its elders.

In this sermonette, Romero seems to be quietly echoing and combining Christ's remark in John 12:23–24 about the seed that does not germinate and "remains itself alone" and his parable in Mark 4:3–9 (and parallels: Matthew 13:3–8 and Luke 8:5–8) about the seed sown on the various sections of a large field. The preacher identifies the thorns that grow up and choke off the wheat in the third region of the field with the "thick roots" of Roman Catholic "superstition, ignorance, fanaticism, and wickedness." The authentic interpretation, probably developed in the early decades of the Church and put in Christ's mouth by the evangelists (Mark 4:19, Matthew 13:22, and Luke 8:14), speaks instead of "the cares of the times, desire for wealth, and all other kinds of desire"; but as a licensed evangelist, Vicente Romero was clear about the source of his own problems in his apostolic field: those rascally Roman Catholics, from the Pope on down.

Passing out tracts to visitors was a small quiet man whom I afterwards knew better. His name was Mr. Vicente F. Romero, and he was the son of Father Martinez of Taos. Father Martinez was a progressive priest who had brought the first printing press into New Mexico and established the first coeducational school. He had broken with the Roman Church after the coming of the French priests and would have been an Episcopalian had there been such a church in our part of the world. He had also married, and his children . . . had taken their mother's name, Romero.

Myra Ellen Jenkins, "New Mexico—1863," *Historical Magazine of the Protestant Episcopal Church* 32 (1963), 221-23, tells the story of Padre Martínez's flirtation with Episcopalianism which is also mentioned by Weatherby, p. 14, and Buell, p. 3.

2. Perry Miller, *The Life of the Mind in America* (New York: Harcourt, Brace and World, 1965), p. 65.

Necesidad de Cultivar la Mente y el Corazón

Caros hermanos:—Mientras no podamos crecer ni adelantar en nuestros deberes religiosos, somos semejantes a la buena simiente tirada en un desierto, faltándole el agua y buen temporal. Pues aunque la semilla sea buena y la tierra buena, faltándoles estas dos cosas, no puede crecer ni multiplicarse. Lo que principalmente nos falta para poder aumentar y crecer mientras vivamos en este desierto de grande ignorancia, fanatismo, superstición y maldad, es el gran cultivo tanto de nuestra mente como de nuestro corazón. Pues sólo con éste y la ayuda del todopoderoso Dios que hizo los cielos y la tierra, podemos cortar las grandes raices de tanta superstición, ignorancia, fanatismo y maldad, que desgraciadamente heredamos del Pontificio Romano, quien por tan largo tiempo dominó sobre nosotros subyugándonos a él, y conservándonos en la mas crasa y pérfida ignorancia de la luz del Evangelio: no dejándonos examinar por nosotros mismos, las Sagradas Escrituras, que son las que nos hacen conocer el camino que nos conduce al cielo.

Mientras no tengamos o no procuremos tener este cultivo, en lugar de crecer descrecemos. Pues faltándonos éste estamos sin vitalidad y sin fuerza. No pasamos de ser la misma semilla que aunque buena, pero tirada en un desierto seco aunque la tierra también sea buena, sólo se naturaliza con aquel mal temporal, y no pasa de estar brotando y saliendo la misma cosa, pero sin ningún aumento. Esto es lo que acontece, amables hermanos, faltándonos la cultivación del entendimiento y del corazón que es lo que mas necesitamos.

Roguémos pues a Dios que es nuestro autor, pidiéndole en nombre de Jesucristo, que él nos dé la capacidad y el poder de cultivar tanto nuestra mente como también nuestro corazón. Y cuando ya consigamos esto, entónces serémos semejantes a la buena semilla, tomada en la mano del cultivador, llevada y sembrada en buena tierra; la cual teniendo su verdadero cultivo, dándole todos sus beneficios, y acompañada del agua y buen temporal, desde luego se aumenta, se extiende, crece y multiplica su fruto copioso y admirablemente. Así es como todas las cosas producen, andando con tino, regla y buen orden.

Mientras nos falta el cultivo de nuestra mente y de nuestro corazón, la ley de Dios no cabe en nuestro interior. Esta ley se nos impone no sólo por su propia excelencia, cuanto por la autoridad de Dios. El desprecio de esta autoridad es el mayor crimen que la criatura es capaz de cometer. El desprecio de esta autoridad, es negar la fe de Jesucristo, apartarse del reino de Dios y unirse al de Satanás. No hay término medio entre Dios y Satanás. Cada uno se hace siervo de Dios o siervo del diablo. La santidad es la

The Necessity of Cultivating the Mind and the Heart

Beloved brothers: So long as we cannot grow or advance in our religious duties, we are like the good seed sown in a desert, lacking water and a good climate. For although the seed is good and the earth is good, lacking those two things it cannot grow or multiply. What keeps us from increasing and growing during our lifetime in this desert of immense ignorance, fanaticism, superstition, and wickedness is the broad cultivation of our mind as well as our heart. For only with this and the aid of God almighty who made the heavens and the earth can we cut the thick roots of so much superstition, ignorance, fanaticism, and wickedness that we have unfortunately inherited from the Roman Papacy which for such a long time has ruled over us, subjugating us, and keeping us in the grossest and most perfidious ignorance of the Gospel's light, not allowing us to examine for ourselves the Holy Scriptures which show the way that leads to heaven.

For as long as we do not have this cultivation or endeavor to get it, instead of growing we dwindle. Lacking cultivation, we lack vitality and strength. We do not go beyond being like the seed which, though the seed be good enough, is sown in a dry desert; and though the earth also be good enough, the seed simply acclimatizes itself to that bad environment and does not go beyond sprouting and staying in the same state, not maturing at all. This is what we face, beloved brothers, when we lack cultivation of the understanding and the heart which is what we need most.

Let us beseech the Lord, who is our author, asking in the name of Christ Jesus, to give us the ability and the strength to cultivate both our minds and our hearts. And when we achieve this, then we will resemble the good seed, cast abroad by the hand of the farmer, brought and sown into the good earth, which receives its true cultivation, giving it all possible benefits. Accompanied by moisture and good weather, it forthwith grows, stretches itself abroad, increases and multiplies its abundant and admirable fruit. Thus it is that all good things are produced, proceeding with prudence, rule, and good order.

For as long as we lack the cultivation of our minds and hearts, the law of the Lord does not find a home within us. This law imposes itself not so much through its intrinsic excellence as through God's authority. Disregarding this authority is the greatest crime a creature is capable of committing. The rejection of this authority is the denial of faith in Christ Jesus, separating oneself from the Kingdom of God and joining that of Satan. Each man must be either a servant of God or a servant of the devil. Holiness is our obedience through the loyalty and submission we owe to our

obediencia de nuestra lealtad y sumisión que debemos a nuestro Criador. El pecado es el servicio de Satanás.[3] Si fuera posible formar una idea de ambos reinos; de la excelencia intrínseca del uno, y de la maldad absoluta del otro; de la felicidad que acompaña al uno y de la miseria unida al otro; en una palabra, si fuera posible establecer entre los cielos y el infierno un contraste inmediato, desde luego podríamos tener una idea propia de lo que es la grave culpa de negar a Dios. La tendencia natural de nuestra conducta es degradarnos a nosotros mismos y también a otros, hacer el Edén semejante a Sodoma y encender donde quiera el fuego que nunca se apagará. Esto no se puede negar, porque la maldad moral es la mayor de todas las maldades y la causa cierta de todas las demás. Por tanto, el que peca, no es solamente rebelde a Dios, sino también malhechor y enemigo de bien estar público de sus semejantes.

En fin, caros hermanos, y todos los que aman y temen a Dios, si no dáis a vuestro entendimiento y a vuestro corazón el verdadero cultivo que deben tener, por introducir entre ambos la palabra de Dios, que es la joya mas preciosa que debemos obtener, jamás arreglaremos nuestras malas costumbres, conversaciones y acciones; jamás cortaremos el hilo de nuestras concupiscencias carnales y vicios desordenados; jamás cambiaremos lo pernicioso del corazón engañoso. Pero tan pronto como el espíritu de Dios se establezca, more y reine en vuestro entendimiento y en vuestro corazón, quedaremos enteramente disueltos y limpios de todas nuestras concupiscencias, deseos y vicios desordenados; por cuanto hemos confiado y hallado gracia delante de Aquél que nos rescató, librándonos de la muerte, del pecado y del infierno: el cual es nuestro amparo, nuestra plena consolación, el remedio universal de todas nuestras enfermedades, la curación eterna de todos nuestros males, y la victoria preciosa, llena del constante amor, para salvar a los mortales, redimiéndolos con su copiosa sangre, de la muerte y del pecado.

V.F. Romero

---

3. These three sentences echo John Calvin, *Institutes of the Christian Religion*, trans. John Allen (1813; reprint Philadelphia: Presbyterian Board of Christian Education, 1928), I:265-66: "If a necessity of doing well impairs not the liberty of the Divine will in doing well; if the devil, who cannot but do evil, nevertheless sins voluntarily; who then will assert that man sins less voluntarily, because he is under a necessity of sinning?" (2.3.5).

Creator. Sin is slavery to Satan.[3] If it were possible to form an idea of both kingdoms, of the intrinsic excellence of the one and the utter wickedness of the other, of the happiness that accompanies the one and the misery conjoined to the other—in one word, if it were possible to draw a vivid contrast between heaven and hell, then we could have a proper idea of how serious a sin it is to deny God. The natural tendency of our conduct is to degrade our very selves and others as well, to make a Sodom out of Eden, and to kindle everywhere the fire that will never burn itself out. This is undeniable, for moral evil is the worst of all the evils and the certain cause of all the rest. Indeed, the sinner is not merely a rebel against God, he is also an evildoer and an enemy of the public well-being of his fellows.

Finally, beloved brethren and all who love and fear God, if you do not give your understanding and your heart the true cultivation they need by introducing into each the word of God, which is the most precious jewel we ought to acquire, we will never subject our bad habits, conversations, and actions to regulation. [We will] never cut the thread of our carnal desires and inordinate vices, never alter the perversions of our deceitful hearts. But as soon as the Spirit of God dwells within us, inhabits and reigns over your understanding and your heart, we will be entirely dissolved and become cleansed of all our concupiscences, desires, and unruly vices, to the extent that we trust and find grace in his presence who has redeemed us, delivered us from death, from sin, and from hell: he who is our protection, our complete consolation, the universal remedy for all our illnesses, the precious victory filled with continual love that saves mortal men by redeeming us with his abundant blood from death and from sin.

V.F. Romero

Rev. Elijah McLean Fenton

The 1900 U.S. Census records 38-year-old Elijah M. Fenton, a wife, and two children in the tiny settlement of Cebolla Village; his younger brother and his wife lived in the house next door. Elijah had come into the Territory of New Mexico in 1881, just after the railroad arrived, served the Presbyterian church in various towns, and became pastor of a Jémez Pueblo mission in 1892 with responsibility for Nacimiento (today called Cuba), Capulin, and Archuleta (later named Perea and since 1904 called Jémez Springs). Though Fenton had retired from the active ministry—the 1900 census identified him only as a farmer—he had long been an ordained Presbyterian minister on Sundays and a surveyor on the weekdays. It must have been this last occupation that enabled him to identify that part of the beautiful Cebolla River Valley as open for homesteading. He dammed the river to build stock ponds, and when he sold out to the state in 1940, the New Mexico Game and Fish Department built the present Fenton Lake. Fenton died in 1945 and lies buried on a hill overlooking his homestead.[1]

Christ's Sheep

A surveyor ought to have a good sense of place, and Rev. Fenton does a fine job in this sermon of making Christ's parable at home in the regional landscape. The sermon reflects the maximalist interpretation of Original Sin current among nineteenth-century Presbyterians. Man's fallen human nature is incapable of resisting temptation because it is oriented to evil, and to apparent (but false) good rather than to real good. That Spanish was Fenton's second language is reflected in the frequent errors with regard to gender and preposition use.

---

1. Robert Julyan, *The Place Names of New Mexico* (Albuquerque: University of New Mexico Press, 1996). See also 1900 Census, Bernalillo County, sheet 162A; David E. Reiter, "History of the Presbyterian Church in the Synod of New Mexico," (unpublished, 1963), p. 10; Dennis Wall, "Fenton Lake," *New Mexico Magazine* 72, no. 4 (April 1994), 20-21, mistakenly identifies Fenton as an Episcopalian minister.

11. *Grave marker of Elijah McL. Fenton.
Author photograph.*

Las Ovejas del Christo

"Yo soy la puerta; El que por me [mi] entrara sera salvo; y entrará, y saldrá, y hallará pastos."

La Pais [El país] de Palestina es muy semejante a ésta aqui. Es muy montoso. Hay muy poco [poca] lluvia. Los laboradores [labradores] tienen que regar como aqui. Los frutos y granos, y verdaduras son casi las mismas, y casi todo la gente fueron en tiempos antiguos pastores de ovejas y cabras. VV. [Ustedes] pueden entender estas ilustraciones de nuestro Señor mucho mejor que yo. VV. saben muy bien el cuidado que necessita una rebaña de ovejas. Es necesario a guardarlos de los animales, como hizo David el Salmista, quien escribio las palabras - "El Señor es mi pastor yo no faltará. En lugares de yerba me hará yacer, junto a aguas de reposo me pastoreará." David fué pastor de ovejas, y vinieron un oso y un leon y tomaron cada uno un cordero de su ganado, el les siguió y mató con su honda, y su cayado [1 Samuel 17:34–37; Eclesiástico 47:2]. El era buen pastor.

Pero no son unicamente las [los] animales que son enemigos de las ovejas. El seco es grande enemigo a ellas, y los ladrones tambien hacen mucho mal a las rebañas. Es deber del pastor a pastorear sus ovejas en "lugares de yerba" y junto a las "aguas de reposo" asi que no se mueran de sed y de hambre. VV. [saben] cuan dificil es, en veces, a hallar lugares buenas, en donde hay zacate en abundancia y aguas copiosas, y cuan grande es el perdido [la pérdida] en tiempos secos cuando estas son escasos.

Hay en Palestina los hombres, no muy ricos, que tenian no mas pocas ovejas—eran muy cariñosos y tiernos con sus animales. Les trataban casi el mismo como tratarian sus niños—conocian cada uno por su propio nombre. Y las ovejas con[o]cieron la voz del pastor y siguieron a el sin temor ninguno. En la noche es deber del pastor a encerrar seguramente en el aprisco o el redil, las ovejas, asi que no sea molestado por las lobos y los ladrones. El que no hace esto, no es buen pastor. Yo sale un dia de Santas Claras[1] y encontre un muchacho corriendo en el llano, buscando su ganado. Era pastor de un hombre rico hay en Ocate.[2] Hay tema una vaile anoche en Santas Claras y el ha dejado su ganado y se fué por el baile. Cuando volvio, no halló su ganado. Al fin se halló, pero mucho carneros fueron matado por los coyotes— El era asalariado. El no queria por las ovejas. El no era buen pastor.

---

1. On the northwest shoulder of the Spanish Peaks just south of Walsenburg (La Plaza de los Leones) in Huerfano County, Colorado.

2. Ocate is in Mora County about twenty-five miles west of Wagon Mound (Santa Clara).

Christ's Sheep

"I am the sheepgate; whoever enters through me will be saved; and he will come in and go out and find pasture."

The land of Palestine is very much like this land here. It is very mountainous. It gets very little rain. The farmers need water for irrigation. The fruits and grains and vegetation are like ours, and in the olden times just about everybody spent some time herding sheep and goats. You can understand these illustrations of Our Lord far better than I can. You know quite well the care needed for a flock of sheep. You have to protect them from wild animals just like David, the Psalmist who wrote these words: "The Lord is my shepherd; I shall not want. In grassy places he makes me lie down, and he pastures me by still waters." David was a shepherd of sheep, and a bear and a lion came and each of them took a lamb from his flock, and he followed them and killed them with only his slingshot and his shepherd's crook [1 Samuel 17:34–37; Sirach 47:2]. He was a good shepherd.

But it is not animals alone that are enemies of the sheep. Drought is one of their great enemies, and robbers also do a great deal of harm to the flocks. The shepherd must pasture his sheep in "grassy places" near the "still waters" so they do not die of thirst or hunger. How difficult it is at times to find good places, where there is an abundance of grass and plenty of water, and how great a loss there is in dry years when those things are scarce.

In Palestine there are some men, though not rich, who have lots of sheep; they have been very loving and gentle with their animals. They treat them almost in the same manner they treat their children, knowing each one of them by its special name. And the sheep know the shepherd's voice and follow him without any fear at all. At night the shepherd has to shut the sheep safely in their fold or pen so that no robber will harm them. Whoever does not do so is not a good shepherd. I set out one day from Santas Claras[1] and came upon a youngster running across the plains in search of his flock. He was the shepherd for a rich man in Ocate.[2] There had been a dance the night before in Santas Claras, and he had left the flock and gone to it. When he returned, he could not find his sheep. When he finally found them, the coyotes had killed a lot of the wethers. He was a hired man. He did not care about the sheep. He was not a good shepherd.

¿Que dice Jesus? "El asalariado, que no es el pastor, cuyas no son propias las ovejas, ve al lobo que viene, y deja las ovejas, y huye: y el lobo arrebata y dispersa las ovejas: Así que el asalariado huye porque es asalariado y no tiene cuidado de las ovejas—["]

Esta figura o ilustracion (en comun con todas las ilustraciones de nuestro Señor) tomó Jesus de los empleos, y costumbres del pueblo, y es muy facil para intender. Nosotros somos las ovejas del Señor. Jesus es el Buen Pastor. El guardanos y preservanos de todo mal. El dio su vida por sus ovejas.

Encuentremos muchos peligros en este mundo. Nuestros vidas son llena de tentaciones. No podemos resistirles en nuestro propio fuerza. Nuestros corazones estan muy malos. Nuestro naturaleza es pecaminosa. Queremos mas lo que es malo que lo que es bueno. VV. padres de familia saben este muy bien. Cuan dificil es, muchos veces a enseñar los niños a hacer lo que es bueno y derecho! La naturaleza pecaminosa que haremos de nuestro primero padre Adam, es muy fuerte y duro, y causa a sufrir nosotros in [en] esta vida mundanal. Todos estamos imperfectos, llenos de manchas y impureza. ¿Como, pues, podemos entrar en el aprisco celestial en donde no sea permitido entrará ningun cosa impuro, imperfecto o pecaminoso? ¿Podremos entrar por razon de nuestros meritos?—No porque no hay ningun merito en nosotros, digno para salvarnos. ¿Podemos hacer alguna obra, o penitencia para asegurar nuestro entrado allá? No, porque pudiesemos vivir vidas puras y santos desde ahora, hasta que mueremos, esta no quitará las pecados ya cometido. Si queremos ser justificado por la alianza de obras, es necesario a guardar la ley perfectamente, y cumplir con sus obligaciones enteramente [Gálatas 5:3]. No hay ninguno que puede hacer esto. No podremos entrar por media de nuestras propias obras.

¿Puede la iglesia darnos entrada? No, porque no hay hombre o hombres que puede hacer por nosotros, lo que pertenece a nosotros individualmente. La salvacion es cosa individual o particular, por cada y uno persona. No hay quien puede comer por nosotros ni beber, ni pensar, ni creer. ¿Si tuviese yo hambre, que vale a mi, lo tanto que come V.? ¿Si es necesario que yo aprendiese alguno cierto cosa, que vale a mi el pensar de algun otro hombre? ¿Si es necesario que yo creyese en Dios para ser salvo, que vale a mi lo tanto que crean VV.?

La iglesia puede ayudamos [ayudarnos] en vivir vidas puras y buenas. El sacerdote o el ministro puede enseñarnos y guiarnos (y debe enseñar por ejemplo tambien como palabras) pero no puede salvarnos ni perdonar nuestros pecados.

¿Como, pues, entraremos en esta lugar celestial? Oid estas palabras de Jesus, por la boca de la profeta—

What is it that Jesus says? "The hired man, the one who's not the shepherd and who does not own the sheep, sees the wolf coming, leaves the sheep, and runs away, and the wolf tears and scatters the sheep. The hired man runs because he is a hired man and the sheep do not matter to him."

Jesus takes this image or illustration (as he does all the rest of his illustrations) from the work and the customs of his people, and it is easy to grasp. We are the Lord's sheep. Jesus is the Good Shepherd. He guards us and protects us from all evil. He gives his life for his sheep.

We encounter many dangers in this world. Our lives are filled with temptations. We are unable to resist them simply with our own strength. Our hearts are very wicked. Our nature is sinful. We desire what is evil rather than what is good. You parents of children know this very well. How difficult it is, so much of the time, to teach your children to do what is good and right! The sinful nature that we have received from our forefather Adam is very strong and obstinate, and it causes us to suffer in this earthly life. We are all imperfect, full of stain and impurity. How then can we enter into the heavenly sheepfold where nothing impure, imperfect, or sinful is allowed? Can we enter by reason of our own merits? No, because we have no merit of our own valuable enough to save us. Can we do some work, some penance, to assure our entrance there? No, because if we lived pure and holy lives from this moment until we died, they would not remove the sins we have already committed. If we wish to be justified by the covenant of works, we have to keep the Law perfectly and comply entirely with all its requirements [Galatians 5:3]. No human being can do that. We cannot enter [heaven] by means of our own [good] deeds.

Can the church grant us entrance? No, because no other man or men can do for us what we have to do for ourselves individually. Salvation is an individual or particular thing for each and every person. Nobody can eat for us, drink for us, think for us, believe for us. If I am hungry, what good does it do *me* how big a meal *you* eat? If I have to understand a certain thing myself, how does some other man's knowledge help? If I have to believe in God to be saved, what good does it do me how deeply you believe?

The church can help us to live good and pure lives. The priest or minister can teach us and guide us (and he ought to teach by example as well as with words), but he cannot save us or pardon our sins.

How then can we enter this heavenly place? Listen to the word of Jesus, spoken through the mouth of the prophet: "Look unto me, and be saved, all the ends of the earth" [Isaiah 45:22]. He and he alone can save us and admit us into our heavenly home. He holds the keys of the gate. He himself is the gate, and whoever does not enter through Christ but desires instead to crawl in some other way is a thief or a robber who has neither a

"Mirad a mi y sed salvos todas las términos de la tierra" [Isaías 45:22]. El, y El solo puede salvarnos, y admitirnos en nuestro hogar celestial. El tiene las llaves de la puerta. El mismo es la puerta y el que no entrará por Cristo, mas quiere subir por otro parte, es ladron y robador y no tiene ni parte ni derecho con las ovejas del Señor. ¿Y como recibió Jesus esta poder? En primero vez—El es Dios. Dios puede hacer toda su voluntad.[3] En segundo vez, Dios Padre hizo con El La Alianza de gracia para redimirnos del muerte si creyesen en El. El ha cumplido con la ley—Ha hecho expiacion por nosotros en su muerte en la cruz, y ahora esta al mano derecha de Dios padre en el cielo, listo para recibir todos que creen en El y hallen en El la salvacion por fé. Porque no hay otro manera para ser salvo. No hay otro puerta para que entrar en el hogar de los redimidos.

¿Estamos rodeados con peligros grandes y espantuosos? Vamos a Cristo y El nos protegira. Dice el Salmista—"El Señor es mi roca y mi castillo y salvador. El es mi Dios y mi fuerte. Confiarme hé en El me escudó y el cuerno de mi salud; mi refugio" [Salmo 18:2].

¿Son las tentaciones tan fuerte que no podemos resistirles? Vamos a Cristo Quien ha prometido, "No os dejará ser tentados mas de los podais, antes dará tambien salida con la tentacion, para que la podais lleva," y "estara con vosotros para siempre aun hasta el fin" [1 Corintios 10:13; Mateo 28:20].

¿Estamos muy tristes y descansados, listos para caer en desconfianza? Vamos a Cristo, Quien dice, "Ven a mi y yo te dare consolacion, reposo y paz." "Venid a mi todos los que estais trabajados y cargados, que yo os dare descansar. Llevad mi yugo sobre vosotros, y aprended de mi, que soy manso y humilde de corazon, y hallareis descanso para vuestros almas. Porque mi yugo es suave, y ligera mi carga." Matt. 11:28–30.[4]

¿Parece que el diablo, que va al rededor la rebaña de Jesus, como un leon, buscando los que pueda devorar, esta haciendo todo lo que puede para halagarnos lejos de nuestro Señor y Pastor, digamos a el en las palabras de Jesus—"Vete Satanás; que escrita está: Al Señor tu Dios adoraras y a El solo serviras" [Deuteronomio 6:13; Lucas 4:12], y adheriramos aun mas cerca a nuestro Buen Pastor.

Dijo Jesus, "Tambien tengo otras ovejas, que no son de este redil: Aquellos tambien he de traer, y oirán mi voz, y habra un rebaño y un pastor."

---

3. By a unilateral decision of predestination, which resembles sorting strawberries by telephone, John Calvin's God elects each individual for salvation or damnation, and if for the former, God henceforth knows the person *as if* justified and imputes justification to an actually sinful human being.

The result of this doctrine is a church largely inactive. Sacraments do not cause anything; they

share in nor rights to the Lord's sheep. And how does Jesus receive this power? In the first place, he is God. God can do whatever he chooses.³ Secondly, God the Father formed the Covenant of Grace with him to redeem us from death if we believe in him. He has complied with the Law, he has made expiation for us by his death on the cross, and he now sits at the right hand of God the Father in heaven, ready to receive all those who believe in him and find in him salvation though faith. For there is no other way to be saved. There is no other gate through which to enter into the home of the redeemed.

Are we surrounded by great and terrifying dangers? Let us turn to Christ, and he will protect us. As the Psalmist says, "The Lord is my rock and my fortress and my deliverer. He is my God and my strength. I trust in him, my buckler, the horn of my salvation, and my refuge" [Psalm 18:2].

Are the temptations so strong that we cannot resist them? Let us turn to Christ who has promised, "He will not allow you to be tempted above what you are able to bear, but with the temptation he will grant you beforehand a way to escape, so you can endure it," and "He will be with you always, even to the end" [1 Corinthians 10:13; Matthew 28:20].

Are we very sad and disheartened, ready to lapse into discouragement? Let us turn to Christ, who says, "Come to me and I will grant consolation, rest, and peace—Come to me all who are exhausted and burdened, and I will give you rest. Take up my yoke, and learn of me that I am gentle and humble of heart, and you will find rest for your souls. For my yoke is easy, my burden light."⁴

Should it seem that the devil, who lurks round about the flock of Jesus like a lion seeking whom it may devour [1 Peter 5:8], is doing whatever he can to lure us away from our Lord and Shepherd, let us tell him in Our Lord's words, "Leave, Satan, for it is written, 'The Lord your God you shall adore and him only serve'" [Deuteronomy 6:13; Luke 4:12], and let us then stay close to our Good Shepherd.

Jesus says, "I also have other sheep who do not belong to this fold. Those also I must lead, and they will hear my voice, and there will be one fold and one shepherd."

---

rather resemble a badge or button someone dons to affirm and publicize an event already over and done with: "I voted" or "I gave blood."

In 1903, the Presbyterian Church moved away from this strict Calvinist interpretation.

4. Fenton gives the citation, Matthew 11:28-30. The first sentence within the quotation marks seems to be a fair-use paraphrase of the scripture verses that follow.

Entonces tendran paz todos los naciones del mundo. ¿Teneis os hambre? Ven a Cristo y comais del pan vivo que ha descendido del cielo, y viveremos para siempre—

¿Teneis sed? Ven a Cristo y bebemos del agua de la vida de balde.[5]

¿Quereis entrar al redil celestial? Ven a Cristo, Quien dice Yo soy la puerta: el que por me entrare, será salvo; y entrará, y saldrá, y hallará pastos. Ven mis amigos, a Cristo la fuente de toda bien y recibid de El las mas ricas bendiciones de su gracia—vida, paz y gozo eterno.

—*fin*—

---

5. In Fenton's words "bebemos del agua de la vida de balde," the final two-word idiom which is translated "free of charge" literally means "from a bucket." There might have been some grins in the chapel.

Then all the nations of the world will be at peace. Are you hungry? Come to Christ and Eat of the living Bread that has come down from heaven, and we will live forever.

Are you thirsty? Come to Christ and drink of the water of life free of charge.[5]

Do you wish to enter the celestial sheepfold? Turn to Christ, who says "I am the sheepgate. Whoever enters through me will be saved; and he will come in and go out and find pasture." Come, my friends, to Christ the fountainhead of all that is good and receive the richest blessings of his grace—life, peace, and joy everlasting.

—*end*—

PART VI

*Methodist Christianity on
the Western Frontier*

✠

✠

In the beginning, John and Charles Wesley's "method" was simply "to live a life according to the method laid down in the Bible." But as the Methodist movement within the Anglican Episcopal Church continued, it developed a tradition of revivalist preaching to the unchurched along with a theology that remained more practical than dogmatic. After the American Revolution, John Wesley himself drafted the Twenty-Four Articles of faith that formed the movement in this country into a separate denomination and freed it from many of the Calvinist threads in the Anglican Thirty-Nine Articles. British Methodism became a separate denomination after Wesley's death in 1791.

Methodism in New Mexico began in 1853 with an eccentric spin when the renegade Franciscan Benigno Cárdenas arrived fresh from England, licensed as a Methodist preacher and ready to convert the Catholic Río Abajo that had followed him and Father Nicolás Valencia into schism a few years previous. When Cárdenas returned to Catholicism two or three years later, Methodism went dormant and remained so for a decade and a half, until Thomas and Emily Harwood arrived and made a success of it with their energy and ability. The number of members and ministers peaked around the turn of the century, then diminished as the Harwoods' energy declined.[1]

---

1. Santa Fe *Weekly Gazette* (3 September 1853), quoted in Arnold Rodríguez, O.F.M., "New Mexico in Transition," *New Mexico Historical Review* 24 (1949), 295; Fray Angélico Chávez, "A Nineteenth-Century New Mexico Schism," *New Mexico Historical Review* 58 (1983), 35-54; Randi Jones Walker, *Protestantism in the Sangre de Cristos, 1850–1920* (Albuquerque: University of New Mexico Press, 1991), pp. 73, 76.

12. *Reverend Thomas Harwood.
Courtesy of the Museum of New Mexico,
negative number 50137.*

Thomas Harwood

Thomas Harwood (1829–1916) came to New Mexico with his dedicated and well-educated wife Emily (1842–1902) at the invitation of his friend the famous Father John L. Dyer, the "snow-shoe" missionary priest for the Methodist Church in southwestern Colorado. Arriving in New Mexico in 1869, the Harwoods went to Mora County where Emily started a school; Bishop Lamy was so concerned with the intrusion that he sent some Jesuits to the vicinity to go head-to-head with the Harwoods. The couple soon closed their school and moved to Valencia County, where the eccentric ex-Franciscan Benigno Cárdenas had gotten New Mexico Methodism off to a strange start. The Harwoods also worked in Socorro and Sierra counties and in Albuquerque.[1]

Randi Jones Walker noted that although Harwood spoke Spanish as well as anyone, the fact that he never tried to "live Spanish" must have suggested to potential converts that becoming Methodist entailed the adoption of an Anglo lifestyle.[2]

With Harwood, we come to a brief respite from the free-form sermons of the romantic period. A brief glance at the sermons of John Wesley (1703–91) with their frequent explicit headings will make clear that Wesley's eighteenth-century neo-classical formalism influenced Harwood in his manner of dividing and numbering his material. Hillsboro, where Harwood preached this sermon, was a silver-strike town in Sierra County about thirty-five miles southwest of Truth or Consequences.

---

1. Harriet S. Kellogg, *The Life of Mrs. Emily J. Harwood* (Albuquerque: El Abogado Press, 1903); Thomas Harwood, *History of New Mexico Spanish and English Missions of the Methodist Episcopal Church from 1850 to 1910* (Albuquerque: El Abogado Press, 1908, 1910); Martin Rist, "Methodism Goes West" in *The History of American Methodism* (New York: Abingdon Press, 1964), pp. 443-45.

2. Randi Jones Walker, *Protestantism in the Sangre de Cristos* (Albuquerque: University of New Mexico Press, 1991), p. 93. In much the same way, some of Lamy's priests may have suggested by their attitudes that to be *really* Catholic was to be French.

Transfiguración de Cristo

Introducción. Texto. Mateo 17:2. "Y se transfiguró delante de ellos; y resplandeció su rostro como el sol; y sus vestidos brillantes como la luz."

Es imposible para el hombre mortal é ignorante, añadir algo a la sublime discripcion [descripción] de esta vision ó esta gloriosa manifestacion de la divina gloria de Jesu Cristo.

1. Es muy probable que el lugar de esta notable manifestación fué el monte Hermon y el tiempo en la noche, porque dice San Lucas 9:37, "Y aconteció el dia siguiente, que bajándo ellos de monte, un gran gentío le salió al encuentro." Entonces por de que ellos habian pasado la noche en aquel lugar.[1]

2. Las personas que estuvieron allá. Jesu Cristo, Pedro, Juan, Santiago, Moisés y Elías. Los testigos de la transfiguración fueron Pedro, Juan y Santiago.

3. Una descripción de esta extraordinaria ocasion. No hay alguna mejor que la de Biblia. San Mateo dice "Y despues de seis diás [días] Jesus toma a Pedro, y a Santiago, y a Juan su hermano, y los saca aparte a un monte alto. Y se transfiguró delante de ellos; y resplandeció su rostro como el sol, y sus vestidos brillantes como la luz. Y, he aquí, les aparecieron Moisés y Elías, hablando con ellos." Lucas dice, Se fueron par orar. "Y entre tanto que oraba, la apariencia de su rostro se hizo otra; y su vestido blanco y resplandeciente. Y, he aqui, dos varones que hablaban con él, los cuales eran Moisés y Elias." San Mateo dice "Estando aun hablando el, he aqui, una nube de luz que los cubrió; y he aqui, una voz de la nube que dijo este es mi Hijo amado en el cual tomo contentamiento a él oíd." San Lucas dice que Moisés y Elias aparecieron en gloria y hablaban de su salida, la cual había de cumplir en Jerusalem.

Y Pedro y los que estaban con él, estaban cargados de sueño, y como despertaron, vieron su gloria, a los dos varones que estaban con él. Y aconteció que apartándoce ellos de él, Pedro dice a Jesus; Maestro, bien es que nos quedemos aqui; y hagamos tres cabañas, una para ti y otra para Moisés y una para Elias; no sabiéndo lo que se dicia. Y estando el hablando esto, vino una nube y vino una voz de la nube, que decia: Este es mi Hijo amado, a él oid. Y pasada aquella voz, Jesus fué hallado solo."

4. Pocas lecciones para ser derivadas de esta vision.

(1.) Primera, que Cristo era el Salvador del mundo, el Hijo de Dios: porque la voz resonó desde la nube que decia; "Este es mi querido Hijo, en quien tengo puesta toda mi complacencia: oidle."

---

1. Harwood probably got this idea from Adam Clarke (c.1760–1832), a Methodist scripture scholar to whom he refers by name later in the sermon.

Transfiguration of Christ

I. Introduction: A. Text

Introduction. Text. Matthew 17:2—"And he was transfigured before them; and his face did shine as the sun, and his raiment was white as the light."

B. Proposition

It is impossible for an ignorant mortal to improve upon the sublime description of this vision, this splendid manifestation of the divine glory of Jesus Christ.

Setting in Time and Place

1. It is quite probable that the place of this remarkable manifestation was Mount Hebron and that the time was night, for Saint Luke says (9:37), "And it came to pass that on the next day, when they were coming down from the hill, many people came to meet him" because they had passed the night in that place.[1]

Persons

2. The persons who were there. Jesus Christ, Peter, John, James, Moses, and Elijah. The witnesses of the transfiguration were Peter, John, and James.

Narration

3. A description of this extraordinary occasion. None surpasses that of the Bible. Saint Matthew says, "And after six days Jesus takes Peter, James, and John his brother and brings them up onto a high mountain apart and was transfigured before them, and his face did shine as the sun, and his raiment was white as the light. And behold, there appeared unto them Moses and Elijah talking with them." Luke says that they went to pray: "And as he prayed, the fashion of his countenance was altered, and his raiment was white and glistening. And behold, there talked with him two men, which were Moses and Elijah." Saint Matthew says, "While he yet spoke, behold a bright cloud overshadowed them, and behold a voice out of the cloud which said, 'This is my beloved Son in whom I am well pleased. Hear him.'" Saint Luke says that Moses and Elijah appeared in glory and spoke of the departure he should accomplish at Jerusalem.

"And Peter and they that were with him were heavy with sleep, and when they awakened, they saw his glory and the two men that stood with him. And it came to pass as they departed from him, Peter said to Jesus, 'Master, it is good for us to be here. Let us make three tabernacles, one for thee and one for Moses and one for Elijah.' He did not know what he was saying. And while he thus spoke, there came a cloud . . . and a voice came

(2.) La segunda leccion es que no necesitamos tener miedo cuando Cristo esta cerca. Y el es siempre cerca y les dijo "Levantaos y no temais."

(3.) La tercera leccion es, que bueno que quedemos donde esta Cristo[.] Pedro dijo "Señor, bien es que nos quedemos aqui, sí te parece, formemos tres tabernáculos, uno para ti otro para Moises, y otro para Elias."

Tenemos aqui pocas inferencias. Una es, que es bien para los Cristianos vengan al lugar de oracion y culto. Porque Cristo ha prometido estar alli. "Porque donde estan dos ó tres congregados en mi nombre allí estoy en medio de ellos." Otra inferencia es, que es bien para nosotros seamos juntos en un lugar aparte del mundo porque Cristo tomó a Pedro, y a Juan y a Santiago y "los saca aparte a un monte alto," y ellos vieron a Cristo en toda su gloria; y tambien el fiel Cristiano frecuentemente puede tener vision de la gloria de Dios cuándo se separa del mundo.

4 Que hay una existencia futura, ó en otras palabras que el alma no muere con el cuerpo. Porque Moisés había sido muerto como 1482 anos. Deut. 34:5. "Y murió alli Moisés siervo de Jehova, en la tierra de Moab conforme al dicho de Jehova" "Y enterrole en el valle en tierra de Moab enfrente de Bet-pehor; y ninguno supo su sepulcro hasta hoy." Mientras su sepulcro fue escondido de la vista del hombre, su espiritu, su alma fue tomado con los angeles y él apareció con Elias y Cristo y habia venido sin duda del cielo, dando prueba clara que el alma no había muerto con el cuerpo.

Tambien Elias estuvo con ellos. El no murió, pero fué tomado al cielo en un torbellino.

La Biblia da una historia de Elias llena de interes y hermosura. Lease toda la historia en el Libro Primero y el Segundo de Los Reyes, en diferentes partes y para la historia de su traslacion leanse los dos capítulos del libro segundo y especialmente II Reyes 2:11, que dice, "Y aconteció que yendo ellos hablando, he aqui que un carro de fuego con caballos de fuego apartó a los dos (quienes son Elias y Eliseo) y Elias subió al cielo en un torbellino." "Y viendolo Eliseo, clamaba Padre mio, padre mio, carro de Israel y su gente de a caballo, y nunca más lo vio."

Estos dos hombres notables en la historia de los ancianos aparecieron ser hombres representativos. Moises un representativo de la ley y Elias de la profesia. El Doctor Clarke, en su Comentario ha dado esta interpretacion.[2]

---

2. Adam Clarke, *Commentary on the Holy Bible* (Grand Rapids: Barker Book House, 1967), p. 804; the six or eight-volume work by Clarke (c.1760-1832) was the standard Methodist commentary during the nineteenth century. Reverend Christopher Newman Hall (1816-1902) was a British Congregationalist whose anti-slavery stance probably recommended him to the GAR (Grand Army of the Republic—the Union Army) veteran Harwood.

Harwood's mention of "representative men" is probably a nod at Ralph Waldo Emerson's book of essays from 1850.

from the cloud saying 'This is my beloved Son. Hear him.' And when that voice fell silent, Jesus was there alone" [Luke 9:32–36].

Lessons

4. A few lessons to be derived from this vision.

(1.) First, that Christ is the Savior of the World, the Son of God, for the voice resounded from the cloud and said, "This is my beloved Son, in whom I am well pleased. Listen to him."

(2.) The second lesson is that we need have no fear when Christ is near us. And he is always near us saying, "Arise and be not afraid" [Matthew 17:7].

(3.) The third lesson is that it is good for us to spend some time with Christ. Peter says, "Lord, it is good for us to be here; if thou wilt, let us make three tabernacles, one for thee and one for Moses and one for Elijah" [Matthew 17:4].

II. Body: Logical inferences

We have here a few inferences. One is that it is good for Christians to come to a place of prayer and worship, for Christ has promised to be there: "For where two or three are gathered together in my name, there am I in the midst of them" [Matthew 18:20]. A second inference is that it is good for us to meet in a place apart from the world, for Christ took Peter, John, and James and "brought them onto a high mountain apart," and they saw Christ in all his glory; and furthermore [3] the believing Christian can often witness the glory of God when he withdraws from the world.

4 That there is a future existence, or in other words that the soul does not die when the body does. Moses indeed had been dead for about 1482 years; Deuteronomy 34:5[–6]: "So Moses the servant of the Lord died there in the land of Moab, according to the word of the Lord. And he buried him in a valley in the land of Moab across from Beth-peor, but no man knows of his sepulchre unto this day." Though his tomb was hidden from the knowledge of men, his spirit, his soul, was borne off with the angels, and he appeared with Elijah and Christ, having doubtless come from heaven, giving clear proof that the soul had not died along with the body.

Elijah was with them as well. He had not died but was taken up into heaven in a whirlwind.

The Bible gives a most interesting and beautiful account of Elijah. Read the whole story in various parts of the First and Second Books of Kings, and for the account of his translation read the two chapters of the second book and especially 2 Kings 2:11[–12], where it says, "And it came to pass as they still went along and talked, behold there appeared a chariot of fire and horses of fire and parted them both (Elijah and Elisha) asunder, and Elijah went up by a whirlwind into heaven. And Elisha saw it and cried,

El Doctor Newman Hale dice tambien que Moisés, cuando apareció con Cristo y con sus tres dscipulos representó a los muertos porque el habia clasificado con los muertos. "El murió y fué enterrado en al valle en tierra de Moab." Y habia sido muerto por tan largo tiempo que pudiera ser bien llamado un representativo de los muertos, mientras Elias habia sido tomado, sin morir, de la tierra hasta a los cielos, pudiera ser bien llamado un representativo de los vivos.

Pero en mi humilde opinion, la gran doctrina de esta gloriosa apariencia de Cristo y de estos dos ilustres hombres es, que Cristo es el Hijo amado de Dios; y que el alma no muere con el cuerpo; y la vida futura y finalmente la gloriosa doctrina de la ínmortalidad del alma.

El rostro de Cristo resplandeció como el sol y su vestidura adquirió la blancura como la nieve, indicandola naturaleza pura, celestial y la divinidad de Cristo-Dios manifestado en la carne, y la apariencia de Moisés y Elias nos enseñan que los muertos vivirán.

"Enoch fué trasladado para que no viese muerte; y no fué hallado, porque—antes de su traslacion tuvo testimonio de haber agradado a Dios" Heb. 11:5.[3] Y nuestro Señor dijo, "y no tengais miedo de los que matan el cuerpo, mas al alma no pueden matar[;] temod ántes a aquel que puede destruir el alma y el cuerpo en el infierno." Mat. 10:28. En otra ocasion, cuando Pedro, Juan y Santiago fueron presentes, la hija de un príncipe de la sinagoga llamado Jairo, había muerto. Cristo vino y le dijo, "Tu hija no es muerta mas duerme." La inferencia y la esperanza de todo esto, es que nuestros queridos amigos y parientes, no están muertos, pero están viviendo.

¡Oh gloriosa esperanza de la vida eterna! ¡Oh, el pensamiento felíz de morar muy pronto en aquella bonita ciudad celestial con Cristo, con los angeles y los arcángeles y con nuestros buenos amigos, los que han pasado delante de nosotros! Y ahora en conclusion, con las palabras de otro, quiero decir, "Allí, en los cielos, discurren los ángeles, ministran los arcángeles, triunfan los principiados, y alégranse las potestades, enseñoreanse las dominaciones, resplandecen las virtudes, relampaguéan los tronos, lucen los querubines, y arden los serafines, y todas cantan alabanzas a Dios."[4] Amen.
T.H.

—*fin*—

3. For more on Enoch, see Genesis 5:22-24.
4. I cannot discover the author of this quotation, but all its content derives from Pseudo-Dionysius' early-sixth century neo-platonic speculations on the nine choirs of angels in *The Celestial Hierarchies*. This schema entered western Christianity with Gregory the Great (d. 604), especially his Homily 34 (*PL* 76:1246-59).

'My father, my father! The chariot of Israel and the horsemen thereof!' And he saw him no more."

These two men, notable in ancient history, seem to have been representative men, Moses of the law and Elijah of prophecy. In his *Commentary*, Doctor Clarke has given this interpretation.[2] Doctor Newman Hall says further that Moses, when he appeared with Christ and his three disciples, represented the dead since he was classified among them. "He died and was buried in a valley in the land of Moab." And he had been dead for such a long time that he could well have been called their representative, while Elijah had been taken, without dying, from the earth up into heaven and could well be called a representative of the living.

Summary of doctrine

But in my humble opinion, the great teaching of this glorious appearance of Christ and these two renowned men is [1] that Christ is the beloved Son of God, [2] that [a] the soul does not die with the body, [b] there is a future life, and finally [c] the glorious doctrine of the soul's immortality.

Repetition

[1] Christ's face shone like the sun and his clothing took on a whiteness like that of snow, indicating his pure heavenly nature and the divinity of Christ-God manifested in the flesh, and [2] the appearance of Moses and Elijah teaches us that the dead live.

"Enoch was translated that he should not see death; and he was not found, for . . . before his translation he had testimony that he pleased God" (Hebrews 11:5).[3] And Our Lord said, "And fear not them which kill the body but are not able to kill the soul; but rather fear him who is able to destroy soul and body in hell" (Matthew 10:28). When Peter, John, and James were present on another occasion, the daughter of Jairus, the synagogue leader, had died. Christ came and said to him, "Your daughter is not dead but sleeps." The inference and the hope of all this is that our beloved friends and relatives are not dead but are alive.

III. End or peroration

Oh glorious hope of life everlasting! Oh the blest thought of dwelling quite soon in that beautiful heavenly city with Christ, with the angels and archangels, and with our good friends, those who have gone on before us! And now in conclusion, I wish to quote another man's words: "There in the heavens the angels speak, the archangels minister, and the principalities triumph; the powers rejoice, the dominations reign, and the virtues shine; the thrones illuminate, the cherubim enlighten, and the seraphim burn; and all sing the praises of God."[4] Amen.   —*end*—

Blas Chávez

Born in about 1838, Blas Chávez converted from the Baptist Church to the Methodist in 1873 at Old San Marcial in southern Socorro County. At the time he was a well-to-do merchant with a wife and five children. Thirty years later he was living with a second wife and three little children in Kingston, Sierra County, about forty-five miles southwest of Truth or Consequences, nine miles west of Hillsboro.[1]

---

1. Thomas Harwood, *History of New Mexico Spanish and English Missions of the Methodist Episcopal Church from 1850 to 1910* (Albuquerque: El Abogado Press, 1908), 1:201; Harriet S. Kellogg, *The Life of Mrs. Emily J. Harwood* (Albuquerque: El Abogado Press, 1903), p. xi.

Fúnebre del niño

Fúnebre pronunciado por Blas Chavez, en la esquias del niño, Salomón Padilla, el dia 10 de Abril de 1893.

Caros hermanos; Todos somos hermanos en este mundo, hijos de un solo Padre que es Dios, y por lo mismo deberíamos vernos como hermanos, llevando las cargas los unos de los otros, en nuestras aflicciones y desgracias.

Es la costumbre en todas naciones civilizadas en acontecimientos como el presente, teniendo lugar un funeral, que alguna persona piadosa a falta de un ministro del Evangelio se dirija al pueblo con palabras edificantes y que sirven de consuelo a los dolientes en particular, y a todo el auditorio en general, pues caros hermanos. Yo he sido esa persona designada por los dolientes del niño, y aunque incapas [incapaz] para desempeñar ese dever cristiano lo hago solamente instigado y compelido para cumplir con la humanidad. Aqui teneis caros hermanos delante de vosotros a un parvulito cuyos restos mortales estarán debajo de la tierra dentro de unos minutos, cuyo espíritu voló al cielo a exhalar el último aliento de su vida cuando entregó su preciosa alma al señor, pues el Redactor del mundo a dicho "Dejad a los niños venid a mi porque de los tales como ellos es el reino de los cielos" [Mateo 19:14]. ¡Que consuelo para un padre y para una madre aflijida oir tan preciosas palabras pronunciadas por el Redentor del mundo, pero al mismo tiempo por desgracia estamos revestidos de la carne humano, llena de pecados, la cual nos hace flaquear algunas veces y aun hasta descenfiar de las misericordias de Dios por nuestra poca fé por eso debemos estar apersividos y hacer fuerza que no suseda tal cosa entre nosotros los cristianos, antes al contrario, debemos ser mas vigilantes y confiar más en su fiel promesa y llena de fé, esperanza y caridad debemos acompañar a los serafines del cielo y dar voces de loor y de alabanza a Dios diciendo: "Santo, Santo, Santo. Señor Dios de los ejércitos [Isaías 6:3] llenos están los cielos y la tierra de tu gloria por los siglos de los siglos amen."

Nada tan hermoso como el Evangelio! ¡Nada que haya hecho tanto bien a la humanidad como el evangelio! ¡Nada que pueda reemplazar al Evangelio! El pueblo que lo rechaza no puede ser feliz porque rechaza su bien temporal y eterno.

Los enemigos del Evangelio tienen su inteligencia muy obscurecida, y su corazon muy pervertido. La experiencia nos ha demostrado que los hombres, mas viciosos son los que se oponen mas al Evangelio, pero nosotros que nos preciamos de cristianos debemos siempre defender la verdad sin miedo, ni temor para poder conseguir que nuestros nombres sean inscritos en el libro de la vida del cordero.

A Child's Funeral

Delivered by Blas Chávez at the burial of the child Salomón Padilla on 10 April 1893

Dear brethren: We are all brothers in this world, children of the one Father who is God, and therefore we ought to recognize each other as brothers, bearing each others' burdens in our afflictions and misfortunes.

It is the custom in all civilized nations at times like the present, when a funeral is taking place in the absence of any minister of the Gospel, for some devout person to address the public with some edifying words which might serve to console the bereaved family in particular and the entire assembly in general. And so, dear brothers, I have been the person designated by those who mourn for this child, and although I cannot discharge this Christian duty [as well as I should], I am incited and impelled to comply out of simple humanity.

My dear brethren, here you have before you a little boy whose mortal remains will be buried under the earth within a very few minutes. His spirit has flown to the heavens to emit the last breath of his life when he hands over his precious soul to the Lord, for the Redeemer of the world has said, "Suffer little children, and forbid them not, to come to me, for of such is the kingdom of heaven" [Matthew 19:14]. What a consolation for a father and for an afflicted mother to hear such precious words spoken by the Redeemer of the world, but at the same time unfortunately we are dressed in human flesh, filled with sins, which makes us weaken at times and almost despair of God's mercies because of our weak faith. Wherefore we ought to be prepared and strive to see that such a thing does not happen among us Christians. Quite the opposite, let us be most vigilant and trust yet more in his faithful promise; and filled with faith, hope, and charity let us join our voices to those of the seraphim of heaven in praise and honor of God, saying, "Holy, Holy, Holy is the Lord of hosts [Isaiah 6:3]. The heavens and earth are full of his glory for ages and ages. Amen."

Nothing is so beautiful as the Gospel! Nothing has done the human race as much good as the Gospel! Nothing can replace the Gospel! The nation that rejects it cannot be happy because it rejects its own temporal and eternal good.

The enemies of the Gospel possess very weakened intellects and very perverted hearts. Experience has shown us that the most sinful of men are those who most oppose the Gospel, but we who value being Christians must always defend the truth without fear and without cowardice so that our names may be inscribed in the Lamb's book of life.

Dichoso el pueblo que tiene la palabra de Dios por su guia. En esa Palabra Divina hallamos toda clase de consuelos espirituales. "Venid a mi" dice el Señor "todos los que estais aflijidos trabajados y cargados que yo os haré descansar. Llevad mi llugo [yugo] sobre vosotros que sois humilde y manso de corazon y hallareis alivio para vuestras almas" [Mateo 11:28–29]. ¿Que pueden ofrecer los sabios del mundo en reeplazo de estas promesas? conqué podremos quedar satisfechos en vida y consolarnos en la muerte?

En vano nos ofrecen los mundanos un paraiso de bien estar y comodidades, pues asi lo llamareis pero nosotros sabemos que es un paraiso lleno de lagrimas, de enfermedades y muerte, y esa cruz cuyo nombre nosotros quicierais borrar, es el emblema verdadero de la humanidad.

Ved aqui al pobre padre a esa aflijida madre que han perdido al hijo de sus entrañas a quien seguramente amaban mucho, ¡que duelo que desesperacion! ¿qué podremos decirles? ¿Cómo los consolaremos? Podemos decirles de este modo, vuestro hijo nació mortal, lloren es natural llorar, pero que vuestro llanto no llegue a la desesperación porque seria contra Dios, lloren sí, porque es necesario llorar, pero estoy seguro que el tiempo borrará su recuerdo y dará consuelo a vuestros corazones. Todo esto podemos decirles nosotros los mortales, pero Jesu Cristo vá más allá y el mismo les dice algo mas: "consuelate hijo mio y tu tambien hija mia: yo lo haré glorioso é inmortal. Acordáos que está escrito en mi Evangelio: "Dejad a los niños venir a mi porque de ellos es el reino de los cielos."

Tambien está escrito para los cristianos que cuando Dios los visite quitandoles a algun ser querido de la familia deben de conformarse y decir: "El Señor lo quitó hagase la voluntad del Señor" [Job 1:21]. Amen.
B. Chavez

—fin—

Happy the people who take the word of God as their guide. In this Divine Word we find every sort of spiritual consolation. "Come unto me," says the Lord, "all you that labor and are heavy laden, and I will give you rest. Take my yoke upon you . . . for I am meek and lowly in heart, and you will find rest for your souls" [Matthew 11:28–29].

What can wise worldlings offer in place of these promises? With what can we remain satisfied in this life and console ourselves at the time of death?

In vain those worldlings offer us a paradise of well being and conveniences, for that is what they call it, though *we* know that it is a paradise full of sorrow, sickness, and death, and that the cross, whose name they wish to erase from our souls, is the true symbol of humanity.

See here the poor father and that afflicted mother who has lost the child carried in her womb whom they have loved so much. What a struggle, what despair! What can we say to them? How will we console them? We might speak after this fashion: your son was born mortal. They weep; it is natural to weep, but indeed your weeping should not become despair (for that would be contrary to God). They weep indeed, for it is necessary to do so, but I am confident that time will soften your memory and grant consolation to your hearts. We mortals can say this much, but Jesus Christ goes much further, and he himself says ever so much more: "Console yourself, my son, and you also, my daughter, for I have made him glorious and immortal. Remember what is written in my Gospel: 'Suffer little children, and forbid them not, to come to me, for of such is the kingdom of heaven.'"

It is also written for us Christians that when God visits them to take away from their family some beloved family member, they ought to resign themselves and say, "The Lord has taken him away. May the Lord's will be done" [Job 1:21]. Amen.
B. Chávez

—end—

Lauriano Vargas

Lauriano Vargas was born in Placita, near Vadito, southern Taos County, in about 1846, the eldest son of a large family. Thomas Harwood offers a brief account of his Methodist years:

Rev. Lauriano Vargas, Taos.
Brother Vargas came to us in 1883 from the Presbyterian church. He served several charges [ministries], but finally left us and went off with the Seventh Day Adventists and is now [1910] residing at Costilla without employment by any religious denomination.

Harwood adds elsewhere that Vargas was active in the Methodist ministry from the first year of his conversion and that he was ordained an elder in 1885.[1]

This historical sketch perhaps suggests why the following sermon sounds less Methodist and incarnational than it does Calvinist, Puritanical, iconoclastic, and Old-Testament.

It is oddly coincidental that as this book of sermons began with an exemplary cat, so it ends with another cat, the latter feline perhaps fifteen or twenty generations later than the cat in the first of the Franciscan sermons—and far less comprehensible.

---

1. Census of 1860, Taos County, p. 79; Census of 1870, Taos County, p. 671; Thomas Harwood, *History of New Mexico Spanish and English Missions of the Methodist Episcopal Church from 1850 to 1910* (Albuquerque: El Abogado Press, 1908, 1910), 2:398, 66; 1:368, 378.

Falsas Dioses

by Lauriano Vargas, Prado de Taos, N.M. *El Abogado Cristiano Neo-Mexicano* 12, no. 11 (Nov 1896), 208.

Oigan, oigan Católicos Romanos, a Vds. que fabrican imágenes y confían en ellos, es a quienes se refiere el Salmo 115 de David, versos 4–8. Si teméis a Dios escuchad lo que dice; porque en verdad que a vosotros la voz de Dios habla.[1]

Siendo Vds. los que fabrican imágenes y confían en ellas, la sentencia de Dios es, que como vuestras imágenes no hablan, no ven, no oyen, no palpan ni andan, asi, sean Vds. que las hacen y confían en ellas.

Yo no lo sé otra interpretacion quieran Vds. darle a esta parte de la Sagrada Escritura. Pero ella declara la verdad con respecto a Vds. en la materia a que se refiere: porque si vuestras imágenes no ven, tam poco [tampoco] Vds. no ven en lo que conflictan vuestras imágenes con la única imágen de Dios, que es el hombre.

Sí ellas no oyen, vosotros tam poco no oís cuando el Señor os dice, que no hagáis imágenes, ni os inclineis a ellas, ni las adoréis. Si ellas no hablan, vosotros tampoco no podeis hablar con Dios en oración, sino con Maria y los santos. Y esto es con los santos de palo en la tierra y no con los santos del cielo, por que al cielo no puede ir ni uno sólo de Vds. que adorais los santos de palo en la tierra. Si vuestras imágenes no palpan con sus manos, tampoco vosotros no palpais el libro de Dios (la Biblia) ni lo tomais en vuestras manos para leerlo; porque su lectura está en lucha abierta con vuestra práctica de hacer imágenes y de inclinaros a ellas y en contra de todo vuestro sistema religioso. Si lo palpais y lo tomais cuando por mandado de vuestros curas, lo arrojais al fuego.[2]

Si vuestras imágenes tienen piés y no andan, vosotros os asemejais a ellos. Cuando no andáis por el único camino que guía al cielo, que es Cristo, sino que quereis brincar y andar por sobre tanto garrote y palo como tambien piedra y demás materia, con que atestais vuestros templos y casas de oración y hasta vuestros hogares personales.

No es estraño para mi que vuestras imágenes no hablan, no vean, no oígan, no palpen y no anden; porque siendo construidas de madera y demás

---

1. Psalm 115:4-8 runs as follows:
Their idols are silver and gold, the word of men's hands.
They have mouths, but they speak not; eyes have they, but they see not;
They have ears, but they hear not; noses have they, but they smell not;
They have hands, but they handle not; feet have they, but they walk not; neither speak they through their throat.
They that make them are like unto them; so is everyone that trusts in them.

False Gods

Hear ye, hear ye, Roman Catholics, you who fashion images and trust in them, it is to you that Psalm 115 of David refers, verses four to eight. If you fear God, listen to what it says, for it is in truth that the voice of God speaks to you.[1]

Since you are the people who make images and trust in them, it is the sentence of God that just as your images neither speak, nor walk, nor hear, nor feel, nor move about, so will you be who make them and trust in them.

I do not know any other interpretation that you could wish to give to this part of Sacred Scripture. But it states the truth in regard to yourselves about the material to which it refers: for if your images do not see, neither do you see that your images conflict with the unique image of God, which is man.

If they do not hear, neither do you hear when the Lord tells you not to make idols, not to bow down to them, and not to worship them. If they do not speak, neither do you speak to God in prayer, but rather you talk to Mary and the saints. And your speech is with the wooden saints on the earth and not with saints in heaven, because not one of you will be able to go to heaven, you who worship wooden saints on earth. If your images cannot feel with their hands, neither can you feel the book of God (the Bible), nor do you take it in your hands to read it, for your reading is in open conflict with your practice of making images and bowing down to them and contrary to your whole religious system. If you touch the Bible and deal with it in the way your pastors order you, you throw it into the fire.[2]

If your images have feet and do not walk, you make yourselves like them. For you do not walk along the unique way which leads to heaven, which is Christ, except that you would rather skip along beside some cudgel, some log, or for that matter some stone or some other material object with which you fill up all your churches and oratories and even your private homes.

It does not seem strange to me that your images neither talk nor see nor hear nor feel nor walk; since they are made of wood and other such stuff, they pertain to the neuter gender. What seems really strange to me is that you rational beings do not use all the faculties the Supreme Being has freely given you, since by using them you would give glory to God and to him alone. For his word says, "Whether you eat or drink or whatever you do, do all to the glory of God" [1 Corinthians 10:31]. But you do not do so, for if you say a prayer you say it for the glory of Mary and the Saints and not for the glory of God. If you look, you do not look up to heaven where God

---

2. The introduction to the previous group of sermons by Presbyterians quotes Bishop Lamy's reasons for bitterly opposing the King James Version of the Bible.

/213

materia, pertenecen al genero neutro. Lo estraño para mí es, que Vds. siendo seres racionales, no hagan uso de todas esas facultades que les han sido dadas gratuitamente por el sér supremo, para que con el uso de ellas deis gloria a Dios y sola a él. Porque su palabra dice que, si comemos, ó bebemos, ó cualquiera otra cosa que hacemos, lo hagamos todo para la gloria de Dios [1 Corintios 10:31]. Mas vosotros no así, sino que si hablan en oracion, lo hacen para dar gloria a Maria, y a los santos, y no a Dios; si mirais, no mirais al cielo donde está Dios, sino a las paredes donde esta colgadas vuestros ídolos. Si ois, no ois la palabra de Dios, sino lo que dice el cura y su tradición.

Si palpais, no palpais la verdad sino la mentira; y si andais, no andais en el camino de Dios, y no sólo andais pero hasta correis en camino de Diablo. Porque este es él que se los llevará, si continuais fabricando imágenes y confiando en ellas.

Vds. me dicen que no confían en ellas, pero considero vuestro dicho como una hoja de higuera de que hacéis uso meramente para cubrir vuestra desnudez, porque desnudos estáis, ante la masa inteligente, de que verdaderamente confías en ellas, en vista de lo cual, a ellos prometeis velorios, rosarios y novenas. Todas estas cosas y muchas otras prometais a vuestras imágenes con la condición que le traigan lluvia y de que les hagan tal ó cual otro milagro; pero nada de milagros que hacen en vuestro favor, sino que todo el resultado de toda esta tragedia viene en favor de los comerciantes de quienes compráis el café, arroz, azúcar, chile para hacer tamales, y demas cosas que preparáis para empantanar a la gente la noche de sus velorios.

Los cantineros tambien tocan parte de milagro de vuestros santos, cuando los velan por el whiskey que les compran para dar a los cantadores de alabados, ¿y no reflejan ni ven todas estas cosas, amigos? Pues bien dice la palabra de Dios, que como ellas sean los que los hacen y confían en ellos.

Finalmente, y para concluir por esta vez. Les digo, que sí no se apartan de sus ídolos tan féos y abominables, vendrá el Diablo cuando ménos esperan y hará carga con Vds. tan ciegos como vuestros ídolos. Y les sucederá la que le sucede al gato, cuando lo traen de otra parte. Con los ojos tapados para que no se vuelva así a vosotros, no vereis por donde vais a las cavernas infernales. Y mucho ménos por donde volvéis y espero que vuestros frailes no se quedarán sin parte de estas moradas. Por ser ellos los que como enseñadores por tantos años en este país, han tolerado todas estas monerías y muñecas en los templos. ¡Que Dios les pagué segun sus obras!
Prado de Taos, N.M.

—*fin*—

is but at the walls where you hang your idols. If you listen, you do not hear God's word because you hear only what your pastor says and what your tradition says.

If you feel, you feel not the truth but a lie; and if you walk, you do not walk along the way of God—and you do not merely walk, you practically run along the road of the Devil; for that is the one who will carry you away if you continue to make images and trust in them.

You tell me that you do not trust in them, but I consider your statement like a fig leaf you use simply to cover your nakedness, for naked you are before a whole crowd of intelligent people. For you truly trust in them, and for this reason you promise them vigils, rosaries, and novenas. All these things and many others you promise to your images on condition that they bring rain and perform some or another miracle for you. But never a miracle do they work in your favor, for the only outcome of this whole tragedy consists of profit to the store owners from whom you buy coffee, rice, sugar, chile for making tamales, and all the other things you prepare to stuff people with on the night you hold your vigil.

The bartenders also get their share of your saints' miracle during the vigils because of the whiskey you purchase to give the men who lead the alabados, and do they neither reflect upon nor notice all these things, my friends? For the word of God well says that those who make them and trust in them become like them.

Finally, and to conclude for now, let me say to you that if you do not get rid of your idols, which are so ugly and such abominations, the Devil will come when you least expect and take hold of you, since you are as blind as your idols. And what will happen to you is what happened to the cat when they took it to the other place. With eyes shut so you do not look at yourselves, you will not see that you are going to the infernal caverns, and much less how to turn back from there; and I hope that your friars will not lack a place in those dwellings. For these are the men who, as the teachers for so many years in this land, have tolerated all these puppet shows and dolls in the churches. May God reward them according to their works!

—*end*—

Conclusion
Old World and New World

This book has been an armchair (or padded-pew) excursion through the cultural history of the religious groups in New Mexico who left sermons in writing prior to the end of the nineteenth century. The Franciscan friars who staffed the many New Mexican pueblo missions and parishes have embodied for us the late-medieval mainstream spirituality of saints Bernard of Clairvaux and Francis of Assisi. Father Antonio José Martínez and Reverend Thomas Harwood represent the neo-classical stage of Renaissance culture, Martínez because he passed his formative years while New Spain still suffered a culture lag of several decades, Harwood because of the pervasive influence of the eighteenth-century founder of Methodism, John Wesley. Our remaining orators—French diocesans, Italian Jesuits, Catholic laymen, and the other Protestant ministers—can be identified with the Romantic period that had begun in Europe around the middle of the eighteenth century and percolated even to European seminaries by the 1830s and to literate Americans—as far away as distant New Mexico—a few years later.

Our roster of speakers suggests, as do many other lists, that the cultural history of New Mexico can be told best in terms of the groups of outsiders who came here. Very few of them were educated solely in New Mexico—only José Vicente Ferrer Romero and the two Hispanic Methodists went to New Mexico schools and no others. Rafael Romero attended Princeton, and of course all of the Catholic priests and all of the Anglo Protestant ministers had seminary training outside the Territory.

Late-twentieth-century readers probably find themselves less at home with the oratory of their own denominations than they would listening to sermons delivered today in other churches. Ecumenism within the mainstream Christian denominations has made the churches less adversarial.[1] The World Council of Churches and Vatican II have certainly brought all the mainstream denominations to greater understanding and civility, if not always to greater agreement. The Protestant churches have moderated some of their American sense of primacy and prerogative and relinquished much of their unlovely puritanism, and Roman Catholicism has maintained its inner authority even while lightening up on its former "Pay, Pray, and

Obey" Christianity. Interchurch biblical scholarship has helped all the denominations to refrain from beating each other over the heads with "proof texts," single verses or parts of verses torn out of context and used more like crude blunt instruments than like fine two-edged swords.

Consider the daunting number of major transitions that New Mexican Hispanics (and Native Americans) had to undergo from the beginning to the end of the nineteenth century: from Spanish Empire to Mexican Republic to United States possession approaching statehood; from mercantilist closed-border economics to capitalist free-trade liberalism; from farm-and-ranch agrarianism which does not reward literacy to industrial-revolution commercialism which demands it; from established church to freedom of religion. It may be that the successive waves of Spanish and viceregal Franciscan friars, Durango diocesans, French and Italian priests, and Anglo Protestants, by the very fact of their preaching one after the other to the people of New Mexico, enabled New Mexicans to adjust creatively to each of the new economic, political, social, and cultural movements, maintaining control of their destiny and preserving their integrity as a people.

---

1. Randi Jones Walker, *Protestantism in the Sangre de Cristos, 1850–1920* (Albuquerque: University of New Mexico Press, 1991), pp. 104-05: "While both Protestants and Catholics misunderstood each other much of the time, on the whole the Catholics had a better grasp of Protestant doctrine and practice than the Protestants of Catholic doctrine. The Protestants faced the same problem in New Mexico that they faced in other mission fields: their own division.... When *Revista Católica* left the field in 1918, Roman Catholicism was still the form of religion practiced by the Hispanic New Mexicans."

Sources Of Religious Oratory In Spanish From Nineteenth-Century New Mexico

Proceeding section by section, this list will give both the source of each sermon in the present book and the location of other sermons and religious addresses of interest but not included in this volume.

Franciscan Period

The anonymous sermon against superstition is in the Martínez-Sandoval Papers in the New Mexico State Record Center and Archives (NMSRCA). There are two García del Valle sermons in the Archives of the Archdiocese of Santa Fe (AASF): the one printed here, loose document 1825 (a misreading of 1821), no. 15, and loose document 1823, no. 16, a first-mass sermon for Father Rafael Ortiz.

A 1791 written exhortation by Vice-Custos fray Santiago Fernández de Valle appears in several books of *patentes*; see Fray Angélico Chávez, *Archives of the Archdiocese of Santa Fe (AASF)*, p. 166. It may have at some point been delivered as a sermon.

Padre Martínez

The first-mass sermon and the Hidalgo panegyric come from the Santiago Váldez *Biografía* in the Ritch Papers, original ledger in the Huntington Library, no. 2210, microfilm reel 8, supplemented by drafts, no. 2209, reel 5, and Read Collection, I:193. I am grateful to the Huntington Library for granting permission. The English translation (often little more than a brief summary), no. 2210, reel 8, is occasionally helpful. The Fourth of July talk is from the Alvarez Papers of the Benjamin Read Collection, NMSRCA, II:192.

The Spanish text of an 1862 sermon from the Martínez-Romero 1858–62 broadside series appears in *La Aurora* 5, no. 11 (1 June 1904), and the English appears in 5, no. 14 (15 July 1904). Many items in the series (*AASF*, pp. 127–28) probably derive from sermons. There is also a devotional sermon in private hands that is almost certainly by Padre Martínez and probably dates from about 1833; it narrates the Way of the Cross and serves as text for some tableaux presented in a Holy Week ritual.

Governor Pérez

Pérez's ominous inaugural address of 1835 has certain religious passages that might qualify it as religious oratory. The original broadside, published on the Abreu-Barreiro-Martínez printing press, is in the NMSRCA, Benjamin Read Collection, I:240. It appears in *New Mexico Historical Review* 12:14 and in the Mexican Archives of New Mexico microfilms 19:621.

Father Machebeuf

Machebeuf's surviving sermons are in the Archives of the Archives of Denver. His handwriting is extremely difficult to read. The unpublished sermons: a retreat talk on Hell from 1855; First Sunday after Epiphany and The Word (perhaps Sexagesima Sunday), both about 1855; Monday of Holy Week, 1856; First Sunday of Advent 1856; and Third Sunday of Advent 1856.

Bishop Lamy

All the sermons and instructions published here are from AASF except the 1860 sermon, which is from NMSRCA, Sermons of Archbishop John B. Lamy.

There are two dozen more brief Spanish sermons in AASF, along with a few dozen in English. There are two more sermons in the same NMSRCA group. And judging from the extracts in Paul Horgan, *Lamy of Santa Fe*, pp. 423–25, the Sisters of Loretto Motherhouse in Kentucky may have texts of some Spanish sermons delivered in Mexico in 1884. I am grateful to the Archdiocese of Santa Fe for permission to publish the two Lamy sermons and the García del Valle sermon in their Archives.

Academic Addresses

These talks appeared in *Revista Católica* an issue or two after being delivered; Tromby's talk appeared first in William McGuinness's Albuquerque *Review*.

The unpublished talks: Charles A. Blanchard at the Academía de Inmaculada Concepción in Las Vegas; Diego Archuleta at the Colegio de Las Vegas; José Desiderio Sena at the Colegio de Las Vegas; Severino Trujillo at the Colegio de Santa María in Mora; Leandro Sánchez at the Colegio de Anunciación in Mora; and Father J.B. Guerin and Eleuterio Baca at the Colegio de Las Vegas.

Later European Priests

The Regis Jesuit History Library, Regis University, Denver has the Spanish text of a retreat talk on the Agony in the Garden given probably in

the 1880s by Jesuit Father Biaggio Schiffini; there are no other talks in Spanish, but the collection includes dozens of items in Italian, French, and English as well as a large amount of support material, mostly in Latin.

Diocesan Father Ignace Marie Grom published an intermittent series of seven in Félix Martínez's Las Vegas *Voz del Pueblo* between 7 April and 30 June 1894. The occasions are: Low Sunday; the Second, Fourth, and Fifth Sundays after Easter; the Sunday after Ascension; Trinity Sunday; and the Fifth Sunday after Pentecost.

Presbyterians

The Menaul History Library at Menaul School, Albuquerque, generously allows my use of the two Presbyterian sermons. José Vicente Ferrer Romero's talk (which may have been a school talk like those from *Revista Católica*) was run in *El Anciano* 3, no. 17 (27 September 1884), 132–33.

The Fenton sermon published here comes from a small set of original manuscripts. Other complete Fenton sermons deal with John 6:68–69, 1 Corinthians 1:1–17, and 1 John 3:1, and there is an additional fragmentary manuscript. Rev. José Inés Perea of the prominent Bernalillo family translated a temperance sermon by Rev. F.S. Brush of Las Vegas that was printed in *El Anciano* 14, no. 3 (17 January 1894), 3.

Methodists

All these sermons derive from Thomas Harwood's *El Abogado Cristiano Neo-Mexicano* 9–12 (1893–96) in the UNM Center for Southwest Research. Unpublished here are a sermon by Leandro Martinez on matrimony, a funeral eulogy for a young child by Cruz J. Martínez, and three sermons by Harwood, one on redemption, another on matrimony, and the third at the funeral of José Antonio Baca y Pino, which turns first into a eulogy and finally into a news article.

Index of Biblical References

GENESIS
3:5	103
5:22–24	202
28:10–22	112n.

EXODUS
14:20	27
15:21	49
17:8–16	112

NUMBERS
24:30	112

DEUTERONOMY
6:13	189
34:5	203
34:5–6	201

1 SAMUEL
17:34–37	185

2 KINGS
2:11–12	201

JOB
1:21	209

PSALMS
12:6	47
18:2	189
23	185
25:10	29
64	37n.
85:11	23
115:4–8	211n.

PROVERBS
3:12	60n. 10
8:14–15	83
8:16	81
13:21	60n. 10
23:26	107
27:21	60n. 10

SIRACH
27:6	60n. 10
47:2	185

ISAIAH
6:3	207
14:5	61
40:3	115
41:1	60n. 10
42–53	28n. 6
45:22	187
45:6	66n. 15
53:11	28n. 6
53:2–5	139
53:3	105
53:6	27
64:4	63

JEREMIAH
31:33–34	85

EZEKIEL
18:20	87

HABAKKUK
3:2	29

MALACHI
1:11	85
2:7	112n.

MATTHEW
10:28	203
11:28–29	207
11:28–30	189n. 4
13:3–8	177
13:22	177
16:27	60n. 9
17:2	199
17:29	138n.
17:4	201
17:5	27
17:7	201
18:20	201
18:27–33	100n. 4
19:14	207, 209
27:19	34n. 12
27:40	99
27:45	29n.

27:51–53	29n.
28:19	115
28:20	189

Mark

4:3–9	177
4:19	177
6:18	114n. 8
14:34	139
15:18	138n.
15:37	101
15:39	107, 141

Luke

1:78	31
2:11	131
2:34	107
4:12	189
8:14	177
8:5–8	177
9:32–36	201
9:37	199
10:16	117
22:15	107
23:28	97
23:34	100n. 3
23:42	32n. 9
23:43	100n. 3
23:46	100n. 3
23:47	141
24:19	37

John

1	131
3:16	32n. 10, 33
3:19	104n.
4:34	127
10:12–13	187
10:18	101
10:32	37n.
11:50	35n. 12
12:13	104n.
12:23–24	177
14:30–31	137
19:26–27	32n. 9, 100n. 3
19:30	72n. 22
19:34	23, 25

Acts

2:14–40	1
3:12–26	1
4:26–27	100n. 4
10:28–43	1
13:16–41	1
17:34	29n.

Romans

1:16	97
2:2	104n.
2:6	99
13:14	125

1 Corinthians

1:22–24	97
2:9	63
10:13	189
10:31	213

Galatians

2:20	31
4:12	52n. 6
5:3	187
6:14	97

Ephesians

3:18	103, 105
4:24	125
5:6	16
5:19	17
5:25–26	110n. 4
6:10–17	52n. 5

Philippians

2:5	125
2:5–11	124
2:6	131
2:8	105
2:10	101

Colossians

2:9	25
2:13	33
2:14	31

Titus

1:16	131
2	131

Hebrews

8	85
9:28	28n. 6
11:5	203
12:6	60n. 10
13:12	28n. 6

James

2:13	31
5:14–15	111n.

1 Peter

2:24	27
3:9	103n. 7
4:17	104n.
5:8	189

2 Peter

3:16	175

1 John

2:16–17	105
5:4	99

Index of Topics

Abajo, Rio, 195
Abimelech, 113
Allende, Ignacio, 66n. 16, 67, 69
Amalek, 112
Aquinas, Saint Thomas, 10nn. 1, 2, 111
Aristotelian analysis by causes, 48n.
Atonement, The, 25, 189
Augustine, Saint, 13, 37n., 111n.
Augustinian Platonism, 174
authority: appeal to, 3; performing sacred duties without, 11; submission to, 159
Axtell, Samuel B., 148; compared to Pilate, 155; forced resignation of, 149n. 2

Baptist criticism, 93
Barreiro, Antonio, 54
Bent, Charles, 42
Bernard of Clairvaux, Saint, 19, 36n., 37, 216
Blanchard, Carlos, 146
Bonaventure, Saint, 174
Bossuet, Jacques-Benigne, 1
Bourbons, 75
Bravo, Miguel, 73n.
Bravo, Nicolás, 73n.
Briggs, Charles, 2
Brotherhood of Our Father Jesus the Nazarene, 43
"Burlesque on Christianity, A", 94

Caiaphas, 34n. 12
Calvin, John, 174
Calvinism, 90, 174
Cárdenas, Benigno, 195, 197
cat analogies, 13, 210, 215
catechism, 167
cathedral interior (Santa Fe), *129*
Cather, Willa, 121
Catholicism, French, 90
Cebolla Village, 182

Cerco House, 160
Chávez, Blas, 204, 205
"Child's Funeral, A" (Chávez), text of, 205–209
"Christ's Sheep" (Fenton), text of, 184–91
Christian Brothers, 123
"Christmas" (Lamy), text of, 130–33
Christmas, 128
church figures, notable historic: Aquinas, Saint Thomas, 10nn. 1, 2, 111n.; Augustine, Saint, 13, 37n., 111n.; Bernard of Clairvaux, Saint, 19, 36n., 37, 216; Bonaventure, Saint, 174; Calvin, John, 174; Clarke, Adam, 198n., 200n., 203; Dionysius, 29n.; Edwards, Jonathan, 1; Ferrer, Saint Vincent, 111; Francis of Assisi, Saint, 6, 19, 216; Gregory the Great, 202; Ignatius of Loyola, Saint, 155; Joachim de Fiore, 6; Knox, John, 174; Leo I, Pope Saint, 102n.; Marcion, 100n., 101; Martin of Tours, Saint, 111; Pseudo-Dionysius, 29n.; Tertullian, 103; Wesley, Charles, 195; Wesley, John, 1, 195, 197, 216
Clarke, Adam, 198n., 200n., 203
Clermont Seminary, 120
College of Las Vegas, 148, 159
Constantine, 111
contextuality-textuality scale, 2
Cortés, Hernando: casualties inflicted by, at fall of Tenochtitlan, 64n. 14; conquest of America by, 63; slaughter by, graphically described, 67
Covenant of Grace, 189
cross, meaning of, 97
crucifix, dismantling of, 19
Crucifixion, description of, 23, 29
cult, false, 11, 12n. 4
cultivation of minds and hearts, 179, 181

darkness, 105
Dávila Padilla, Agustín, 20
Death Comes for the Archbishop, 121

deceptions, 11
definitor, 19n.
Denys of Paris, Saint, 29n.
deposition from the cross, 35–39, 93
De Smet, Pieter Jan, 91
devotion, improper, 15
Dionysius, Saint, 29
Dionysius the Areopagite, 28n. 7
discourse, event-oriented, 2
"Distribution of Prizes, College of Las Vegas" (R. Romero), text of, 150–59
divine protection, 49–51
Dolores celebrations, 54, 56
Dyer, John L., 197

ecumenism, 216
Eden, 181
education, 151; importance of, 171
Edwards, Jonathan, 1
Elijah, 199, 201, 203
Elisha, 201
Emerson, Ralph Waldo, 200n.
emigration, 85
Enoch, 202n. 3
Episcopalianism, 43, 177n. 1
essentialism, 8
existentialism, 8

fakery, 11–17
"False Gods" (Vargas), text of, 211–15
fanaticism, 85
fathers, uncaring, 169
Fenton, Elijah McLean, 182; grave marker of, *183*
Fernández de San Salvador, Felix, 73n.
Fernández de Sierra, Santiago, 8
Ferrer, Saint Vincent, 111
"First Mass" (Martínez), text of, 47–53
formation vs. information, 2
"Fourth of July" (Martínez): dating of, 79; text of, 79–87
Francesco de Hieronimo, 1
Franciscans, missionary drive of, 6
Francis of Assisi, Saint, 1, 6, 19, 174, 216

García del Valle, Manuel Antonio, 1n., 8, 19
Gasparri, Donato, 148

gate, 187
Gilchrist, J. J., 176
God and Hidalgo, 77
"Good Friday" (García del Valle), text of, 23–39
"Good Friday" (Machebeuf), text of, 96–107
good shepherd, 185–87
Grant, Ulysses, 16n. 17
Grant Peace Policy, 146
gratitude, 49
Gregory the Great, 202
"Grinch Theology", 128
Grito de Dolores, 54
Guadalupe Church (Taos), *45*
Guerin, J. B., 146

Habakkuk, 29
Harwood, Emily, 195, 197
Harwood, Thomas, 195–97, *196*, 210, 216; influence of John Wesley on, 197
"headless" sermons, 90
heart as tomb, 107
Herod, 114n.
Herodias, 114n.
Hidalgo revolution, 57
hidalgos, 155
Hidalgo y Costilla, Miguel, 42, 54, 56, 61–75, 76–78; compared to Jesus Christ, 73, 77; compared to Maccabees, 71, 77; execution of, 57; God's will worked through, 61; as hero-liberator, 63; martyrdom of, 63; as secondary agent to God, 76
Hillsboro, New Mexico, 197
holiness, pretended, 13
Home Mission Record (Baptist), 93
House Made of Dawn, 3

idols, 213, 215
Ignatius of Loyola, Saint, 155
images, 211
Indian reservations, 146
individualism, 86n. 9
indulgences, 13
Inquisition, 9, 11, 85
"Instruction on the Passion" (Lamy), text of, 136–41
insurrection of the clergy, 57
Iturbide, Agustín de, 73n.

Jackson, Sheldon, 90
Jairus, daughter of, 203
James, Saint, 199, 201, 203
Jansenism, 90, 120
Jefferson, Thomas, 84n. 7, 146
Jesuits, 123, 155, 159; and tax exemption, 148
Jesus Christ, 199, 201; honor of, 139; humanity of, 19; options facing, 31; passion and death of, 137; and refusal to save self from crucifixion, 99, 101; reputation of, 139; seven last words of, 33, 100n. 3; as victim, 25, 29–31
Jewish religious practice, 11
Joachim de Fiore, 6
Job, 31
John the Apostle, Saint, 131, 199, 201, 203
John the Baptist, Saint, 114n.
Joseph of Arimathea, 107
Josephus, 99
Judas, 141
justice, 87; of God, 29

King James Bible, 146; opposition to, 175
Kingston, New Mexico, 204
Knox, John, 174

Lafayette, 83
Lamy, Jean Baptiste, 42, 79, 90, 120, *122*: concern about Harwoods, 197; Jansenist tendencies of, 128; niece of, 123; sister of, 123; statue of, 135
La Parroquia (Santa Fe), 55
las posadas, 132
LaTour, Archbishop, 121
Leo I, Pope Saint, 102n.
Leone, Alessandro, 160
liberty: attainment of, 83; in North America a result of God's will, 61
Loretto Sisters. *See* Sisters of Loretto
Lucero, Mariano de Jesús, 79

Maccabees, 67, 71
Machebeuf, Joseph P., 2, 42, 79, 90, 93–95, 120, 123; 108; accused of breaking seal of confession, 92; and development of his speaking skills, 92; engraving of, 109; physical description of, 91
Madariaga, Francisco Ignacio de, 19
magic as target of sermon, 9

Marcion, 100n., 101
Martin of Tours, Saint, 111
Martínez, Antonio José, 42, 76, 90, 176, 216; excommunication of, 42; gives thanks, 53; and his declaration of service to God, 47; priesthood of, a result of God's will, 47, 49; and use of abstractions and Latinisms, 44
Mary (mother of Jesus), 107, 213; and her apostrophe dramatically enacted, 37; three necessities of, 34n. 11
Mary Magdalen, 107
mass, guidelines on celebration of, 14n. 8
massacres, 69
Matamoros y Orive, Mariano, 73n.
"maximalist" Mariology, 36n.
Maximian, 111
medievalism, decline of, in New World, 7n. 2
mercy, 31
Methodism, 195, 204
Mexican Revolution, 77, 57
Mier y Terán, Manuel, 73n.
miracles, 101
Miriam the Prophetess, 49
Moby Dick, 3
Montezuma, 64n. 13; failure of, 65
moral evil, 181
Morelos y Pavón, José María, 72n. 23
Moses, 199, 203
music, 15–17, 16 n. 15

"Necessity of Cultivating the Mind and Heart, The" (J. V. F. Romero), text of, 178–81
New Mexico, Catholic influence on, 153
New Mexico founders, character of, 153
"New School Building at San Felipe Neri, The" (Tromby), text of, 162–71
novelties, 11, 17

oppression, 65, 67
Original Sin, 25, 182
Our Lady of Solitude statue, 19, *40*
Our Lady of the Angels School (Albuquerque), *161*

Padilla, Salomón, 205
Palestine, 185

"Panegyric in Praise of Padre Miguel Hidalgo" (Martínez): structure of, 58–59; text of, 60–78; two surviving copies of, 59
passion play, 20–21, 93
Paul, Saint, 27, 85, 97, 131, 175
Pelagianism, 134
persuasive speech, 2
Peter, Saint, 141, 175, 199, 201, 203
Pieta, 19; enactment of, 33
Pilate, Pontius, 34n. 12, 35, 107, 155, 157, 159
Placita, New Mexico, 210
plaza of Las Vegas, 147
Portrait of the Artist as a Young Man, 3, 108
Poverello, 1, 174
power of God, 99
prayer effectuating outcome, 53
prayer or hymn during sermon, 23, 25, 47, 63
preaching traditions, 1, 216
predestination, 175, 188n.
Presbyterianism, 174, 182, 210
"Priesthood, The", (Machebeuf): compared to Joyce's *Portrait of the Artist as a Young Man*, 108; text of, 111–17
priesthood as magic, 108
priests: compared to angels, 113; as mediators, 113; recruitment of French, 120; role of, 115; as superior to kings, 111
private schools, Catholic, 145
proof texts, 95, 217
Pseudo-Dionysius, 29n., 202
public schools, religious influence on, 145–46
purgatory, 13

Ratio Studiorum, 164n. 3
Rayón, Ignacio López, 73n.
Regis Jesuit High School (Denver), 148
Regis University (Denver), 148
religion: and morality, 157; and schools, 175
religious academic address, 145
religious life defined, 125
"Religious Profession" (Lamy), text of, 124–27
religious toleration, 85

Rencher, Abraham, 148
Rendon, Gabino, 149n. 1, 176n. 1
Revista Católica, 147, 149, 217, 220, 221
revivalist preaching, 195
rhetoric, 57–58
rigid observance, 15
Rimbaud, Arthur, 3
Roberts, J. M., 176
Romanticism, 90, 176, 216
Romero, José Vicente Ferrer, 176–77, 216
Romero, Rafael, 148, 216
Romero, Trinidad, 148

sacraments, 111n.
sadness, mortal, 139
Saint Francis of Assisi Church (Santa Fe), 21
saints, wooden, 213
Salome, 114n.
salvation, individual nature of, 187
Sánchez, Leandro, 146
Sánchez, Pedro, 43
Santo Entierro, 21
"Santo" statue (San Felipe Neri Church, Albuquerque), *119*
Scarlet Letter, The, 1
school at San Felipe Neri: appeal for support of, 169; described, 163; methods of instruction at, 165–167; needs of, 165; subjects of study at, 167
schools, sectarian, 145–46
seed analogy, 179
self-government, 83
separation of church and state: as alien concept, 1, 58, 146; lack of understanding of, 154n. 4
sermons: examples of, from literary classics, 3; as performances, 2; style differences of, 90; tradition of publishing, 3
Serra, Junípero, 6
servant, 179
seven last words of Christ, 33, 100n. 3
Seventh Day Adventists, 210
sin, remission of, 33
"Sinners in the Hands of an Angry God", 3
Sisters of Charity of Cincinnati, 123, 161n.
Sisters of Loretto, 123, 134, 148; formal name for, 136n.
Sixteenth of September, 54, 63

Smith, Lewis, 93
Sodom, 181
"Soledad" statue (San Felipe Neri Church, Albuquerque), *118*
songs, 17
"Songs of the Suffering Servant of Yahweh", 28n. 6
soul, immortality of, 201, 203
Sound and the Fury, The, 3
Spanish domination, 63
spiritual consolation, 207
spirituality, late-medieval, 6
statuary, 19–21
suffering, 137–41
"Superstition" (anonymous): dating of, 8; structure of, 8–9; text of, 10–17
superstition, 6, 179; species of, 10n. 1
"Superstition Rampant", 93

Taladrid, Dámaso, 79
Taos uprising, 42
Terán, Manuel Mier y, 73n.
Tercio-Millennial Exposition, 152n.
Tertullian, 103
theology: dogmatic, 76, 174; grinch, 128; textbook, 8–9, 10n. 1, 11n. 4, 95
Tlaxcaltecans, 64n. 14, 65
tolerance of cults, 85, 85n. 8
tolerance of religions, 83
tomb, 107
"Transfiguration of Christ" (Harwood), text of, 198–203
transformation of nature, 51
transitions, 217
Trent, Council of, 14n. 8
Tridentine Seminary of the Diocese of Durango, 42, 44, 90
Tromby, Vito, 160
Trujillo, Severino, 146

Váldez, Santiago, 59
Valencia, Nicolás, 195
Vargas, Lauriano, 210
Verdusco, José Sixto, 73n.
vice, remedies to, 105
Victoria, Guadalupe, 73n.
Virgin of Guadalupe, 69
vows, 125

Washington, George, 81–87
Washistong. *See* Washington, George
Wesley, Charles, 195
Wesley, John, 1, 195, 216; and neo-classical formalism, 197
Western Reserve, 157
Wroth, William, 20